This journal belongs to

....

She Will
Be Blessed

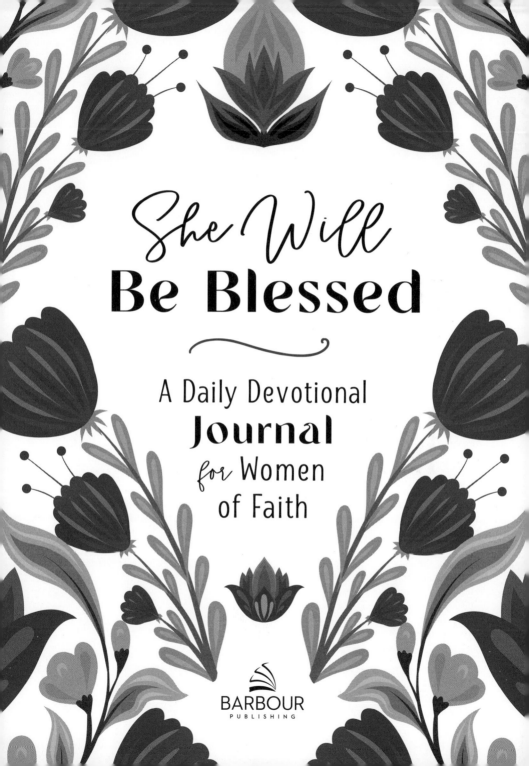

She Will Be Blessed

A Daily Devotional
Journal
for Women
of Faith

BARBOUR
PUBLISHING

© 2024 by Barbour Publishing, Inc.

Print ISBN 978-1-63609-944-6

Text previously appeared in *Blessed Is She Who Hopes*, *Blessed Is She Who Prays*, and *Blessed Is She Who Believes*.

Scripture quotations marked KJV are taken from the King James Version of the Bible.

Scripture quotations marked MSG are taken from *THE MESSAGE*, copyright © 1993, 2002, 2018 by Eugene H. Peterson. Used by permission of NavPress, represented by Tyndale House Publishers. All rights reserved.

Scripture quotations marked NIV are taken from the HOLY BIBLE, NEW INTERNATIONAL VERSION®. NIV®. Copyright © 1973, 1978, 1984, 2011 by Biblica, Inc.™ Used by permission. All rights reserved worldwide.

Scripture quotations marked NLT are taken from the *Holy Bible*. New Living Translation copyright © 1996, 2004, 2015 by Tyndale House Foundation. Used by permission of Tyndale House Publishers, Inc., Carol Stream, Illinois 60188. All rights reserved.

Scripture quotations marked VOICE are taken from The Voice™. Copyright © 2008 by Ecclesia Bible Society. Used by permission. All rights reserved.

Published by Barbour Publishing, Inc., 1810 Barbour Drive, Uhrichsville, Ohio 44683, www.barbourbooks.com

Our mission is to inspire the world with the life-changing message of the Bible.

 Member of the Evangelical Christian Publishers Association

Printed in China.

Day 1
Taste and See

*I prayed to the Lord, and he answered me. He freed me from
all my fears. . . . Taste and see that the Lord is good.*
PSALM 34:4, 8 NLT

David wrote this psalm before he became king, after a situation when he was so scared of his enemies that he pretended to be a drooling madman in order to escape. After his life was spared, he didn't say, "See how clever I am that I managed to get away!" Instead, he gave God all the credit.

Notice that David didn't say, "Pray and be spiritual, and then you'll experience God's goodness." Not, of course, that praying is ever wrong! But David implied that when life seems scary and hopeless, our physical senses may give us glimpses of God and renew our hope. It might be the flavor of homemade bread, the rosy light of a sunrise, or the scent of new-mown grass that brings hope to our hearts. It could be a child's laughter or a loving hug. Our favorite song, a warm bath, or even a comfy old sweater can all be opportunities to "taste and see" God. And through each of these small sensual pleasures, God whispers hope into our hearts.

....

....

....

....

....

....

....

....

Today, Lord, open my eyes to the beauty of Your world. Remind me to take
a moment to listen, smell, taste, and feel all the wonderful things
You have created. May I taste and see You and find new hope.

Day 2
Memories

"Don't you see, you planned evil against me
but God used those same plans for my good."
GENESIS 50:20 MSG

Neuroscientists tell us our brains handle negative and positive memories differently. We tend to spend more time thinking about painful experiences, which means these memories may become deeply ingrained, shaping how we think about both the present and the future. Often, like hamsters circling endlessly on their wheels, we relive again and again the hurts we have received—the times we felt insulted or rejected, the times when someone made us feel small or ashamed—and in the process, we remain stuck in the past. We can't change how our brains work, nor can we change what happened in the past, but we can allow God to transform how we think about painful memories.

Ask the Spirit to reveal to you how God might use your painful memories to help you grow. Be open to exploring new possibilities that might arise from even the most hurtful experiences. Believe that God's creative power can continue to work through what has already happened to you. Let hope have the final word!

....

....

....

....

....

....

....

Heavenly friend, as I look back at my past, show me Your presence
and love even in the most painful moments. Give new meaning to
these old memories so I can face the future with fresh hope.

The Gift of Friendship

Wounds from a sincere friend are better than many kisses from an enemy.
PROVERBS 27:6 NLT

Talking with a friend, sharing your life with someone who understands, is one of life's great blessings. After you talk with a wise friend, life usually makes more sense. Seemingly unsolvable problems no longer seem as overwhelming. A faithful friend's words—even when you don't want to hear them!—can help you understand yourself and can also point you toward the eternal meaning that's hidden in your life. Friendship teaches you new perspectives. It strengthens your belief in God's power and allows you to see yourself as God sees you.

....
....
....
....
....
....
....
....
....
....
....

Thank You, heavenly friend, for the earthly friendships You have
given me. Please use my friends to nurture my belief in
You—and use me to encourage my friends as well.

Day 4
Burning Bushes

*There the angel of the LORD appeared to him in a blazing
fire from the middle of a bush. Moses stared in amazement.
Though the bush was engulfed in flames, it didn't burn up.*

EXODUS 3:2 NLT

Moses was out in the desert doing his ordinary, everyday work. In his case, his job was to tend his father-in-law's sheep. In our case, our work might be sitting in front of a computer for eight hours, or it might be teaching children or caring for sick people, managing a business, or making meals for our families. Whatever our daily responsibilities are, we don't usually expect our workday to be interrupted by a vision of God's presence. We assume that if God is going to visit us in some spectacular way, it's not likely to be in the middle of our ordinary routine.

In the Bible, though, that is often how God turns up—by surprise, somewhere people aren't expecting to find Him. God startles us out of our mental ruts so we can confront a larger reality, a world that blazes with His hope and power. When we look at the world with the eyes of hope, we may be amazed by a "burning bush" of our own.

....

....

....

....

....

....

....

....

*God of hope and power, may I never be so busy that I'm
not startled to awareness by the fire of Your love.*

Day 5

A New Day

God is within her, she will not fall; God will help her at break of day.
PSALM 46:5 NIV

We may start the day full of energy and hope but end the same day with weariness and discouragement. Sometimes the events of the day batter our hearts and minds to the point that our hope begins to ebb away. Other times, our minds and bodies are simply tired, and tired minds and bodies are more easily discouraged. Meanwhile, God never changes. He doesn't blame us for our physical and emotional reactions to a long day; instead, His love holds us steady through each day's ebb and flow. And every morning, He gives us a chance to begin again.

No matter how tired or discouraged you feel, God's Spirit never abandons you. Regardless of what happened yesterday or today, you can have hope for tomorrow because God is *within you.*

....

....

....

....

....

....

....

....

....

I can't quite grasp, God, what it means to have You live within me, but I believe
that no matter how I feel physically and emotionally, You are holding me,
helping me. Thank You for the opportunity to begin again each new day.

Day 6
A Good Word

Anxiety weighs down the heart, but a kind word cheers it up.
PROVERBS 12:25 NIV

We all get discouraged. It's just one of those normal human emotions. We get excited about the hopes we have for the future, not realizing that we've confused "hope" with "goal-setting." Then, when we realize there are obstacles in our way and it's going to take longer than we expected to reach our goals, our hearts grow heavy and our shoulders slump. Even people who are spiritually mature and emotionally strong go through times when they feel like giving up. "Why bother trying?" we ask ourselves. "If I'm just going to fail, why not give up?"

Times like that, we need an encouraging word from someone. And when we notice that someone else is going through a discouraging time, we can be the ones who offer encouragement and hope. Sometimes it only takes something very little—an understanding smile, a hug, or a listening ear—to renew someone's energy and help them get back on track.

What "good word" can you share with someone today?

....

....

....

....

....

....

....

*Show me, Lord, if someone in my life needs encouragement today.
And when I've gotten off track and feel like giving up, please
send someone to lift my heart and restore my hope in You.*

Pray for Absolutely Everything

Jesus was matter-of-fact: "Embrace this God-life. Really embrace it, and nothing will be too much for you. This mountain, for instance: Just say, 'Go jump in the lake'—no shuffling or hemming and hawing—and it's as good as done. That's why I urge you to pray for absolutely everything, ranging from small to large. Include everything as you embrace this God-life, and you'll get God's everything. And when you assume the posture of prayer, remember that it's not all asking."

MARK 11:22–25 MSG

You have the freedom to pray for whatever it is you want or need. When you talk to God, He invites you to ask without fear and without insecurity. You can talk to Him about anything and everything. Big or small, God wants you to bring it to the throne room and share it with heartfelt authenticity. Are you worried you won't find the right job? Do you struggle with how to best raise your kids in today's culture? Are you lonely and unsure if you'll ever find companionship? Are the signs of aging beginning to take their toll on your self-worth? Do you need to defeat the Goliath in front of you? No matter what's going on in your life, God wants in on it. And it's His power through your prayers that brings hope and healing to a defeated soul in need of restoration.

Father in heaven, You know the reasons my heart is heavy.
I need Your help. In the name of Jesus I pray. Amen.

Day 8
Resting in Belief

And we know that in all things God works for the good of those
who love him, who have been called according to his purpose.
ROMANS 8:28 NIV

When catastrophe strikes your life, you're faced with the reality of how fragile life truly is. There you are, going along like normal, when without warning something painful happens. Your sense of safety and security is shattered. Life suddenly feels shaky, as though danger is lurking around every corner. Your belief in God's love and power is shaken.

But regardless of your feelings in this moment, God's love remains strong and creative. The same amazing energy that made the world is still at work in every event of your life. What seems like catastrophe will be swept up by His power and made into something that—somehow, in some way—will bless you and those you love. You can rest in that belief!

....

....

....

....

....

....

....

....

Lord, when life seems frightening and unpredictable, remind me that
Your creative power is always at work, weaving together even life's
challenges and disasters into a fabric of blessing. As my belief in
You is tested by life's painful events, may it grow sturdier.

The Hope of Eternal Life

God's gift is real life, eternal life, delivered by Jesus, our Master.
ROMANS 6:23 MSG

Our culture doesn't like to talk about death. Instead, we pretend that death is not an ordinary part of life. We act as though it is the ultimate tragedy—and yet it will happen to us all. A century ago, by age fifty, most people had lost many loved ones: their parents, aunts and uncles, brothers and sisters, children, and possibly a spouse. Until relatively recently, normal life contained a succession of funerals. People were born in the home and they died at home, making death both visible and familiar. These days, death is often hidden away in hospitals or nursing homes.

But no matter how we may hide it, the fear of death still haunts us. We may perceive it as a shadow lying over our lives, something terrible that robs us of hope. After all, if death awaits us all, what hope do we have? But Jesus brought a new perspective to our world. Because He conquered death on the cross, we no longer need to fear the end of this life. Instead, we can face even death with hope's joyful anticipation, trusting that God has even more wonderful things in store for us in eternity.

....

....

....

....

....

....

....

Thank You, Jesus, for the hope I have in You.

Day 10
Hope That Triumphs over Fear

"Lord, there is no one like you to help the powerless against the mighty. Help us, Lord our God, for we rely on you, and in your name we have come against this vast army. Lord, you are our God; do not let mere mortals prevail against you."

2 Chronicles 14:11 niv

When we read verses like this from the Old Testament, we can claim the spiritual symbolism found in these stories of long-ago armies. We too sometimes feel powerless as we confront a situation that seems too vast for us to overcome. The Living One, the God of Israel, is also our God, and He will give us the hope and strength we need to triumph over fear. Historical author Amy Harmon once referenced this in her writings. She wrote about her belief that faith and hope have victory over fear and that choosing to find beauty in hope is an act of rebellion against fear itself.

....

....

....

....

....

....

....

....

....

Living one, You know how scared and powerless I feel sometimes.
Thank You that hope in You gives me the strength I need to keep
taking tiny steps forward. I know that step by step You are
leading me into the abundant life You have planned for me.

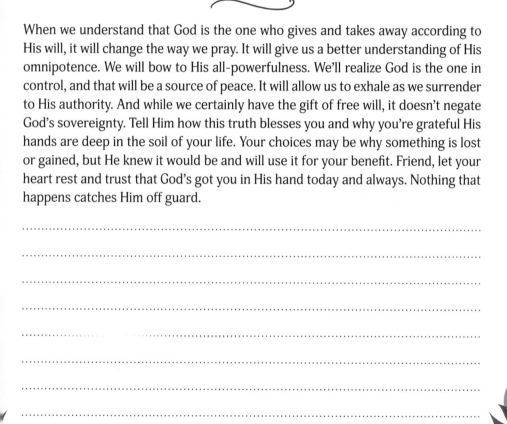

Day 11
He Gives and Takes Away

I was naked, with nothing, when I came from my mother's womb;
and naked, with nothing, I will return to the earth. The Eternal has given,
and He has taken away. May the name of the Eternal One be blessed.

JOB 1:21 VOICE

When we understand that God is the one who gives and takes away according to His will, it will change the way we pray. It will give us a better understanding of His omnipotence. We will bow to His all-powerfulness. We'll realize God is the one in control, and that will be a source of peace. It will allow us to exhale as we surrender to His authority. And while we certainly have the gift of free will, it doesn't negate God's sovereignty. Tell Him how this truth blesses you and why you're grateful His hands are deep in the soil of your life. Your choices may be why something is lost or gained, but He knew it would be and will use it for your benefit. Friend, let your heart rest and trust that God's got you in His hand today and always. Nothing that happens catches Him off guard.

....

....

....

....

....

....

....

....

Father in heaven, it blesses me to know You're in control. I'm grateful You
have the insight to give and take away so I benefit in the end. Help
me keep the right perspective on this powerful truth, even when
I may not understand. In the name of Jesus I pray. Amen.

Day 12
Thank You!

*Give thanks for everything to God the Father
in the name of our Lord Jesus Christ.*
Ephesians 5:20 nlt

"Don't forget to say thank you," we teach our children (just as our parents taught us). Too often, though, we're just being polite; we may say the words without truly feeling grateful. When Paul wrote his letter to the Ephesians, telling them to be sure to give God thanks for everything, he wasn't talking about rules of courtesy. God doesn't need us to be polite to Him. It's our own hearts that need to experience gratitude.

Gratitude shifts our attention away from ourselves and our narrow, self-centered concerns. As it affirms all that God has already done, it opens the door to hope for the future.

....

....

....

....

....

....

....

....

....

Thank You, God, for the many gifts You have given me—a home,
family, friendships, work, the beauty of the world, and so many other
things. Thank You for everything. May my gratitude for all You
have done in the past and are doing in the present give me
joyful confidence in what You will do in the future.

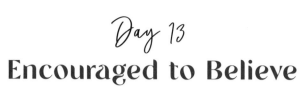

Day 13
Encouraged to Believe

If your gift is to encourage others, be encouraging.
ROMANS 12:8 NLT

The word *encourage* comes from Latin words that mean to put heart or inner strength into someone. The Greek word originally used in this verse adds even deeper meaning, for it implies that the person who encourages others comes close by their side; she becomes so intimate with another person that her words are trustworthy, motivating, and inspiring. Others can believe in what she says. When God encourages you, His own heart reaches out to you, and His strength becomes yours. He enters into an intimate relationship with you so that you can have confidence in His promises. Then, as you rely on this blessing, you will be empowered to reach out to those around you, lending them your own heart and strength as you inspire them to believe in the power of God's love.

....

....

....

....

....

....

....

....

....

Thank You, God, for all the ways You encourage me and
bless me. May I, in turn, encourage and bless others.

God's Words at Home in You

*"But if you make yourselves at home with me and my words are at home in you,
you can be sure that whatever you ask will be listened to and acted upon."*

JOHN 15:7 MSG

The Lord wants to bless your requests, but only when they are aligned with His will for your life. Sometimes people read today's verse and are frustrated when the new and improved husband isn't who walks in the door after work. They're angry when money isn't pouring in like they requested. When the cancer doesn't immediately disappear, some walk away from their faith. They give up on God when pregnancy continues to elude them. But when the Lord's words *are at home* in us, it means we understand that His will and ways are above ours. In faith, we choose to trust them over our own. And when we do, our language in prayer will reflect it. We will share our hopes and dreams with God, ending with "But Your will be done, not mine." God hears your heart and has plans already in place to bless you with the right answer at the right time.

Father in heaven, let my requests reflect my faith in You. Let Your
words be on my tongue so I am asking in alignment with Your will
and ways. I know You hear my prayers, and I want Your blessings
to abound in my life. In the name of Jesus I pray, Amen.

Day 15
New Life

"Look, I am making everything new!"
REVELATION 21:5 NLT

Do you ever feel as though you are old and worn out? Even if you're not actually old in years, you're so tired you feel as though you can barely keep going. When you are looking around at your life, everything looks stale, nothing is fresh; you're in a rut, and you don't know how to get out. And right about then, when you're at your weakest, disaster strikes. It could be a financial crisis, a health situation, or a family problem. Whatever it is, it just doesn't seem fair that you have to go through this now!

Sometimes, though, a crisis is exactly what we need to get us out of our ruts. It's not that God is punishing us for feeling tired and hopeless; it's more like He's giving us a wake-up call so we can see what He is trying to do in our lives.

"Look," says Jesus, "I'm making everything new!"

....
....
....
....
....
....
....
....
....

Lord Jesus, show me the green new growth You are bringing from my
life's scorched soil. May my hope in You never falter, even when I'm
weary, even when I'm in the midst of a crisis. I trust Your love.

Day 16
In the Dark Valleys

Even though I walk through the darkest valley, I will fear no evil,
*for you are with me. . .and I will dwell in the house of the L*ORD *forever.*
PSALM 23:4, 6 NIV

Our culture often equates darkness with evil. However, God is with us just as much in the dark as He is in the light. This means that both the dark and light experiences in our lives have things to teach us about hope. Remember, just as a baby grows in the darkness of a womb so do seeds sprout and grow in the darkness of the soil. Transformation and new life rise from the darkness into the light.

But it's hard to remember all that when we're walking through a "dark valley." God is still with us, but we may not be able to sense His presence. We feel as though we're all alone, stumbling blindly through the dark. In times like that, here are some suggestions for finding glimmers of light even in the darkest valleys:

- Be grateful and express your gratitude in prayer or creative work.
- Be patient with yourself.
- Reach out to help others.
- Seek support from friends and family or a pastor or therapist. Don't be embarrassed to ask for help.
- Spend more time reading scripture and in prayer.

....

....

....

....

....

....

Amid my life's darkest valleys, good shepherd,
may I still see stars of hope.

Day 17
Roots

"This year you. . .will take root below and bear fruit above."
2 KINGS 19:29–30 NIV

Our lives go through many seasons. We have fruitful seasons when it's easy to be filled with hope, as well as dry, bleak seasons when we feel as though we are withering inside and out. Changes come relentlessly into our lives: children grow up, beloved older folks leave this earth, and our bodies feel their limitations as they age, while in the larger world, trends come and go, political parties rise and fall, and triumph and despair seem to take turns having the upper hand. So, amid so much change and turmoil, how do we keep our hope steady?

Our roots in God and His love are the source of our hope, and they never change—no matter how many times the world spins around. What's more, the psalmist assures us that even while our inner root systems are spreading out in God's love, down in the soil where no one can see them, our outer lives are also growing tall and strong, bearing fruit that benefits everyone.

*Heavenly gardener, nourish my roots with Your love so that
I am filled with the hope that will one day bear fruit.*

Day 18
Eternity

*"There is plenty of room for you in my Father's home. If that weren't so,
would I have told you that I'm on my way to get a room ready for you?"*

JOHN 14:2 MSG

People have various beliefs about eternity, but the fact is none of us *knows* exactly what lies on the other side of death's dark door. But you can be certain of this: death will take you home. Jesus promised that. He wouldn't have said it just to make us feel better, because Jesus wasn't one for telling polite lies. He didn't make up stories just to make Himself look better either. So you can rest in the belief that right now He is getting your home in heaven ready for you, filling it with everything you need to be happy. When the day comes that you enter the door, you'll find it's exactly right for you, the place you've always longed for.

....

....

....

....

....

....

....

....

....

....

Jesus, I'm grateful for Your promises. When death seems like
something dark and frightening, help me believe that it
is a homegoing. Thank You that You are creating the
perfect home for me for all eternity.

The Open Door of Forgiveness

"If you enter your place of worship and, about to make an offering, you suddenly remember a grudge a friend has against you, abandon your offering, leave immediately, go to this friend and make things right. Then and only then, come back and work things out with God."

MATTHEW 5:23–24 MSG

Sometimes we believe we can excuse our own failure to forgive. "But they hurt me too badly," we say. Or "They never said they were sorry." Or even, "I did try to express my apologies, but they refused to accept them." Jesus, however, didn't include an exception clause in His instructions. He made clear that we cannot be close to God when our relationship with another person has broken.

Forgiveness is to start fresh, to have a new beginning. This new beginning doesn't apply only to the other person. It also applies to us. A lack of forgiveness is like a closed door that prevents us from going any further, but forgiveness opens the door to new possibilities. In other words, when we forgive, we bring new hope into the world.

....

....

....

....

....

....

....

You know, Jesus, how hard it is for me to forgive certain people in my life. Teach me the words to say and the actions to take that will lead to a restoration of this relationship. Show me how to set healthy boundaries even as I forgive. Bring new hope to this relationship, I pray.

Day 20

When You Live by His Plan

*Don't you know that He who pursues and explores the human heart
intimately knows the Spirit's mind because He pleads to God for His saints
to align their lives with the will of God? We are confident that God is able
to orchestrate everything to work toward something good and beautiful
when we love Him and accept His invitation to live according to His plan.*

ROMANS 8:27–28 VOICE

When you ask the Lord to help you live out His plan for your life, heaven celebrates. A woman who embraces her purpose brings delight to the heart of God. And it's that sweet surrender and deliberate decision to align her life with His that unlocks blessing, the blessing of God's intention to orchestrate everything in her life for good. Good or bad, He will bring beauty. That means the Lord can recycle a divorce, a bankruptcy, a season of sinning, a moral failure, or a bad parenting moment. You're not disqualified. So pray for the courage to walk out God's will for your life with purpose and passion. Ask Him for the confidence to live according to His plan.

....

....

....

....

....

....

....

....

*Father in heaven, I can't do this without Your help because my humanity
limits me. I accept Your invitation. So, now, please bless me with
the supernatural strength and wisdom to follow Your path
every chance I get. In the name of Jesus I pray. Amen.*

Day 21
Thoughts

For as he thinketh in his heart, so is he.
PROVERBS 23:7 KJV

Psychologists tell us that our thoughts shape our lives. Neurological research even suggests that our brains connect negative thoughts and memories in ways that can rob us of hope. For example, a colleague at work says a cross word to you, and you find yourself feeling discouraged about your weight. You get in a fight with your husband, and for the rest of the day, you worry you might lose your job. These things have nothing to do with each other in reality, but if we allow ourselves to dwell on our hurt feelings and discouragement, they can create a spreading network of brain-cell connections that are easily triggered every time we encounter even the most trivial negative situation.

Fortunately, the opposite is also true: we can create positive thought habits that will empower our faith and fill our lives with hope. Beginning every day with gratitude fills our hearts and minds with the hope that we find in Jesus.

....

....

....

....

....

....

....

....

You know, Lord, how easily I can sink into negative thoughts. I need Your help
with this. Teach me to replace those self-defeating, hope-robbing thoughts
by meditating on You and the many blessings You have given me.

Day 22
Hope in Possibility

Is any thing too hard for the LORD?
GENESIS 18:14 KJV

One night God told Abraham to look up at the night sky and count the stars. There were too many stars for Abraham to count, of course—and then God made an amazing promise to Abraham: "You'll have as many children as there are stars in the sky" (see Genesis 15:5). At the time, though, Abraham and his wife, Sarah, had no children at all, and they were old—much too old to have children. Abraham might have thought he had dreamed his conversation with God. He would have found it hard to believe in a promise so enormous. And yet, God kept His word. When Abraham was one hundred and Sarah was ninety, their son, Isaac, was born. Isaac was the beginning of the Jewish people, who now are more than can be counted.

When you look at the challenging situations in your own life, remember what God did for Abraham and Sarah. Believe in what God can do. The word *impossible* is not in His vocabulary!

....

....

....

....

....

....

....

....

God of Abraham and Sarah, help me believe in
Your power of possibility at work in my life.

Day 23
Rooted in Christ's Love

Despite all these things, overwhelming victory is ours through Christ, who loved us.
ROMANS 8:37 NLT

Hope doesn't mean we look at the world through rose-tinted glasses, nor does it require that we live in a state of denial about the cold, hard facts of life. Instead, we know that Christ's love is the foundation of all our love.

As we learn to believe more fully in that love, trusting that Christ will never leave us or let us down, our sense of hope grows. Love is what gives us the ultimate victory. In fact, love transforms reality. In a vision, John heard Jesus say, "Look, I am making everything new!" (Revelation 21:5 NLT), and that is what He is continually doing—transforming our cold, hard realities into joyful, blooming gardens with His love.

Jesus, come into my life and make it new. May I
send deep roots down into Your love so that I can
grow a hope that never stops blossoming.

Day 24

Jesus Pleads for You

Who has the authority to condemn? Jesus the Anointed who died,
but more importantly, conquered death when He was raised to sit
at the right hand of God where He pleads on our behalf.

ROMANS 8:34 VOICE

It's hard to imagine that the God who created the heavens and the earth and everything in them cares enough about us to sit and listen to His Son plead on our behalf. At the same time, it's unbelievable that the Jesus who stepped out of heaven to become man, died on a cross for our sins, and rose again after three days is the same Jesus who leans over to the Father and mentions our names. But scripture says it's true. We know the Bible is complete truth, so we accept the blessing with a full heart. You have been part of the plan from the very beginning. Your name has been on God's heart forever, even before He formed something out of nothing. He watched you take shape in your mother's womb. And just because Jesus pleads on your behalf doesn't mean the Lord isn't delighted to hear you share what's on your heart too.

....

....

....

....

....

....

....

Father in heaven, to know the Godhead cares so much for me speaks
volumes of value into my heart. Thanks for all the ways I see Your love
for me. It doesn't go unnoticed. In the name of Jesus I pray. Amen.

Day 25
The Truth

"If you stick with this, living out what I tell you, you are my disciples for sure.
Then you will experience for yourselves the truth, and the truth will free you."
J OHN 8:32 MSG

The truth Jesus is talking about in this verse is the message He came to bring us from the Father: God loves us, and through Jesus we have hope, not only for this life but for all eternity. This is a truth that can't just be believed with our minds alone; it needs to be experienced, "lived out," as Jesus says here.

In other words, experiencing truth for ourselves is often a process. Although some of us (the apostle Paul, for example) have amazing, instantaneous conversions, even then we need time for the truth to do its work in us. Paul, after his experience on the road to Damascus, did not instantly begin his ministry for Christ; he needed to spend three years in the desert, allowing the truth of Christ to do its work, experiencing it for himself. This is a process we must each go through, discovering for ourselves that Christ's truth has set us free to hope, even amid the world's darkness and despair.

Jesus, I want to follow You. May Your truth set me free to hope.

Paths of Hope

Speak encouraging words to one another. Build up hope so you'll all be together in this, no one left out, no one left behind.

1 THESSALONIANS 5:11 MSG

The word *encouragement* comes from older words that meant "put courage into." When we speak encouraging words, as Paul recommends in this verse, we are doing more than simply complimenting someone or building up their self-esteem. Our words have the power to strengthen each other's hearts, to give each other hope.

Parakaleó, which is the Greek word used in this verse, had to do with walking close beside someone, teaching them, strengthening them, and comforting them. A similar word—*Paraclete*—refers to the Holy Spirit, who is the divine encourager, our companion, and helper throughout life. Here, once again, we see that God uses relationships to build His kingdom. As we make our spiritual journeys, mutually helping each other, together we create paths of hope for others to also see and follow.

....

....

....

....

....

....

....

....

....

Jesus, may I encourage others, even as they encourage me.
May we work together to build paths of hope that lead
us—and others too—into Your presence.

Day 27
The Answer Is Always Prayer

Are any in your community suffering? They should pray. Are any celebrating? They should sing praises to God. Are any sick? They should call the elders of your church and ask them to pray. They will gather around and anoint them with oil in the name of the Lord.
JAMES 5:13–14 VOICE

No matter what is happening in your life right now—good or not so good—the answer is always to pray. If you're struggling in your marriage, pray for wisdom. If you are grieving the loss of a parent, pray for comfort. If your child passed a math test after studying hard, share a prayer of thanksgiving. If your seasonal allergies are getting the best of you, pray for immediate relief. If your annual review came with an unexpected raise in salary, praise God for provision. If you're feeling alone, pray for community. Prayer is hands down the most powerful weapon in your arsenal because it provides you direct access and constant communication with God. And from it flows abundant blessings as the Lord responds, meeting every need and celebrating each victory.

Father in heaven, what a relief to know I can pray to You no matter what comes my way, be it happy celebrations or hard challenges. Thank You for making a way to talk directly to You. It's my privilege to share my ups and downs with You. In the name of Jesus I pray. Amen.

Day 28
Loving Friends

Dear friends, let us love one another, for love comes from God.
1 JOHN 4:7 NIV

Left to yourself, you might spend much of your time spinning around in your own head, buzzing in tiny circles like flies caught inside a window. Friendship throws open a window and lets those dizzy flies escape. It lets in the fresh air of new beliefs, perspectives, and ideas. Through your friends, you catch a glimpse of God's love. He speaks to you through their voices. He loves you with their smiles and kindness and understanding. Each time they send you a text or email, each time you sit and talk with them over a cup of tea or coffee, and each time you get the giggles over something one of your friends said to you, you are experiencing God's love. And as you return that love to your friends, you allow God to use you to bless them too. Your belief in God will begin to widen and extend itself into the world.

Thank You, heavenly friend, for the human friends You have
brought into my life. I am so grateful for the love You
show me through the friendship we share. Through them
I am learning to believe in You more deeply.

Day 29
The Past

GOD guards you from every evil, he guards your very life.
. . . He guards you now, he guards you always.
PSALM 121:7-8 MSG

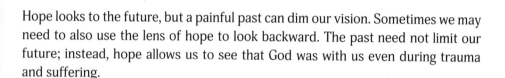

Hope looks to the future, but a painful past can dim our vision. Sometimes we may need to also use the lens of hope to look backward. The past need not limit our future; instead, hope allows us to see that God was with us even during trauma and suffering.

This perspective may not come easily or quickly, though. We may need the help of wise counselors and friends. Then, as we also open our hearts to the working of the Holy Spirit, we can begin to see something we may not have realized at the time: God was there with us, even in the midst of the pain, guarding us then just as He guards us now and as He will guard us in the future, all the days of our lives and into eternity.

....

....

....

....

....

....

....

....

....

Lord, help me see my past in new ways, through the
eyes of hope. I know You are always with me.

Day 30

Even in Hard Times

*That person is like a tree planted by streams of water, which
yields its fruit in season and whose leaf does not wither.*

P SALM 1:3 NIV

We all have seasons in our lives when external circumstances are so bleak and cold it seems as though we're living through an Ice Age winter. And yet, we may discover that external conditions don't need to rob us of our inner hope.

The biblical world had different seasonal patterns than many of us experience in North America. In Bible times, people worried about times of drought rather than the bitter cold of winter. So, when the psalmist wrote that we can be like trees bearing fruit with lush green leaves despite the dry seasons that so easily stunt or destroy plant life, he was expressing that hope can keep our hearts alive and growing even during external hardship. The psalmist also knew the source of that hope. In the previous verse, he indicated that it comes from focusing our thoughts on God's teaching and instruction. When we make a habit of reading God's Word, hope flourishes in our hearts. As we ponder scripture, hope grows sturdy and tall, able to resist even the most frigid winter and the deadliest drought.

....

....

....

....

....

....

....

*Teach me, Lord. Water my thoughts with Your Word and shine the light
of Your Spirit on my heart so that my hope thrives and bears fruit*

Day 31
God's Foolishness

For the foolishness of God is wiser than human wisdom.
1 CORINTHIANS 1:25 NIV

In a world where the rich and the powerful often seem to be the winners, while ordinary people suffer oppression and hardship, some of the Bible's promises can seem silly. "Blessed are those who mourn," for example, and "Blessed are those who are persecuted" (Matthew 5:4,10 NIV) don't seem to make much sense. It's almost as though Jesus was looking at a completely different reality from the ordinary world we inhabit. And it's true; He *was* seeing a different world, the world of His Father's realm. But Jesus wasn't hallucinating; He wasn't crazy or delusional. He knew the kingdom of heaven was *real*. And as foolish as God's promises may sound in *this* world, in the Father's kingdom, they make perfect sense.

Anne Frank once wrote that she clung to her hopes and ideals even in the most difficult of times. If Anne Frank could cling to hope, even while she and her family were hiding from the Nazis, living in desperate fear for their lives, we can too. For it is the eyes of hope that see past this world's grim reality. It is the eyes of hope that perceive the light and splendor of God's realm.

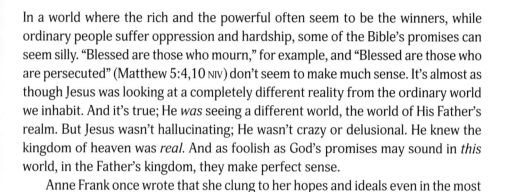

When Your promises seem foolish and impossible,
Lord God, remind me to look through the lens Your
hope gives me. Teach me to see Your kingdom.

Day 32
The Future

There is surely a future hope for you, and your hope will not be cut off.
PROVERBS 23:18 NIV

Mindfulness experts tell us to live in the present moment rather than the past or the future. While there is wisdom in this advice (for God does meet us in the right-now), we also cannot deny that we are creatures who live in time. Scientists aren't exactly sure what time is or if it exists outside the human mind or even if it moves at the same speed in all parts of the universe, while the Bible tells us that in eternity, time will be no more. It's nearly impossible to wrap our minds around those ideas! For now, with our limited understanding, we must settle for our concept of past, present, and future.

Hope is the Bible's word for thinking about the future. Hope believes God has good things in store for us in the days and years ahead. Hope also calls us to cooperate with God *now*, doing whatever it takes to make that future possible. Without hope, our lives would be fearful and miserable. But thanks to Jesus, we have infinite hope!

Thank You, Jesus, for bringing Your hope into our world. May I anticipate my future with You with joyful confidence, resting on Your promises.

Day 33

The New Creation

*Therefore, if anyone is in Christ, the new creation
has come: The old has gone, the new is here!*
2 Corinthians 5:17 niv

Following Christ doesn't mean we won't still experience the world's pain and suffering. At the same time, however, we don't have to wait until after we die to experience the new creation of Christ. It's almost like we live in two dimensions at once—and Christ's dimension is in the process of transforming the world's dimension. It is our hope and faith in Christ's transformative power that is what changes the world around us and creates a ripple effect. This is a perspective we need to grasp and experience for ourselves. When we do, we will have hope on even the most difficult days.

Christ Jesus, help me to remember today that I live in Your dimension
as well as the world's dimension. Give me glimpses of Your new
creation so that I can live my life with greater hope.

Earthly Tents

For we know that when this earthly tent we live in is taken down (that is,
when we die and leave this earthly body), we will have a house in heaven,
an eternal body made for us by God himself and not by human hands.

2 CORINTHIANS 5:1 NLT

Scripture says that God has "set eternity in the human heart" (Ecclesiastes 3:11 NIV). We have a sense that life goes on beyond what exists on this earth—and yet we cannot see what lies beyond death's door. So we tend to hold on tightly to this life, believing that since this is all we know, this must be all there is. The writers of the New Testament often remind us, however, that life is temporary. In this verse, Paul compares our bodies to tents: dwelling places that are not intended to be permanent. A tent is a useful thing to have on a journey; it can provide shelter, keeping out the wind and rain. But few people would want to settle down and live in a tent for the rest of their lives. If we can hold on to the thought that our bodies are like tents, intended only to be temporary shelters during this life's journey, perhaps we'll find it easier to believe in the eternal bodies God will give us.

....

....

....

....

....

....

....

....

God, I believe my life will not end when my body dies. When the time
comes for me to take down the "tent" that has sheltered me through
this life, may I be ready for the new life You have ready for me.

This World Is Not Your Home

*"Everything comes from you; all we're doing is giving back what we've been
given from your generous hand. As far as you're concerned, we're homeless,
shiftless wanderers like our ancestors, our lives mere shadows. . . . I know,
dear God, that you care nothing for the surface—you want us, our true selves."*

1 CHRONICLES 29:14–15, 17 MSG

We look at the world around us, and part of us believes it's the only home we'll
ever know. We've never experienced any other reality, and we can't imagine the far
greater world God inhabits. But we are not meant to feel too at home in this world.
Maybe that's why time is designed to keep us from lingering too long in one place;
it keeps taking away the things we depended on, pushing us constantly into new
experiences. Each new relationship, each new circumstance, each new role in life—all
come from the God who sees the eternal meaning that lies beneath the surface of
our lives. We are not meant to cling too tightly to anything in this life. Instead, God
calls us to be always moving on, making our way to our forever home in heaven.

Heavenly Father, I believe all my "possessions" are expressions of Your
love. Remind me to let go of them when the time comes, filled with
the joyful anticipation of what You'll do next in my life.

Owning Up to Sin

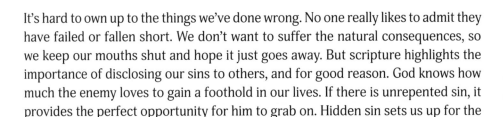

So own up to your sins to one another and pray for one another. In the end, you may be healed. Your prayers are powerful when they are rooted in a righteous life.

JAMES 5:16 VOICE

It's hard to own up to the things we've done wrong. No one really likes to admit they have failed or fallen short. We don't want to suffer the natural consequences, so we keep our mouths shut and hope it just goes away. But scripture highlights the importance of disclosing our sins to others, and for good reason. God knows how much the enemy loves to gain a foothold in our lives. If there is unrepented sin, it provides the perfect opportunity for him to grab on. Hidden sin sets us up for the enemy's trap. But when we reveal, we can heal.

Pray that God gives you courage to come clean, but also invite Him to search your heart for unseen sin. Ask for the blessing of healing and restoration. It may be hard to confess when you've messed up, but nothing compares to the freedom it brings.

Father in heaven, I confess I've fallen short of Your glory so many times.
Thank You for the blessing of Jesus and His finished work on the
cross. Please give me the courage to admit my failures to those
I've offended. I don't want to give the enemy any foothold
in my life. In the name of Jesus I pray. Amen.

Day 37
Belief Instead of Worry

Instead of worrying, pray. Let petitions and praises shape your worries into prayers, letting God know your concerns. Before you know it, a sense of God's wholeness, everything coming together for good, will come and settle you down. It's wonderful what happens when Christ displaces worry at the center of your life.

PHILIPPIANS 4:6–7 MSG

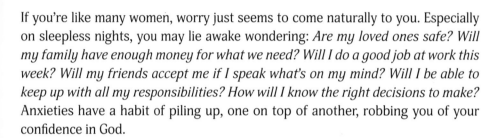

If you're like many women, worry just seems to come naturally to you. Especially on sleepless nights, you may lie awake wondering: *Are my loved ones safe? Will my family have enough money for what we need? Will I do a good job at work this week? Will my friends accept me if I speak what's on my mind? Will I be able to keep up with all my responsibilities? How will I know the right decisions to make?* Anxieties have a habit of piling up, one on top of another, robbing you of your confidence in God.

But anxiety can be transformed into prayer. Each time you find yourself fretting over something, turn that specific set of circumstances over to God. As you make this practice a habit, the presence of Christ will take the place of anxiety in your mind. Your belief in God will grow deeper roots.

....

....

....

....

....

....

....

Thank You, Jesus, that I can give all my worries to You.
I believe You are strong enough to handle them all.

Day 38
Your Wildest Dreams

*"No eye has seen, no ear has heard, and no mind has imagined
what God has prepared for those who love him."*
1 Corinthians 2:9 nit

Hope is a perspective that believes in the potential of future possibilities. That said, hope does not limit itself to what the human mind can imagine. Hope is open-ended; it doesn't insist on a certain outcome. It leaves room for surprise and wonder, as God creates things more beautiful and wonderful than anything we've ever imagined, let alone experienced.

Hope looks outward at the world around us, but it also looks inward, at our own hearts. God has amazing things in store for us. At first, we may feel uncomfortable accepting that God sees so much potential in us. It may seem arrogant or egotistical to lay claim to God's immense plans for our lives. However, this sort of hope is humble, surrendered to God. It accepts that we may never be famous or important in the world's eyes, yet we have an essential role to play in the kingdom of heaven. And we can't even imagine all that will be!

Although you can't know the future shape your life will take, God knows. It may be beyond your wildest dreams!

....

....

....

....

....

....

I am so grateful, God, for all You have in store for me. Keep my mind
open, ready to accept what You are creating in my heart and in
my life. When You see me trying to set limits on Your work in
me, remind me to surrender myself more fully to You

Day 33
Following Jesus

Then Jesus said to his disciples, "If any of you wants to be my follower, you must give up your own way, take up your cross, and follow me."
MATTHEW 16:24 NLT

The words that Jesus spoke to His disciples some two thousand years ago still apply to us today. They give us a step-by-step formula for following Christ. The first step: give up your own way. The second step: take up your cross. Third step: follow Christ.

Notice that the first step asks that we change our attitudes, shifting our focus away from the egocentric, me-first perspective most of us have always had. The second step asks us to take action, doing whatever we need to do to live out our surrender to Christ in our daily behaviors. Each person's "cross" will be something different because we all have individual circumstances with the responsibilities and opportunities that go along with them. Ultimately, though, the "cross" is always a visible, tangible expression of selfless love and hope. And finally, now that we have the right attitude and behaviors, we leave the rest up to Christ; all we must do is follow Him.

....
....
....
....
....
....
....

Christ, I want to be Your follower. I give my life to You. Show me
how to express my commitment to You in my daily life, in acts
of love that give hope to others. Remind me to keep my
eyes on You so that I can follow in Your footsteps.

Day 40
Lift Me Up, Lord

My troubles turned out all for the best—they forced me to learn from your textbook.
PSALM 119:71 MSG

The Bible reminds us that troubles don't need to be hopeless dead ends that lead only to discouragement and failure. Instead, they are learning opportunities. They may even be occasions when our hope in God grows stronger and brighter.

As you look at your life today, what is wounding you? What troubles you? Do you see how God is using these painful situations to lift you up? If not, can you bring these circumstances to God, surrendering them to Him to do what He wills? Our God is an amazing Creator, and as He works in the painful areas of our lives, His ingenuity will take us by surprise again and again. As we allow God to have His way, even seemingly hopeless problems can eventually reveal to us the wonder of God's love.

....

....

....

....

....

....

....

....

....

Creator God, You know the things that are troubling me today. I place each
of these situations, including all the individuals involved, into Your
hands. Work Your miracles, I pray. Create hope where I can see
only pain. Use these wounds to teach me and lift me up.

Day 41
Steps to Forgiveness

Be kind and compassionate to one another, forgiving each other, just as in Christ God forgave you.
 EPHESIANS 4:32 NIV

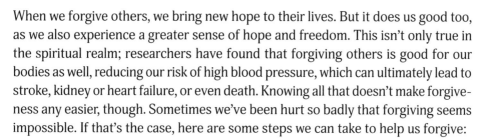

When we forgive others, we bring new hope to their lives. But it does us good too, as we also experience a greater sense of hope and freedom. This isn't only true in the spiritual realm; researchers have found that forgiving others is good for our bodies as well, reducing our risk of high blood pressure, which can ultimately lead to stroke, kidney or heart failure, or even death. Knowing all that doesn't make forgiveness any easier, though. Sometimes we've been hurt so badly that forgiving seems impossible. If that's the case, here are some steps we can take to help us forgive:

- Face the painful memories. Psychologists say that avoiding the hurt can allow it to become like a piece of petrified wood that never changes. Facing those old memories doesn't mean wallowing in them; it means allowing ourselves to process them and work through them with the Holy Spirit's help (and sometimes with the help of a friend, counselor, or pastor).
- Put yourself in the shoes of the person who hurt you. Try to understand what motivated their actions, and allow yourself to feel their pain.
- Make a *choice* to forgive. Don't wait to feel forgiveness emotionally. Ask for God's help, regardless of your emotions.

Holy Spirit, help me to forgive, bringing new
hope to others' lives as well as my own.

Day 42
Nature's Message

The heavens proclaim the glory of God. The skies display his craftsmanship.
Day after day they continue to speak; night after night they make him known.
They speak without a sound or word; their voice is never heard. Yet their
message has gone throughout the earth, and their words to all the world.

PSALM 19:1–4 NLT

The ancient Christian Celts referred to nature as the "second Book of God." They meant that while scripture is God's Word, nature too reveals God's glory—and we do well to take the time to "read" what God is saying in the natural world. We can find powerful spiritual messages there, both in nature's beauty and in its rhythms and cycles.

Again and again, the Bible speaks of God revealing Himself to people when they are "in the wilderness"—in other words, outside in the natural world. Jesus Himself sought out times alone in nature, retreating to those quiet secluded places to restore His connection with His Father (see Matthew 14:13, John 6:15, Mark 1:35, Luke 6:12).

So, the next time you're feeling discouraged with life, try spending some time alone outside. The world of nature can renew your hope in God.

Creator God, may I never be too busy to notice You speaking to
me through a sunrise, birdsong, or the wind in the trees.

Day 43

God Will Answer Your Prayer

While Jeremiah was still locked up in jail, a second Message from G od was given to him: "This is G od's Message, the God who made earth, made it livable and lasting, known everywhere as G od: 'Call to me and I will answer you. I'll tell you marvelous and wondrous things that you could never figure out on your own.'"

JEREMIAH 33:1-3 MSG

This passage of scripture confirms that when you pray to the Lord, He will answer. Every time you ask for strength, it will be given. When you need wisdom or discernment to figure out your next step, God will open your eyes. If you need hope, He will hear your cry for it and deliver. Are you needing peace during a difficult season? God will fill your heart with it. Looking for motivation or endurance to stay present in a relationship? He will bless your request. The Lord knows there are things we cannot figure out ourselves. By design, we need our Creator's help to live and love well. And that is why He promises to listen for our voices and bless us with an answer every time we call out to Him.

....

....

....

....

....

....

....

Father in heaven, I know You can hear me talking to You right now. And I know You're already working on the perfect answer to meet my needs. Thank You for that! In the name of Jesus I pray. Amen.

Day 44
God's Economy

When we get together, I want to encourage you in your faith, but I also want to be encouraged by yours.
ROMANS 1:12 NLT

In the world's economy, we pay a price in order to receive something we want; we have to give up something in order to get something. That belief is deeply ingrained in our minds, but that's not the way things work in God's economy, where giving and receiving are linked together. We need to be open to this divine belief, allowing it to replace what the world tells us. As we accept that whatever good we do for another person is good for us as well, we will begin to understand that we are truly connected to each other, like parts of a body. What blesses me will ultimately bless you—and vice versa. When we encourage others, we too will be encouraged.

Teach me, God of love, not to be stingy with my resources (whether they are physical or emotional). May I share the blessings You give me with others, believing that as I encourage others, I too will be encouraged.

Day 45
Storytelling

Don't copy the behavior and customs of this world, but let God transform you into a new person by changing the way you think.

ROMANS 12:2 NLT

Our world has a whole range of stories it tells. Some stories emphasize courage and kindness and hope, while others focus on hatred, suffering, and despair. Some describe life as vicious and cruel, while others portray the endless possibilities of love. The narrative we believe often depends on our perspective. Even when we accept that the same facts are true, we may reach entirely different conclusions. And each story we tell about the world shapes the way we think and act.

In his letter to the Romans, the apostle Paul reminds us not to copy the world's behaviors. This means we also must be careful about accepting the world's stories. When we hold a particular narrative up to the Bible, do they match up? The Bible is always a story of hope. There's no unhappy ending, no ultimate tragedy, no cliffhanger that leaves us wondering what comes next. The story God tells has plenty of ups and downs, but it ends with love and the eternal companionship of His presence.

Storytelling God, remind me not to soak in the stories the world tells me, for I know they often end with hopelessness and despair. Thank You that Your Word always gives me a reason to hope.

Day 46
Celebrate!

Seize life! Eat bread with gusto, drink wine with a robust heart. Oh yes—
God takes pleasure in your pleasure! Dress festively every morning.
Don't skimp on colors and scarves. Relish life with the spouse you love
each and every day of your precarious life. Each day is God's gift.
ECCLESIASTES 9:7–9 MSG

These verses may not seem consistent with the God many of us were raised to believe in. But the truth is, God longs to make us happy. He knows that happiness is good for us. Mentally and physically, we function better when we are happy. Discouragement and sadness sap our strength. It's like trying to work while carrying a heavy load on our backs: it slows us down and makes everything harder.

Believe that God wants you to be strong and happy! He doesn't want you to creep through life with a pinched look of disapproval and displeasure on your face. No, He wants you to celebrate! He wants everyone to see the joy you feel as you receive His daily blessings.

....
....
....
....
....
....
....
....

God of joy, I believe You take pleasure in my pleasure. Give me a joyful
heart. Remind me to rejoice in the life You've given me. Make my
happiness contagious so that those around me catch Your joy.

Blessing Instead of Cursing

"Bless those who curse you. Pray for those who hurt you."
LUKE 6:28 NLT

When we believe in God's promise, He blesses us; but we are also called to bless others. God wants to show the world His love through us. We accomplish this through prayer—and through our commitment to make God's love real in the world around us. We offer blessings to others when we greet a scowl with a smile, when we refuse to respond to angry words, and when we offer understanding to those who are angry and hurt. Belief in God is never meant to be a private, personal thing. It is always intended to spread out from us, touching everyone we interact with.

Lord of love, I believe You have called me to be Your coworker, sharing in Your work of spreading love to all people. Help me bless instead of curse; may I make a practice of offering loving prayer for those who have hurt me. Please use me in whatever way You can to show Your love.

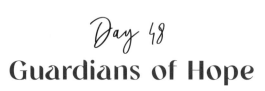

Day 48
Guardians of Hope

"For where two or three gather in my name, there am I with them."
Matthew 18:20 NIV

When Jesus spoke these words, He wasn't saying that there's something magical about a gathering of just any two or three people. Instead, He was referring to the way His Spirit lives in relationships. Friendship can help us in our spiritual lives. And yet in friendship, as in other parts of our spiritual lives, we often "fall asleep": we take a friend for granted, forgetting that friendship, like all relationships, requires steady effort and faithfulness. We need to not only share ourselves in friendship but also be willing to listen deeply. These are the kinds of conversations that allow us to bring to light truths that each of us alone would never have discovered. They encourage us and strengthen us and bring new hope into our lives. This is the perspective on friendship that makes room for the presence of Christ.

....

....

....

....

....

....

....

....

Thank You for my friends, Jesus. May I remember that friendship is about giving as much as it is receiving. May my friends and I experience Your presence in our relationship, and may we guard each other's hope.

Day 49
A Bold Call to Prayer

Pray always. Pray in the Spirit. Pray about everything in every way you
know how! And keeping all this in mind, pray on behalf of God's people.
Keep on praying feverishly, and be on the lookout until evil has been stayed.
EPHESIANS 6:18 VOICE

This is a bold call to pray. Paul isn't mincing words or veiling the truth. He is direct in reminding us to pray feverishly all the time about everything in every way we know to pray. Why is he so insistent? Maybe it's because he knows that the struggles we will face in this life are not against flesh and blood. You may be able to see the Goliaths in front of you, but they are compelled by darkness. These forces stay hidden, tucked away and unseen, but they are wreaking havoc on your relationships. They are trying to destroy the children around you. They are actively working to mess you up. Don't let this scare you, friend! Instead, take Paul's command to stand firm in God's power through prayer and watch as He blesses you. The enemy's threat against us is real, but when we pray, we unleash the Lord's might.

....
....
....
....
....
....
....
....

Father in heaven, thank You for the reminder of how powerful my prayers
are against the forces of evil. They may be plotting against me every
day, but when I pray, Your blessings will abound. You will equip
me for every battle. In the name of Jesus I pray. Amen.

The Willingness to Learn

Intelligent people are always ready to learn. Their ears are open for knowledge.
PROVERBS 18:15 NLT

In one way or another, most of us rely on our intelligence to get us through life. If we're truly intelligent, though, we'll remember that no matter how many years it's been since we were in school, we're never done learning. We need to be open to new ideas, willing to give up old, stale ways of thinking; we need to be willing to accept the possibility that we could be wrong. And then, as we open our ears to new information, we'll find we learn more and more about God and His plan for us. His blessings will be revealed to us in ways we never expected. Our belief in Him will spread out into new dimensions.

....

....

....

....

....

....

....

....

....

....

Show me, Lord, where I've closed my mind to new ideas. Help me be willing to be surprised by something new. Give me the courage to let go of old ways of looking at things so You can reveal to me more about Your kingdom. Remind me that my belief is in You and Your love, rather than in my own opinions.

Day 51
What's Your Name?

"I will make you into a great nation. I will bless you and make you famous, and you will be a blessing to others."
GENESIS 12:2 NLT

When the Bible speaks of making your name great, it doesn't mean you will become famous, your name recognized around the world. In the Bible, a name had to do with a person's inner identity, the very essence of who that individual was. So, what this verse is saying to you is this: "I will enlarge your identity. I will make your inner being strong." And notice that this greatness has nothing to do with ego or pride; we become bigger people not so we become arrogant and fat-headed but so that we can bless others.

And in God's economy (unlike the world's, which is often based on "me first"), as we bless others, we too are blessed. As we encourage others, our hearts grow more hopeful. The more we help others become who they are meant to be, the more we too claim our unique identities in God.

....

....

....

....

....

....

....

....

*Thank You, Lord, for giving me a name, for calling me
to a larger identity. May Your call fill me with hope,
and may I share that hope with everyone I encounter.*

Day 52
Belief in God's Love

"This is how much God loved the world: He gave his Son, his one and only Son. And this is why: so that no one need be destroyed; by believing in him, anyone can have a whole and lasting life. God didn't go to all the trouble of sending his Son merely to point an accusing finger, telling the world how bad it was. He came to help, to put the world right again."

JOHN 3:16–17 MSG

There are different kinds of belief. For example, we believe the sun will rise in the morning; we expect it to happen because it has always happened. We no longer believe in Santa Claus, as we may have once done when we were children; we acknowledge that Santa is probably not a real person. Meanwhile, we may believe in God as an intellectual concept, something distant and almost irrelevant that we take for granted. But the word that's used in John 3:16 is a different sort of belief. The Greek word implies an active involvement rather than a mere matter of the mind. It speaks to the idea that we need to commit our entire lives to belief; we entrust ourselves to God, and in doing so, we participate in making our belief stronger. The Greek word also indicates that God is part of this process. He works within us to increase our belief in Him. According to *Thayer's Greek Lexicon*, the word *belief* as it's used in these verses from the Gospel of John "signif[ies] that one's faith is preserved, strengthened, increased, raised to the level which it ought to reach."

....

....

....

....

....

Jesus, I believe You came to bring me the fullness of life,
the complete potential for which I was created. Thank You
that You are always working in me to increase my belief in You.

Day 53
Buried with Christ

We were therefore buried with him through baptism into death
in order that, just as Christ was raised from the dead through
the glory of the Father, we too may live a new life.

ROMANS 6:4 NIV

When we think of the temptation to sin, we often have in mind the attraction we may feel to illicit and harmful behaviors. If we're not experiencing those attractions ourselves or we find it easy to resist them, then we may think we don't have a problem with temptation. We assume that when it comes to the enemy of our souls, we're doing just fine. Yet, we would do well to remember that temptation can be more subtle. The enemy can tempt us into believing we aren't doing enough for the kingdom, which causes us to quit trying. Or we are tempted to think we are doing just fine on our own and don't need Jesus' redemptive work on the cross.

Christ doesn't want His followers to plod through life with sad and tired faces. That old way of living needs to die and be buried so that Christ can make our lives fresh and new and filled with resurrection hope.

....

....

....

....

....

....

....

....

Christ, I thank You that my old life of discouragement
and despair is buried with You. Help me today to
experience the hope and energy of Your new life.

Day 54

Praying for Those in Government

The first thing I want you to do is pray. Pray every way you know how,
for everyone you know. Pray especially for rulers and their governments
to rule well so we can be quietly about our business of living simply, in
humble contemplation. This is the way our Savior God wants us to live.

1 TIMOTHY 2:1–3 MSG

When we look at the state of our nation and world, it doesn't take much to realize how badly we need to be praying. Regardless of what political party you belong to, which state you reside in, or how you feel about politics in general, the Bible is clear in its call to pray for our rulers and governments. That needs to be important to us. When we pray, it will be a step forward for our leaders to use their authority wisely. It will help them do their job with our best interests in mind. And the blessing will be that we can go simply and humbly about our lives. Just as it is for anyone, anywhere, there are ample opportunities for those in government to fall prey to temptation. Money and power are big lures, especially when a person feels invincible. So be a woman who prays for those in authority regularly. God will hear it and act.

....

....

....

....

....

....

....

....

Father in heaven, I may not be very political, but I understand
the importance of praying for our leaders' integrity. Bless us
all by their choices. In the name of Jesus I pray. Amen.

Day 55
A Passion for Possibility

Jesus looked at them intently and said, "Humanly speaking,
it is impossible. But with God everything is possible."
MATTHEW 19:26 NLT

We often look at a problem and see no possible solution. An adult child's life has gotten so turned around that we don't know how to help him. Illnesses burden our family again and again, and we don't know why. An elderly parent needs help but refuses to accept it. A work situation is full of conflict and stress, but we can't afford to quit our jobs. And then there's the larger world beyond our own lives, a world where wars and pandemics and violence loom large. Problems like these can seem impossible to untangle.

But hope sees past the impossible. Hope believes in unseen possibilities. It knows that all things are possible with God. He's an expert at untangling even the most complicated problems.

....

....

....

....

....

....

....

....

God of hope, give me a passion for possibility. Teach me that
even when I can see no solution to a problem, You are even
then patiently combing out the tangles in my life.

Day 56
The Hope of Following Jesus

Jesus looked around and saw them following. "What do you want?"
he asked them. They replied, "Rabbi" (which means "Teacher"),
"where are you staying?" "Come and see," he said.

JOHN 1:38–39 NLT

Before you can get anywhere in life, you first must make the decision to not stay where you are. This, in effect, is the message Jesus is giving to us in this story from the Gospel of John. If we want to experience the hope and joy of following Christ, then we have to decide to leave our old lives behind—and then we must follow Jesus and see where He lives.

Yet again, Jesus tells us that following Him is something that requires action on our part. Yes, the first step is to make up our minds that we want to leave our old lives so that we can experience the new life of Jesus, but then we must put that decision into action. We have to change the way we live. This means seeing for ourselves where and how Jesus lives and then imitating His pattern of life, making it real in our ordinary daily lives. Then, as we see Jesus more and more clearly, our lives will be made new, filled up with love, joy, and hope.

Jesus, I want to follow You. I want to see
where and how You live. I want to be like You.

Day 57
Let There Be Light!

God said, "Light up the darkness!" and our lives filled up with light as we saw and understood God in the face of Christ, all bright and beautiful.
2 Corinthians 4:6 MSG

In the book of Genesis, God says, "Let there be light!"—and light shines out. Today, in our own lives, God continues to call forth light. That light is not for our lives alone; like the moon that reflects sunlight into the night, we too are called to shine with the hope of Christ. We do this by:

- Demonstrating to others that while we still see the darkness, we don't let it keep us from also seeing the hope and beauty in the world.
- Reaching out to help others in tangible and practical ways.
- Shielding our light from the world's tempests so that it burns steadily, even during the times when we are experiencing troubles of our own.
- Allowing people to see that it's Christ living in us who allows us to remain hopeful, even in the face of challenges and hardship.
- Doing whatever we can to help others see more clearly.

None of these mean we shove our beliefs down other people's throats. We simply live out the love and light that Jesus has given to us.

....

....

....

....

....

....

Let me shine, dear Jesus, with Your light.

Asking Others to Pray for You

*And please pray for me. Pray that truth will be with me before I even
open my mouth. Ask the Spirit to guide me while I boldly defend the
mystery that is the good news—for which I am an ambassador in chains—
so pray that I can bravely pronounce the truth, as I should do.*

Ephesian 6:19–20 VOICE

Paul never shied away from asking those around him to pray on his behalf. He even told them the words to share with the Lord. Paul got very detailed about what he needed from God, trusting people to specifically ask for it. Why? Because he understood the power and blessing it would bring forth. Let his example be what compels you to ask for prayer from family and friends too.

As the Church, part of our burden and privilege is to storm the gates of heaven with petitions and prayers of thanksgiving both for ourselves and those around us. It's the most powerful weapon we have in our spiritual-warfare arsenal. So don't shy away from sharing your requests. Let others know what your needs are. Tell them what to ask God to do for you. And feel the blessing that comes from a praying community of believers.

....

....

....

....

....

....

....

....

Father in heaven, hear the prayers of my warriors!
In the name of Jesus I pray. Amen.

Stop Worrying!

"Can any one of you by worrying add a single hour to your life?"
MATTHEW 6:27 NIV

On the nights when you have insomnia, you probably don't lie awake filled with hope and happiness. If you're like most of us, you're much more likely to lie there consumed with worries. Instead of imagining all the wonderful things God has in store for you, you may find yourself picturing scenarios of doom and gloom. *What if such-and-such happens?,* you think, and then you build a complete picture of just how terrible that "such-and-such" might turn out to be. Your worries shake your belief in God's love and providence. But the Bible says that prayer can be your antidote to worry. When you turn your worrying into prayer, your belief in God's love will grow stronger. As you fix your thoughts on God and His promises, your outlook will change. You'll anticipate blessing instead of disaster. You'll be confident that God has everything under control.

....

....

....

....

....

....

....

....

God, when worries threaten to overwhelm me, remind me to turn my
thoughts away from images of disaster and instead anticipate all
the blessings You have in store for me. May worry no longer
have the power to shake my belief in Your providence.

Day 60
The Path of Life

You make known to me the path of life; you will fill me with joy in your presence, with eternal pleasures at your right hand.

Psalm 16:11 niv

The Bible speaks often about life as a "path" (at least fifty-six times!). The word implies that God sees our lives as journeys, with a beginning point that leads through a progression of vistas and experiences. He doesn't expect us to commit our lives to Christ and then instantly become mature saints; He knows it's a journey.

Few paths are smooth and straight; most of them have rough spots, steep stretches, and twisty curves that keep us from seeing what lies ahead. Sometimes we wonder if we're going anywhere at all. We suspect we might even be going backward. But that's not how God sees things. Even when we feel we are lost, hopeless, and stumbling in the dark, He continues to lead. Look forward with hope. God knows where you're going even when you don't.

....

....

....

....

....

....

....

....

Beloved path-finder, thank You that You are leading me along paths that lead to You. When the way seems dark and full of wrong turns, remind me that You know exactly where I'm going.

Day 61
Love Made Visible

*No one has ever seen God. But if we love each other, God lives
in us, and his love is brought to full expression in us.*

1 JOHN 4:12 NLT

It's hard to believe in something we can't see. As human beings, most of us (those of us who have vision) depend on our eyes to understand the world around us. We've all heard the saying "A picture is worth a thousand words," and the advertising world knows the power of visual images to influence our minds. So do teachers. Abstract concepts are difficult to wrap our minds around—but if we can see something, it instantly becomes easier for us to grasp.

As John points out, none of us have seen God. We know we are told to walk by faith rather than sight (see 2 Corinthians 5:7)—and yet all of us, at one time or another, have had a hard time believing in God's love. In a world where terrible things happen, we can't help but wonder if God's love is real. Is *God* even real? It's hard to believe in something we've never seen. We need a visual image to convince us.

Jesus was that visual image. And now, as His followers, we are called to carry out His work on earth. He wants us each to be a visible embodiment of God's love. Through us, love becomes visible. We are the expression of God to the world.

....

....

....

....

....

....

....

Jesus, I believe You are the embodiment of God's love.
May I too carry divine love out into the world.

Believe in Equality!

The rich and the poor shake hands as equals—God made them both!
Proverbs 22:2 MSG

Americans often affirm their belief in the equality of all people—but at the same time, not all Americans have the same access to privileges and opportunities. This reality rises to the surface again and again throughout our nation's history. Sometimes we try to push it down, out of sight. We'd much rather believe that the American dream is possible for everyone; it's painful to face the fact that some people experience danger, hardship, and unequal opportunities simply because of the color of their skin or some other difference that sets them apart from "the rest of us."

Long before today's struggle for social justice, the Bible reminded human beings that God is the Creator of us all, whether we are rich, poor, dark, light, quick, or slow. We all have the right to breathe, think, act, speak, and live freely.

Lord of justice, I believe You created us all to be equals. Make me aware
of any prejudice within me that interferes with Your all-inclusive
love. Use me as a force for justice in my community.

Day 63

The Anchor of Your Soul

*We who have fled to take hold of the hope set before us may be greatly
encouraged. We have this hope as an anchor for the soul, firm and secure.*
HEBREWS 6:18–19 NIV

Hoping for things that can't possibly happen is not the sort of hope the Bible
describes. We don't hope that we'll grow bird's wings. . .or that our husbands will
wake up one day as perfect individuals who will never frustrate us again. . .or that
our children will never get muddy or tear their clothes. The Bible's hope accepts
the real world with all its limitations. It doesn't have anything to do with fantasy or
make-believe. Instead, it's something real and solid. Although we don't know the
exact shape and size of everything God has in store for us, we are anchored in the
confidence that our futures are steady in His love.

....

....

....

....

....

....

....

....

....

....

....

Lord, may my hope in You hold my life steady even in the
wildest storms. Be my anchor, I pray, today and every day.

Every Word from My Mouth

*Pray diligently. Stay alert, with your eyes wide open in gratitude. Don't
forget to pray for us, that God will open doors for telling the mystery
of Christ, even while I'm locked up in this jail. Pray that every time I
open my mouth I'll be able to make Christ plain as day to them.*

Colossians 4:2–4 msg

What a prayer request by Paul! His hope was that his words would always point to the Lord. Even while in jail—a stressful and uncomfortable situation—he wanted to choose his words carefully. Isn't this also our hope? . . . When we are frustrated with the doctor's care of our aging parents, we can make sure our words are meaningful. When a coworker is mean for sport, we can think before we respond. Every maddening interaction with our loved ones can be met with a thoughtful response.

Our job on planet Earth is for our words and actions to point others to God in heaven. We are the ones to share the gospel with the world. So ask the Lord to bless you with the wherewithal to live and love with intention. The expectation isn't that you are perfect but that you are purposeful.

....

....

....

....

....

....

....

....

*Father in heaven, let my life make a difference for the kingdom so
I can bless You. I want my words to be a neon sign that points
others to You. In the name of Jesus I pray, Amen.*

Day 65
The Windows of Hope

Open my eyes so I can see what you show me of your miracle-wonders.
PSALM 119:18 MSG

Troubles can keep our attention focused on our pain and suffering. Misery can make us blind to spiritual reality. Stumbling along with our heads down and our shoulders hunched, we forget to look up and see the sky. Our lives become small, dismal, and dark, and our depression grows ever deeper.

We don't have to live like that. Instead, we can turn to the one who loves us and ask Him to open our spiritual eyes. We can choose to hope when everything seems hopeless, and we can cling to God even when we can't feel His presence. And then, one day, something surprising happens: we catch a glimpse of the spiritual realm that's all around us. We look at our lives from a new perspective, and we see God's hand at work. We realize creation is filled with miracles and wonder.

....

....

....

....

....

....

....

....

....

Lord, open windows of hope so that I can look
out and see Your miracles and wonders.

Day 66
Belief and Laughter

A cheerful heart is good medicine.
PROVERBS 17:22 NLT

Belief in God and a good sense of humor may seem to have very little to do with one another. As Christians, we may be convinced we need to maintain a sober and serious outlook to be consistent with our religious beliefs. Besides, keeping a sense of humor and a positive perspective isn't easy, not when life is so filled with stress and responsibilities and challenges.

The long-ago author of Proverbs 17:22, however, knew the same truth that modern-day psychologists know: laughter relaxes tension. It allows your body and soul to take a deep, healing breath. It lifts you up when circumstances are pulling you down. It gives you a clearer vision so that you can once more believe in God's grace and love.

God of joy, thank You for the gift of laughter. When life seems
overwhelming, give me reasons to smile. Remind me that a healthy
belief in You will never get in the way of my sense of humor.
Help me to even be willing to laugh at myself.

Day 67

When You're Tired and Weak

The moment we get tired in the waiting,
God's Spirit is right alongside helping us along.
ROMANS 8:26 MSG

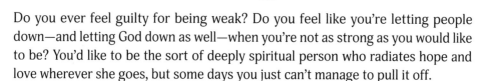

Do you ever feel guilty for being weak? Do you feel like you're letting people down—and letting God down as well—when you're not as strong as you would like to be? You'd like to be the sort of deeply spiritual person who radiates hope and love wherever she goes, but some days you just can't manage to pull it off.

We all have those days. Days when we're tired of waiting for God's blessings to be revealed, tired of hoping when the world seems so dark. . .and just plain *tired*. That's okay. God never said He expects us to be strong all the time. When our hope falters and love seems to be in short supply, that's the moment the Spirit is right there close beside us, hands stretched out to help.

John Calvin, the sixteenth-century Protestant Reformer, once reminded his readers to ask God to build their hope, to awaken and strengthen it. It turns out our weakness is an opportunity to cling even tighter to God!

....

....

....

....

....

....

....

Spirit of God, You know my weakness. You know how easily I get discouraged
when things don't work out quickly the way I'd like. When I get tired
of waiting for Your perfect timing, I ask that You increase my
hope. Wake it up, hold it steady, lift it, and make it strong.

Planting in Tears

Those who plant in tears will harvest with shouts of joy.
PSALM 126:5 NLT

Notice that this verse doesn't say, "Those who retreat from life and sit sobbing endlessly in their bedrooms will harvest with joyful shouts." Instead, the psalmist acknowledges that sometimes we can't help crying—but at the same time, we are called to continue the active work of carrying Christ's hope out into the world. This is the sort of hope psychologists tell us makes optimism so practical; optimism is not mere wishful thinking but rather the belief that our actions can make a difference in the world.

Your tears may water the seeds you plant today, but remember the joyful harvest that lies ahead.

....
....
....
....
....
....
....
....
....

Give me the strength I need, faithful Lord, to continue planting
seeds of hope even when my own heart is breaking, and I'll
trust that one day those tiny, nearly invisible seeds will
grow into hearty, fruit-bearing plants of love.

Day 69

Being Gracious in Your Speech

Use your heads as you live and work among outsiders. Don't miss a trick. Make the most of every opportunity. Be gracious in your speech. The goal is to bring out the best in others in a conversation, not put them down, not cut them out.

COLOSSIANS 4:5–6 MSG

We all need God to help us with our tongues. Sometimes words escape before we can tuck them away, and they get us into trouble. If we're not careful, we'll say what we feel in the moment, which isn't how we really feel. It's hard to be gracious when your child spills orange juice on your computer keyboard. It's hard to be gracious when your friend cancels plans that you rearranged your schedule for. Being kind with your words is difficult when someone cuts you off in traffic. So this call to be gracious with our speech takes God's help.

Pray every day for the Lord to slow your speech so you can measure your words first. Ask Him to bless you with the desire to speak blessings and not curses over people. And choose not to put people down in conversation but, instead, to be intentional to bring out the best in them. Let God help you.

....

....

....

....

....

....

....

Father in heaven, I really need Your help to use my words for good
and not evil. Bless me with gracious words no matter how I
feel in that moment. In the name of Jesus I pray. Amen.

Day 70
Love

"I have loved you with an everlasting love; I have drawn you with unfailing kindness."
JEREMIAH 31:3 NIV

God loves you. There is no better reason to be filled with hope than that! The Creator of the universe loves you, now and forever. He reaches out to you each moment, His hands open to draw you closer to Him and to bless you. A love so big, so deep and wide, is hard to comprehend—especially when we realize it's not merely a generic kind of love for humanity. No, God loves *you,* the one and only individual you are, with all your quirks. He has a unique relationship with *you.*

We may never be able to grasp the fullness of God's love, even in eternity, but we can allow it to fill our lives and hearts with hope. To do that, we must stop focusing our attention on all the empty things we use to try to take the place of God's love. Let's refocus our attention on Him!

....
....
....
....
....
....
....
....
....

Spirit of Love, I want to turn toward You today. I want to live out of Your love. I want to share Your good news with everyone I see. May Your love and hope shine from my face and ring out in my words. Thank You for loving me.

Day 71
Hope for New Paths

"The LORD will guide you continually, giving you water when you are dry and restoring your strength. You will be like a well-watered garden, like an ever-flowing spring."
ISAIAH 58:11 NLT

Hope is not a passive emotion that allows us to curl up and be lazy. Instead, hope pushes us forward onto unexplored paths. It is the voice of God guiding us into new adventures, encouraging us to try new things, grow, and be bold in ways we've never been before.

This doesn't mean there won't be times when we need to take some time out to rest; constant busyness is not what hope in God looks like either. Instead, this hope that is ours relies on God's daily and ongoing sustenance. When our hearts are dry, He waters them. When we feel weak, He restores our strength. When we lack courage, His love nourishes our fearful hearts.

Hope isn't about ego or do-it-yourself self-reliance. We cannot manufacture it on our own or take off running with it in a solo race. Hope depends on God because our hope springs from God.

....

....

....

....

....

....

....

Guide me, Lord. Give me courage and water my heart with Your love. Give me the energy I need to venture out of my ruts into Your plan for my life. All my hope is in You.

Day 72
The Power of Story

He told them a parable, urging them to keep praying and never grow discouraged.
Luke 18:1 voice

Jesus told countless parables during His public ministry as a way of communicating His message. Storytelling is a very engaging and effective method to get a point across because it's relatable. When you tell a story, rather than spout off a ton of facts, to-dos, or rules, it allows listeners to personalize your words. We may not talk in parables much today, but we have our testimonies to share instead. Our stories are powerful ways to reveal God's power in our lives.

Sometimes just hearing that someone else has made it through a difficult time is all we need to cling tighter to the Lord. So pray for the Lord to open doors for you to talk about His role in your life. Ask Him for opportunities to bless others through encouragement. And through your story, urge people to keep their eyes on God as they continue praying for hope and help.

....
....
....
....
....
....
....

Father in heaven, thank You for the example of how significant a story
can be to those who are battling discouragement and hopelessness.
You've done so much for me, so I'm asking for open doors to share
that with others. Bless me with ample chances to boast in
Your omnipotence and to help build their confidence of
faith in You. In the name of Jesus I pray. Amen.

Day 73
God's Victory

When you go to war against your enemies and see horses and chariots and an army greater than yours, do not be afraid of them, because the Lord your God, who brought you up out of Egypt, will be with you. When you are about to go into battle, the priest shall come forward and address the army. He shall say: "Hear, Israel: Today you are going into battle against your enemies. Do not be fainthearted or afraid; do not panic or be terrified by them. For the Lord your God is the one who goes with you to fight for you against your enemies to give you victory."

DEUTERONOMY 20:1–4 NIV

Okay, so you're not likely to ever face an army of horses and chariots—but these verses can still speak to your life. After all, some days the challenges in your life can seem as terrifying and dangerous as any battlefield. So the next time that happens, follow the advice given here in Deuteronomy. First, like the Israelites who recalled how God had helped them escape from Egypt, you too can remember all that God has done for you in the past. Next, remind yourself that God is the one who will fight your battles through you and around you. You can believe in His victory over whatever challenges you face today.

....

....

....

....

....

....

....

God of power, thank You that You are ready and
willing to fight the battles in my life. May my belief
in Your strength make room for Your victories.

Day 74
The Song of Hope

"Very truly I tell you, unless a kernel of wheat falls to the ground and dies, it remains only a single seed. But if it dies, it produces many seeds."

JOHN 12:24 NIV

Do you ever feel as though some aspect of your life has fallen into the mud and died? Maybe it's a treasured role that gave you a sense of identity (whether in your family or your profession). It might be your appearance or your physical strength. Time brings changes to our lives that aren't always welcome; in fact, they feel like losses. They may even feel like little deaths. We may wonder who we are if we can no longer do the same work or if we no longer look the same. We worry we may no longer be as important or as loved. We feel discouraged, and our sense of hope may wither.

But in the Gospel of John, Jesus reminds us that something always must die for new life to be born—and both death and birth happen down in the dirt.

So, the next time you sorrow over the changes in your life—listen to hear the song of hope!

....

....

....

....

....

....

....

....

Jesus, when I feel as though a piece of me has fallen to
the ground and died, remind me to wait and see what
new thing You are bringing to life in its place.

Day 75
You Are Never Forgotten!

But Zion said, "The LORD has forsaken me, the Lord has forgotten me."
ISAIAH 49:14 NIV

Sometimes God allows a long period of pain and hardship in our lives. When that happens, we often start to doubt the promises we once believed. We think God has given up on us. Or maybe we believe that God doesn't actually care about us—or that He doesn't even exist. With our human limitations, we find ways like these to explain to ourselves why God hasn't rescued us from the trouble we're experiencing. If we don't sense He is present with us and we don't see Him saving us from our dilemma, we assume He has forgotten us and given up on us.

But look at what God says in reply when we feel this way: "Can a mother forget the baby at her breast and have no compassion on the child she has borne? Though she may forget, I will not forget you!" (Isaiah 49:15 NIV). What a strong picture of God's love! Then in the next verse, He emphasizes His love even further: "See, I have written your name on the palms of my hands" (see Isaiah 49:16 NLT).

God will never forget you. He will never give up on you. He will never stop loving you.

....
....
....
....
....
....
....

Thank You, Lord, that Your love for me is even greater than
a mother's for her baby. Despite the difficult circumstances
of my life, I believe You will never stop loving me.

Day 76
Give It to God!

Commit to the LORD whatever you do, and he will establish your plans.
PROVERBS 16:3 NIV

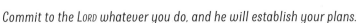

Sometimes when we look at our lives, we see more failure than successes, more endings than beginnings. No one likes to fail; not only are we disappointed that something we cared about did not come to fruition, but also our self-esteem may suffer. We may feel embarrassed or ashamed, especially if we think the failure was our fault. Proverbs' wise author, however, encourages us to look at our lives from a different perspective. When we commit all our efforts to God, then we can let go of our need for success.

We do not know what plan God has for our lives and the world. What to us looks like failure may be the beginning of something new and wonderful. When we depend on God to uphold everything we do, we leave the results in His hands.

....

....

....

....

....

....

....

....

....

All-knowing God, give me hope when failure
and endings are weighing heavily on my mind.
Remind me to give each situation to You.

When You Look with Intention

"For I know the plans I have for you," says the Eternal, "plans for peace, not evil, to give you a future and hope—never forget that. At that time, you will call out for Me, and I will hear. You will pray, and I will listen. You will look for Me intently, and you will find Me."
JEREMIAH 29:11–13 VOICE

God wants us to look for Him with intention and pursue a relationship, investing time and our hearts in it. When we do, God will bless us with His presence. Too often we put Him far down on the list. Our busy days come first, and spending time with God falls in priority. But it's important we remember that He has plans for us. He thought your life through, knowing the impact you'd bring the world. God never planned for evil to invade your life, but peace instead. And when trouble comes, you can cry out to Him through prayer any time of the day or night. What's more, He says that when you seek Him intently, you will know He is right there with you. When you put God first and foremost, you'll see blessings as God powerfully works in your circumstances.

Father in heaven, what a blessing to know You have plans for my life that are for good. Help me seek You with passion so I can walk them out. In the name of Jesus I pray. Amen.

Day 78
Listening

Fools think their own way is right, but the wise listen to others.
Proverbs 12:15 nlt

The Bible is full of practical advice, and the book of Proverbs in particular teaches us ways to get along better with others. The ability to listen is one of the building blocks of any good relationship, whether it's with our spouses, with friends, with our children, or with God. All too often, though, we may find ourselves focusing on the constant chatter inside our own heads rather than listening for what God wants us to hear. Or we may become so focused on our own beliefs that we forget to look outside ourselves to the living world around us. When we cut through our preoccupation with our own thoughts, however, we can begin to listen on a deeper level—and we will gain deeper insights about life, others, ourselves, and God. Our belief in God will be expressed in practical outcomes in the world around us.

....
....
....
....
....
....
....
....
....
....

Thank You, Lord, that You always listen to me. Teach me
to be a better listener to You and to those around me.
I believe You have much You want me to learn.

Day 79
Intentional Love

Love never gives up.
1 CORINTHIANS 13:4 MSG

Love may be a spiritual quality, but it's also as down-to-earth and practical as the air we breathe. As human beings, we need love. In fact, psychologists tell us that love is as necessary to our lives as oxygen. The more connected we are to others and to God, the healthier we will be—both physically and emotionally—and the less connected we are, the more we are at risk.

Our culture tends to believe that love "just happens." If we don't feel enough love in our lives, then we're just not one of the lucky people. If we find it hard to love someone, oh well—that's just the way it is. But love doesn't work that way. Psychologist Erich Fromm called love "an act of will." To feel love in our lives, we have to make up our minds to act in loving ways. We have to put our love for God and others into practice.

....
....
....
....
....
....
....
....

Jesus, I believe You call me to practice Your selfless love
in all my interactions. Teach me to follow in Your
footsteps, no matter how unloving I may feel.

Day 80
Companionship in Suffering

Singing cheerful songs to a person with a heavy heart is like taking someone's coat in cold weather or pouring vinegar in a wound.
PROVERBS 25:20 NLT

We live in a culture that believes we really *ought* to be happy all the time—and if we're not, there's something wrong. This can make it hard for us to interact with those who are suffering. Perhaps you've noticed how uncomfortable it feels to be with someone who just lost her job or is going through a painful divorce. You want to help change her mood. . .but in doing so, you may be denying her right to her painful feelings. Rather than trying to cheer her up, often the most helpful thing you can do is empathize. Listen. Affirm her pain. Verify her disappointment. Your understanding allows her to accept herself so she can eventually move on, in her own time. God ultimately will use this time in her life to bless her. In the meantime, it's not your job to "fix" her or her life. Your job is to simply be her companion through the pain, allowing God's love to use you in whatever way He sees fit.

....
....
....
....
....
....
....
....

God, when my friends are in pain, I believe only You can heal
their hearts. May I be a good friend who is willing to listen,
a faithful companion who will share their suffering.

Don't Believe in Idols!

"Stay away from idols! I am the one who answers your prayers and cares for you. I am like a tree that is always green; all your fruit comes from me."

HOSEA 14:8 NLT

Of course I don't believe in idols, you may say to yourself as you read this verse. You don't pray to a wooden statue or bow down and worship a creature carved from stone. But when the Bible talks about idols, it's referring to anything that takes God's rightful place in your life. The Hebrew word used in this verse refers to something that's been fabricated (something that doesn't occur naturally), but it also has to do with something that ultimately causes pain and suffering. This is the exact opposite of the true God's nature. God always listens and cares. He is like a tree growing at the center of your life, constantly offering you shelter and nourishment. Each one of life's daily blessings is a fruit from this tree; each time you grow and learn, that too is divine fruit ripening in your life.

....

....

....

....

....

....

....

....

Tree of life, I believe only You can satisfy my longings for growth, refreshment, shelter, and nourishment. Show me if I have allowed any idols to encroach on Your place in my life.

Day 82
Shepherd of Hope

"GOD, the Master, says: From now on, I myself am the shepherd. I'm going looking for them. As shepherds go after their flocks when they get scattered, I'm going after my sheep. I'll rescue them from all the places they've been scattered to in the storms."

EZEKIEL 34:11–12 MSG

Sometimes we're hard on ourselves. We realize we've taken a wrong turn in life, and we beat ourselves up for it. We can get so mired in guilt and regret that we feel stuck, hopeless, and unable to see a way forward. But the Bible assures us that God is with us even in our mistakes.

If you've lost your way and found yourself somewhere dark and scary, God doesn't want to punish you, nor does He want you to punish yourself. Instead, He's waiting patiently to rescue you and lead you back onto His path of abundant life. You can never get to the point where your life is hopeless. Even now, no matter what you've done or how impossible circumstances seem, the good shepherd is looking for ways to guide you home.

....
....
....
....
....
....
....
....

Shepherd of my soul, thank You that I can never go beyond
Your love. I know that when my life seems hopeless, You are
still my hope. Thank You that You always rescue me.

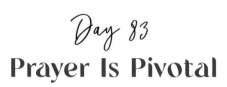

Day 83
Prayer Is Pivotal

And [if] My people (who are known by My name) humbly pray, follow My commandments, and abandon any actions or thoughts that might lead to further sinning, then I shall hear their prayers from My house in heaven, I shall forgive their sins, and I shall save their land from the disasters.

2 Chronicles 7:14 voice

If you've ever doubted the power of prayer, let this verse restore your confidence. When we pray with humility—when we pray understanding that God is God and we are not—our requests will be heard. When we are intentional to live according to His will for our lives by turning away from the sin that entangles us, our choices change things. Every single one of us will face disasters in this life. From broken marriages to the loss of those we love to financial ruin, tragedy is a part of life. But in His infinite love, God made a way for us to be saved and healed. And prayer is pivotal. It's central to God moving on our behalf. It is key to hope and healing. Never underestimate what a Father will do for a child who asks in earnest. Talk to the Lord about what matters to your heart, and be blessed.

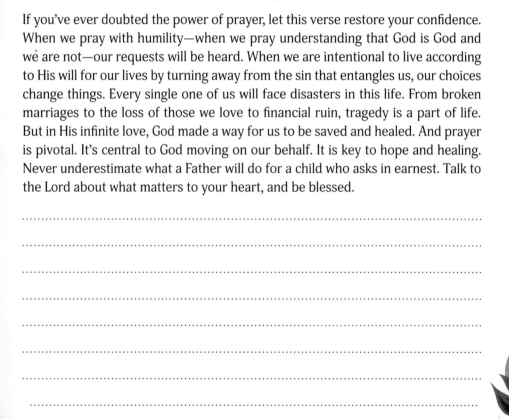

Father in heaven, I'm so grateful You made a way for us to talk to You, because prayer is a powerful way to unlock Your goodness in our lives. In the name of Jesus I pray. Amen.

Day 84
New Paths

"I, the Lord, have called you to demonstrate my righteousness. I will take you by the hand and guard you, and I will give you to my people, Israel, as a symbol of my covenant with them. And you will be a light to guide the nations."

ISAIAH 42:6 NLT

If the choice was left up to us, our friends and loved ones would never leave us. They wouldn't move to new homes across the country, and they would live forever. The choice isn't up to us, though. Sooner or later, we all find ourselves having to say goodbye to someone we love. They leave a hole in our lives when they're gone, and life may seem lonely and strange without them.

We may feel abandoned after a painful goodbye, but God is close beside us. He can use this new, empty space in our lives to reveal doors we never suspected were even there, leading us out onto paths we might otherwise never have dared to follow. We may feel as though we're stumbling in the dark, but one day we will look around and realize He has led us somewhere beautiful and bright and full of hope.

....

....

....

....

....

....

....

....

Thank You, faithful Lord, that You will never leave me.
When I am feeling lonely and sad, missing the people I love,
give me hope. Help me to be open to a new path for my life.

Day 85
Humility and Pride

"God blesses those who are humble, for they will inherit the whole earth."
MATTHEW 5:5 NLT

Do you ever compare yourself to others around you—and when you do, you find you never seem to measure up? Maybe you wish you could be smarter or funnier, prettier or thinner. You wish that you could accomplish as much as your colleague does in a day or that you could make as much money as your friend does or that you were as thin as your sister. You wish you were calmer or more creative. All this wishing shapes your beliefs about yourself. And you might *think* you've ended up with a belief about yourself that is the exact opposite of pride; you might equate your self-criticism with humility. But doubting your own worth is not what God wants for you. When He hears your mind filled with self-dissatisfaction, He longs for you to simply take from Him the gift of yourself. He wants you to humbly accept yourself—both the good parts and the less good—and then offer it all back to Him. When you make peace with being the person you are, He promises to bless that person! You can replace your belief that you're not good enough with the confidence that you are infinitely precious to God.

....

....

....

....

....

....

....

Loving God, help me be humble enough to accept my
imperfections. Remind me that I don't need to be
better than others for You to love me.

Day 86
Required Action

Why, my soul, are you downcast? Why so disturbed within me?
Put your hope in God, for I will yet praise him, my Savior and my God.
PSALM 43:5 NIV

Even when we are at our lowest point, we always have a choice. We can choose to sink deeper and deeper into despair, or we can choose to trust in God. Even when there doesn't seem to be much hope, we need but a mustard seed's worth of faith to persevere and find hope again.

Hope and faith are similar, but they are not the same thing. Hope believes in the future; it looks forward with joyful anticipation to whatever new thing God will do next. Meanwhile, faith means to trust—and *trust* comes from the same ancient word root as *tree*: something that is firm, rooted, solid, and reliable. If we drive across a bridge, we trust it is solid enough to hold our weight. When we leap into someone's waiting arms, we trust they are strong enough to catch us; we also trust them not to turn away and let us fall. And when we trust God, we surrender the full weight of our entire lives into His care, knowing He will never fail us. In all these examples, trust is more than a belief; it requires action.

....

....

....

....

....

....

....

....

Faithful one, on the days when I can
find no hope, help me still to trust You.

Day 87
Deceptive Emotions

Keep a firm grip on the faith. The suffering won't last forever. It won't be long before this generous God who has great plans for us in Christ— eternal and glorious plans they are!—will have you put together and on your feet for good. He gets the last word; yes, he does.

1 PETER 5:10–11 MSG

Despite what our emotions sometimes tell us, the hope of Christ always has the last word. No matter how sad and discouraged we feel, those are only feelings; they say nothing about spiritual reality. Yes, human life is filled with physical, emotional, and spiritual pain—there's no denying that. But even amid suffering, we can cling to the hope we have in Jesus. Even when our prayers seem to go unanswered and we see no evidence that God is in control of the events in our lives, even then we can continue to hope. Our hope is built on trusting God.

Teach me, Jesus, to rely more on You than I do my emotions. Remind me that my feelings can deceive me. They can cloud my perception of spiritual reality. Keep my hope alive as I trust my life to You.

The Kingdom of God

"The kingdom of God is in your midst."
Luke 17:21 NIV

Sometimes Christ's followers forget that God's kingdom is right here, right now, all around us. Since we will one day know the joy of eternity, Christians may act as though we have no responsibility for this world. They talk about how terrible the world is, as though there's no hope for it; sin and rebellion against God are all around, so we might as well forget about trying to make the world a better place.

When Christians focus only on the hereafter, it can lead to indifference to our world's critical problems. Why bother taking care of our planet since God is preparing for us a new earth? Why worry about poverty and sickness when God will wipe away all tears in heaven? But Jesus never had that attitude. He did whatever He could to help everyone he encountered, demonstrating His love by mending crippled legs, restoring sight, healing diseases, feeding the hungry, and seeking out the lonely and forgotten.

Jesus calls us to stop living in the dreary districts of hopelessness and step into His kingdom of active hope, energetic joy, and tangible love.

....
....
....
....
....
....
....

Pull me out of the hopeless regions that have grown so
familiar, Lord, and teach me to live my life in Your kingdom,
empowered by Your Spirit to build a world of hope.

Day 89
It Will Be Granted

I tell you this: if you have faith and do not doubt, then you will be
able to wither a fig tree with one glance. You will be able to tell
mountains to throw themselves into the ocean, and they will obey.
If you believe, whatever you ask for in prayer will be granted.

MATTHEW 21:21–22 VOICE

What do you need from God today? Do you have a sick child who isn't responding to treatment? Have you lost your job and been unable to find another? Are you battling loneliness as an empty nester, desperate for community? Have you been hurt by the Church and need reconciliation? Is your marriage heading in the direction of divorce and you feel helpless to change it? Have you lost a parent and are concerned the grief will never lift? These are the times we should be driven to prayer for God's intervention. This is when we should be on our knees asking for the grace to walk it out. When we place our faith in God, believing He is who He says He is and will do what He says He'll do, we can know with certainty that He will help. When we pray according to His will, we can be assured that our requests will be granted. What a blessing!

....

....

....

....

....

....

....

....

Father in heaven, thank You for reminding me to ask
for what I need. In the name of Jesus I pray. Amen.

Day 90
Faith

Jesus immediately reached out and grabbed him.
"You have so little faith," Jesus said. "Why did you doubt me?"
MATTHEW 14:31 NLT

You can read the whole story in Matthew 14. Jesus was walking on the water, and Peter, impetuous as always, jumped out of the boat and joined Him. Peter was doing just fine, walking along on the surface of the sea, his eyes fixed on Jesus. But then he looked down. He saw his feet stepping over the waves—and instantly he started to sink. In that moment, he forgot everything he believed about Jesus. He was positive he was going to drown.

Jesus didn't let him, of course. He reached out and saved Peter. And He'll do the same for you, each and every time you find yourself swamped with doubts, beginning to sink into life's depths. "Why do you doubt Me?" He'll ask you. "I will *never* let you sink. Have faith in Me!"

....
....
....
....
....
....
....
....
....
....

When doubts torment me, Lord Jesus,
strengthen my heart. Bless me with belief in You.

Day 91
Your Eternal Home

We know that if the earthly tent we live in is destroyed, we have a building from God, an eternal house in heaven, not built by human hands.

2 Corinthians 5:1 NIV

When Jesus spoke about the kingdom of heaven, He always indicated that it wasn't a place far off in some spiritual realm we can only reach after death. Instead, He said His Father's kingdom was right now, right here, even right inside our hearts. At the same time, though, He promised that He would prepare an eternal home for us, a place where we will live forever with Him. This eternal home, where we live united with God, will satisfy all the unmet longings of our hearts, and it is the deepest source of our hope.

By keeping in mind that we have a forever home in eternity, we can gain a better sense of perspective when we encounter trouble and tribulation in this life. If we have this perspective, even death can become a source of hope, for it will be our homegoing day.

....
....
....
....
....
....
....
....

When this world seems dark and bleak, dear Jesus,
remind me that my true homeland is with You in eternity.
Thank You for having my home ready for me there.

Day 92
Hold On!

"This vision-message is a witness pointing to what's coming. . . . And it doesn't lie. If it seems slow in coming, wait. It's on its way. It will come right on time."
HABAKKUK 2:3 MSG

The book of Habakkuk was written nearly three thousand years ago, and yet human nature hasn't changed. The prophet Habakkuk understood how easy it is to have our hope overcome by doubt and impatience. We look around us, and we can't help but wonder if our hope in God is nothing but a lie. In this verse, Habakkuk reassures us that God never lies, and He knows exactly what He's doing even when we don't.

God understands your impatience and doubt. But He asks you to hold on a little longer. Wait and see the amazing things He is doing even now.

When my hope fades, Lord, and all I can feel is fear
and doubt, give me the patience I need to wait for You.

Day 93

A Lot or a Little

*I'm just as happy with little as with much, with much as with little.
I've found the recipe for being happy whether full or hungry, hands
full or hands empty. Whatever I have, wherever I am, I can make
it through anything in the One who makes me who I am.*

PHILIPPIANS 4:12–13 MSG

When you were younger, what did you believe you needed to be happy? Nice clothes? A good job? Lots of friends? And now? What do you believe your happiness requires? Your beliefs can either limit or expand the happiness you actually experience. Day after day, God blesses you—but your happiness does not depend on those blessings. Your joy and contentment depend only on God. When that belief sinks in deep, you no longer have to worry about losing or gaining life's blessings.

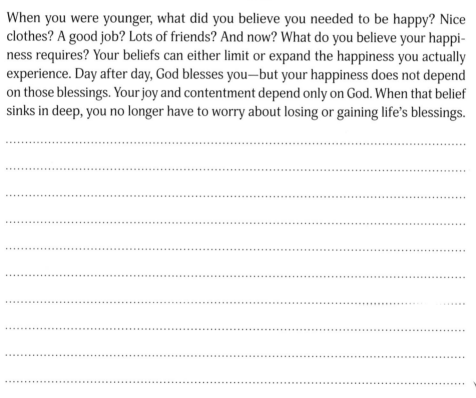

Giver of life, I believe that whether I have a little or a lot,
I will always have enough. Thank You for Your constant
blessing. Thank You for making me who I am.

Day 94
Be a Bold Witness

If you're listening, here's My message: Keep loving your enemies no matter what they do. Keep doing good to those who hate you. Keep speaking blessings on those who curse you. Keep praying for those who mistreat you.
LUKE 6:27–28 VOICE

It is difficult to love others when we keep a scorecard. When we are more focused on keeping track of what others are doing (or not doing), it causes us to take our eyes off what's really important. We begin to justify our nasty and negative responses to their actions. Rather than protect their reputation from the gossip train, we are the ones who drive it. And as things deteriorate, we lose sight of what God expects from those who love Him. We turn our backs on His hope for His followers. We end up looking like everyone else in the world, showing no sign that we carry Jesus in our hearts. But our job is to point others to God. Ask Him to help you shine His goodness unabashedly. Be a bold witness for the Lord, and He will bless you with perspective and purpose so you can glorify His name with your life.

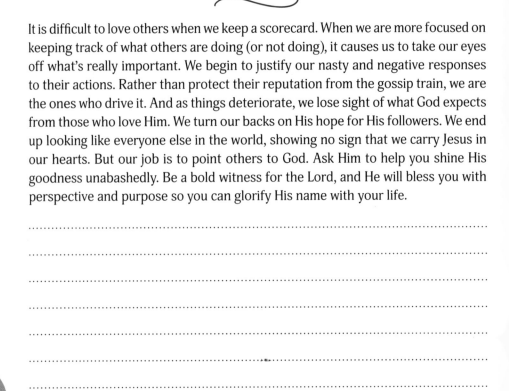

Father in heaven, I most certainly need Your help to love my enemies, do good to those who hate me, and speak with kindness when mistreated. I know with Your blessing through prayer, I can shine brightly for the kingdom. In the name of Jesus I pray. Amen.

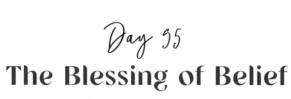

Day 35
The Blessing of Belief

For we live by believing and not by seeing.
2 CORINTHIANS 5:7 NLT

Modern-day Western culture was shaped by the scientific method, which tells us that only what can be seen, measured, and proved is truly real. But twenty-first-century scientists know reality is far bigger than what our five senses can take in. Our own hearts know this as well. Every day, we depend on the things we can't see and yet believe—our faith in God and in our friends and family, our commitment to give ourselves to God and others—and it is these invisible beliefs that daily bless our lives with richness and depth.

....
....
....
....
....
....
....
....
....

Lord of love, I can't see You—but I believe You are present with me:
in the world around me and within my own heart. I cannot prove
Your presence, and yet my belief in You shapes my entire life.
Expand my belief in You, I pray. May it grow stronger and
more certain. Bless me with a growing belief in You.

Day 36

Opportunities to Grow

When troubles of any kind come your way, consider it an opportunity for great joy.
For you know that when your faith is tested, your endurance has a chance to grow.

JAMES 1:2-3 NLT

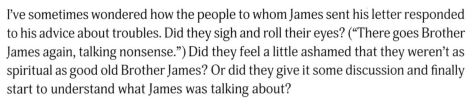

I've sometimes wondered how the people to whom James sent his letter responded to his advice about troubles. Did they sigh and roll their eyes? ("There goes Brother James again, talking nonsense.") Did they feel a little ashamed that they weren't as spiritual as good old Brother James? Or did they give it some discussion and finally start to understand what James was talking about?

Notice that James did not indicate that feeling pain is either avoidable or wrong. We're not supposed to respond to a toothache with a happy smile or give shouts of joy at a funeral. Instead, he asks us to change our *attitudes* and the way we think about trouble. Just as hard exercise makes our bodies stronger, hard experiences can make our souls stronger too. Trouble is an opportunity to grow. It teaches us how to endure, be patient, and hope.

....

....

....

....

....

....

....

....

....

Giver of life, when troubles come, remind me they are opportunities
for You and me to grow closer. Keep my hope in You steady.

Day 97
To Live Extraordinary

If you want to be extraordinary—love your enemies! Do good without restraint! Lend with abandon! Don't expect anything in return! Then you'll receive the truly great reward—you will be children of the Most High—for God is kind to the ungrateful and those who are wicked. So imitate God and be truly compassionate, the way your Father is.

LUKE 6:35-36 VOICE

Imagine how extraordinary our world would be if we lived this way. What if we loved our enemies, treating them with extravagant care? What if we were willing to share what we had with those who needed it? And what if we expected nothing in return? What if, like God, we were kind to those who didn't deserve it? What if we chose to love the one who acted unloving? What if we were known for our compassion? Friend, let's agree that the only way we could live like this is if the Lord infused us with His goodness. And if He did, if He blessed us to live and love with such beautiful intention, it would change the world. But we don't need the whole world to act this way for us to do so. With God's help, through lots of prayer, we can bless the world for Him.

....

....

....

....

....

....

....

Father in heaven, would You bless me with the desire
and ability to be extraordinary and give glory to You
in the heavens? In the name of Jesus I pray. Amen.

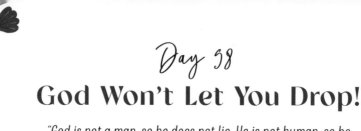

Day 98
God Won't Let You Drop!

"God is not a man, so he does not lie. He is not human, so he does not change his mind. Has he ever spoken and failed to act? Has he ever promised and not carried it through?"

NUMBERS 23:19 NLT

Have you ever done the team-building exercise that's referred to as a *trust fall*? It requires that you deliberately drop backward, blindly trusting that the person behind you will catch you. Most people have trouble doing it the first time, but it gets easier with practice. Each time we fall backward and are caught, our trust builds.

Sometimes, life feels a lot like a trust fall. We can't see God, and yet He asks us to drop our whole life into His hands. The first time we truly lean our entire weight on Him, it can feel scary. What if He's not there? What if He drops us? Augustine, the fourth-century North African bishop, reassured us that that will never happen. He once wrote a line to the effect that God would not offer to support us but then fail to catch us when we need Him most. Our hope in God isn't a wish. Even during the times when we have no sense of His presence, He will never, ever let us fall.

Thank You, God, that You always catch me. You will never drop me. My hope is in You, and I know I can trust You.

Day 55
Your Whole Self

Let all that I am wait quietly before God, for my hope is in him.
PSALM 62:5 NLT

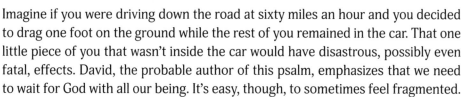

Imagine if you were driving down the road at sixty miles an hour and you decided to drag one foot on the ground while the rest of you remained in the car. That one little piece of you that wasn't inside the car would have disastrous, possibly even fatal, effects. David, the probable author of this psalm, emphasizes that we need to wait for God with all our being. It's easy, though, to sometimes feel fragmented. When we encounter a problem in our lives, part of us may believe that God is still in control, but at the same time, another part of us doubts and wonders if the situation might be hopeless.

Regardless of our emotional reactions, though (for sadness and fear are normal human responses), we can commit our entire lives, every piece of our beings, to God. Even when problems threaten to overwhelm us, we can continue to commit everything to God, waiting for His face to be revealed to us.

....
....
....
....
....
....
....
....

Lord, I want to give You my whole self, every bit of
me. Show me if I am holding anything back. Keep me
hoping, waiting for You to show me Yourself.

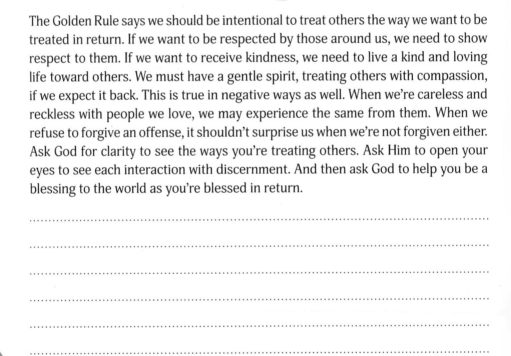

Day 100

The Golden Rule

If you don't want to be judged, don't judge. If you don't want to be condemned, don't condemn. If you want to be forgiven, forgive. Don't hold back—give freely, and you'll have plenty poured back into your lap—a good measure, pressed down, shaken together, brimming over. You'll receive in the same measure you give.

Luke 6:37–38 VOICE

The Golden Rule says we should be intentional to treat others the way we want to be treated in return. If we want to be respected by those around us, we need to show respect to them. If we want to receive kindness, we need to live a kind and loving life toward others. We must have a gentle spirit, treating others with compassion, if we expect it back. This is true in negative ways as well. When we're careless and reckless with people we love, we may experience the same from them. When we refuse to forgive an offense, it shouldn't surprise us when we're not forgiven either. Ask God for clarity to see the ways you're treating others. Ask Him to open your eyes to see each interaction with discernment. And then ask God to help you be a blessing to the world as you're blessed in return.

....
....
....
....
....
....
....
....

Father in heaven, help me check my actions and
attitude toward others so I can be living and loving
in ways that bless. In the name of Jesus I pray. Amen.

Day 101
Our Kind God

*The L*ORD *is righteous in everything he does; he is filled with kindness.*
PSALM 145:17 NLT

The word *kind* comes from the same roots as *kin*. They're both words that originally had to do with family, with intimate shared relationships like the ones that exist between members of the same family. This is what God shows us: the kindness of a good father, the gentleness of a good mother, the understanding of a brother or sister.

The Hebrew word translated as *kind* has to do with mercy and courtesy—the willingness to put oneself last, to forgive and not insist on one's own rights. When you consider the depth of meanings contained within this word, you gain a better picture of the kindness God longs to show you!

....
....
....
....
....
....
....
....
....
....
....

Thank You, Lord, that You are always loving, gentle,
merciful, and forgiving. You are never selfish
or harsh. I believe in Your kindness!

Day 102
Sowing Seeds

The one who sows righteousness reaps a sure reward.
PROVERBS 11:18 NIV

The Bible talks a lot about sowing seeds. This was a metaphor that made sense to communities dependent on farming for their livelihood. Today, farmers still know you can't have a harvest without first planting seeds. Those of us who make our living in other ways, though, may not have learned a farmer's patience.

Our culture often wants big results—fast! When we don't have much to show for our work yet, we may feel discouraged. Whether we're talking about professional work or spiritual, we want to have something noticeable, something impressive, to show for our effort. We haven't learned how to hope and wait for tiny seeds to sprout and grow. Be patient with yourself. Nurture the seeds of hope in your life. Wait for them to grow.

....
....
....
....
....
....
....
....
....
....

Heavenly friend, take my impatience from me
and replace it with Your infinite love and hope.

Day 103
Don't Limit God!

God doesn't come and go. God lasts. He's Creator of all you can see or imagine. He doesn't get tired out, doesn't pause to catch his breath.

Isaiah 40:28 MSG

Human beings shape their expectations by what they have already experienced. We generalize things that may be true, but because our experiences are limited, sometimes our expectations may be false. For example, we've seen the sun rise every day of our lives, so we expect it to rise again tomorrow—and that expectation is justified. But suppose we've been bitten more than once by a dog; are we then correct to assume all dogs are dangerous? Or if we've been betrayed by more than one friend, should we believe that no friendship can be trusted?

We do the same thing with God. Based on our experience with human beings, we find ourselves expecting God to inevitably, sooner or later, let us down. We can't believe He could be loving enough or strong enough to meet all our hopes. Yet, God is not like human beings. He never gets tired, He never gives up, and His love has no end.

....
....
....
....
....
....
....
....

When I place limits on my hope in You, Lord, remind me
that Your love and power exceed anything I have
ever experienced, anything I can even imagine.

Your throne, O Lord, has stood from time immemorial.
You yourself are from the everlasting past.
Psalm 93:2 NLT

Time is a mysterious thing even scientists don't understand. Albert Einstein proposed that time is an illusion, something that depends on human perception. Einstein also came up with the idea that time could be a fourth dimension, as well as the idea that time might move differently depending on our circumstances. Some scientists speculate that time could behave differently in different parts of the cosmos. For most of us, though, time is such a constant part of our lives that we assume we understand how it works. We usually believe it is like a fast-moving river we are caught in, a stream that constantly carries us into the future while the past rushes away behind us. Life keeps slipping away from us like water between our fingers.

But the Bible tells us that time will not exist forever; someday it will come to an end (Revelation 10:6). God is outside time's stream. He holds our past safe in His hands, and His love is permanent and unshakable. Our belief in Him is the lifesaver we cling to in the midst of time's wild waves.

....

....

....

....

....

....

....

Lord, I believe You are greater than time itself.
You hold past, present, and future in Your hands

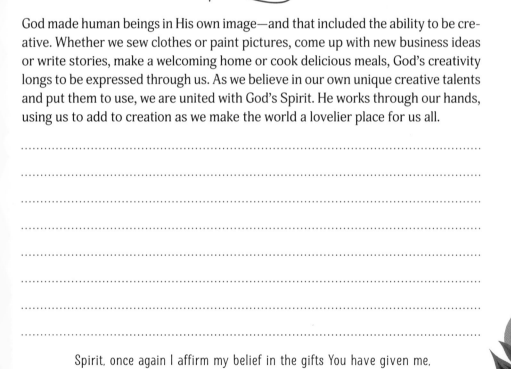

Day 105
Believe in Your Creativity!

*"[God's] filled him with the Spirit of God, with skill, ability, and know-how
for making all sorts of things, to design and work in gold, silver, and bronze;
to carve stones and set them; to carve wood, working in every kind of
skilled craft.... He's gifted them with the know-how needed for carving,
designing, weaving, and embroidering in blue, purple, and scarlet fabrics,
and in fine linen. They can make anything and design anything."*
EXODUS 35:31–33, 35 MSG

God made human beings in His own image—and that included the ability to be creative. Whether we sew clothes or paint pictures, come up with new business ideas
or write stories, make a welcoming home or cook delicious meals, God's creativity
longs to be expressed through us. As we believe in our own unique creative talents
and put them to use, we are united with God's Spirit. He works through our hands,
using us to add to creation as we make the world a lovelier place for us all.

....

....

....

....

....

....

....

....

Spirit, once again I affirm my belief in the gifts You have given me,
including the ability to be creative. Remove any self-doubt that
blocks my creativity. May I take delight in being creative,
allowing Your inspiration to use my talents.

Day 106
Are You Confident He Listens?

My purpose in writing is simply this: that you who believe in God's Son will know beyond the shadow of a doubt that you have eternal life, the reality and not the illusion. And how bold and free we then become in his presence, freely asking according to his will, sure that he's listening. And if we're confident that he's listening, we know that what we've asked for is as good as ours.

1 John 5:13–15 MSG

Do you believe that God listens when you speak to Him? Prayer can be confusing at times. Sometimes it seems our prayers leave our lips and get lost in space. They seem to drift off, unheard by the Father Himself. And when we look at our lives through the eyes of disappointment, we wonder if the Lord is even paying attention. We're sure He's disappointed as well and has gone off to work in greener pastures. Friend, ask the Lord to grow your confidence in knowing you're heard; ask Him to help you trust that your voice matters to the one who created you, because when we have assurance that He's listening and interested, we can know that what we've asked for, according to His will, will be done.

....

....

....

....

....

....

....

....

Father in heaven, thank You for the blessing of being heard by You.
Please build in me the assurance that because You've heard me, You
will act in my best interest. In the name of Jesus I pray, Amen.

Day 107
Joy and Amazement

We were filled with laughter, and we sang for joy. And the other nations said, "What amazing things the LORD has done for them."
PSALM 126:2 NLT

Life is truly amazing. Each day is filled with wonderful blessings. God's love touches you in so many ways: from the sun on your face to each person you encounter, from the love of your friends and family to the satisfaction of your work. Pay attention. Believe that each blessing in your life is a love token from God. Notice the little blessings as well as the bigger ones. Make room for joy as a part of your daily life. Let people hear you laugh more. Don't hide your joy, for it is a witness to God's love and blessing, letting people know what you believe about God. You have an amazing source of joy in your life and heart!

....

....

....

....

....

....

....

....

....

Thank You, amazing God, for all the blessings You shower on me.
Remind me to see joy faster than I see sorrow in my life. Teach me
to believe in Your joyful love. I don't want to take for granted
all the amazing things You do for me each and every day.

The Lord Is Your Helper

So we can say with confidence, "The LORD is my helper, so I will have no fear. What can mere people do to me?"

HEBREWS 13:6 NLT

We sometimes allow our lives to be controlled by fear of what other people will think. Instead of focusing on God's path of love, we wander around, pushed here and there by others' opinions of us. That's not a very hopeful way to live!

Nelson Mandela, the former president of South Africa, once gave a quote to the effect that we should be led by our hope and not by what worries us. Discriminated against, oppressed, and imprisoned, Mandela still chose to align his life with hope rather than with fear—and because he did, he brought positive change to the world. Who knows what we too can do when we rely on God as our Helper! When we stop worrying about what other people think and start trusting God, hope will show us the way.

....

....

....

....

....

....

....

....

....

Dear Lord, when You catch me worrying more about other people's opinions than I do You, draw my attention back to You. I'm so glad that You are my Helper!

Day 105
A New Song

He put a new song in my mouth, a hymn of praise to our God.
PSALM 40:3 NIV

When life seems hopeless, sometimes the best thing we can do to restore our sense of hope is to sing. From a physical standpoint, research has found that singing benefits our nervous systems by helping to reduce stress. One study found that people who sing regularly either improve or maintain good mental health. Singing also encourages us to breathe more deeply, which can heighten our sense of well-being. From a spiritual perspective, the Bible often speaks of the power of song to express praise, lift our spirits, and give us a greater sense of God's presence.

So, the next time you find your hope wavering—sing!

Lord Jesus, when I begin to lose hope, when I see no reason whatsoever to sing, remind me that You Yourself are my song. Even if I can't keep a tune, make Your music in my life.

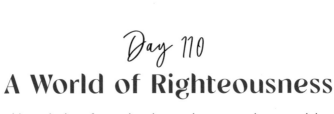

Day 110
A World of Righteousness

*We are looking forward to the new heavens and new earth he
has promised, a world filled with God's righteousness.*

2 Peter 3:13 NLT

God wants us to be actively engaged in this world, with all its problems and challenges. But as we work to build God's kingdom here on earth, we will be encouraged if we balance our outlook with the awareness that, ultimately, God will create a new world that overflows with His goodness and love. This perspective can keep us hopeful, even when everything around us insists that there cannot possibly be any hope. With the assurance of that hope firmly grasped, we will have more strength to do the work that God calls us to in this life.

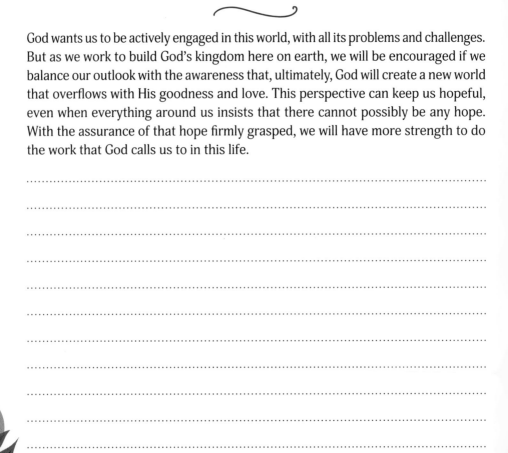

God of goodness, I look forward with joyful anticipation to sharing
with You a new world where nothing is broken, where all are
healed, where love reigns and hatred is banished.

Day 111

The More the Merrier

"Take this most seriously: A yes on earth is yes in heaven; a no on earth is no in heaven. What you say to one another is eternal. I mean this. When two of you get together on anything at all on earth and make a prayer of it, my Father in heaven goes into action. And when two or three of you are together because of me, you can be sure that I'll be there."

MATTHEW 18:18–20 MSG

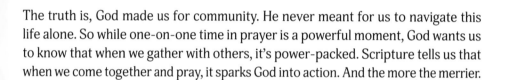

The truth is, God made us for community. He never meant for us to navigate this life alone. So while one-on-one time in prayer is a powerful moment, God wants us to know that when we gather with others, it's power-packed. Scripture tells us that when we come together and pray, it sparks God into action. And the more the merrier.

What a blessing that God sees value in relationship. Do you pray with others? Do you make time to gather together as a church or a small group or a family and lift things up to the Lord? Don't miss the weight that community prayer carries. Imagine how it blesses God to hear a collection of voices storming the gates of heaven!

Father in heaven, I don't think I realized how important it is to pray as a collective. Thank You for scripture that points it out so clearly. Help me facilitate this in my own life and my own communities. In the name of Jesus I pray. Amen.

Day 112
Enemies

"You're familiar with the old written law, 'Love your friend,' and its unwritten companion, 'Hate your enemy.' I'm challenging that. I'm telling you to love your enemies. Let them bring out the best in you, not the worst. When someone gives you a hard time, respond with the supple moves of prayer, for then you are working out of your true selves, your God-created selves.... Live generously and graciously toward others, the way God lives toward you."
MATTHEW 5:43–45, 48 MSG

Sometimes Christians ignore what Jesus says here in the Gospel of Matthew. We make enemies out of the people we don't approve of—the people who disagree with what we believe, who have different politics, different values, different ideas. We might deny that we treat these people like enemies—but do we really act as though we love them? Do we offer them the best of ourselves? Do we pray for them with all our energy? And if we *do* pray for them, are we only praying that they will change their minds and think like we do? Or are we truly praying that God will bless them, no matter what? Jesus tells us we can't enter into our own God-given identities if we don't start treating everyone, including our enemies, with the same love and generosity God has shown us. He wants us to believe He will use even our "enemies" to bless us.

....

....

....

....

....

Lord, remind me that You want to bless me through the people
I don't like, the people I disagree with, the people I disapprove
of. I believe You will teach me more about You, myself,
and others as I open my heart to everyone.

Day 113
God's in Control

"Do not be afraid or discouraged, for the LORD will personally go ahead of you. He will be with you; he will neither fail you nor abandon you."
DEUTERONOMY 31:8 NLT

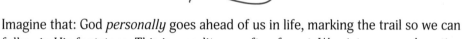

Imagine that: God *personally* goes ahead of us in life, marking the trail so we can follow in His footsteps. This is a reality we often forget. We picture ourselves tip-toeing through the dark all alone, in danger of falling off a cliff at any moment if we take the wrong step—and meanwhile, God is right there, leading the way.

No matter how chaotic or overwhelming life seems, God sees the pattern. No matter how lost we feel, He knows the way. He never steps away for even a moment; His presence is constant, dependable, and powerful. So, there's no need to be afraid or discouraged. If we surrender our lives to God, we can live our lives with hope. He has everything under control.

Lord of my life, when I feel out of control,
remind me to give full control to You.

Day 114
Mystery

My goal is that they may be encouraged in heart and united in love,
so that they may have the full riches of complete understanding,
in order that they may know the mystery of God, namely, Christ.
COLOSSIANS 2:2 NIV

In the Bible, the word *mystery* doesn't refer to a whodunit or a puzzle to be solved. Neither is it something that is completely unknowable. Instead, it indicates something very real that exists outside the box of our previous experience. It's something we can only perceive as God reveals it to us, and when He does, it stretches our understanding and widens our perspective. This verse from the book of Colossians tells us that Christ Himself is the revelation of the divine mystery. Although we still cannot understand all that God is, when we look at Christ, we see the embodiment of God, the full expression of His love, and the ultimate assurance of all our hope.

As we continue to follow Christ, getting to know Him better and better, both our hope and our understanding will grow stronger, wider, and brighter.

....

....

....

....

....

....

....

....

There is so much about You that I still find mysterious, Lord God.
Thank You that the wonder of You not only gives me hope
but also stretches my assumptions to make more
room for Your Spirit in my heart and life.

Light

"The people living in darkness have seen a great light; on those living in the land of the shadow of death a light has dawned."

MATTHEW 4:16 NIV

Imagine you are standing in a shadow that stretches around you in every direction. In the darkness, you can't make out the shape of your surroundings. You can't see anyone, so you assume you are alone. You feel lost, afraid to take a step in any direction and paralyzed by hopelessness and anxiety. You ask yourself, *What if I'm stuck here alone forever?* Your anxiety grows stronger as you become certain there is no way out of this shadowland.

And then, suddenly, a strong wind blows away the clouds. The sun blazes down on you from a blue sky. You blink, and once your eyes adjust to the light, you look around only to discover that the person you love best in all the world is there beside you. He smiles and takes your hand, and together you explore the beautiful land of green hills and valleys that were there all along.

Nothing changed in this scenario except for the presence of light—and in our lives, the light of God makes all the difference.

....

....

....

....

....

....

....

....

Shine Your light on me, Lord, and give me hope.

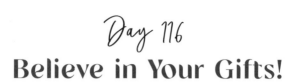

Day 116
Believe in Your Gifts!

God's various gifts are handed out everywhere; but they all originate in God's Spirit. God's various ministries are carried out everywhere; but they all originate in God's Spirit. God's various expressions of power are in action everywhere; but God himself is behind it all. Each person is given something to do that shows who God is: Everyone gets in on it, everyone benefits. All kinds of things are handed out by the Spirit, and to all kinds of people! The variety is wonderful.

1 CORINTHIANS 12:4–8 MSG

Do you ever look around at other people's gifts and talents and believe you don't measure up by comparison? This belief can interfere with what God wants to do through you. God shines through each of us in different ways. One person is good at expressing herself in words; another is good with children; and still another has a gift for giving wise advice to her friends. Whatever our gifts are, they all come from God. They are all tangible expressions of His love, and each one reveals God's Spirit to the world.

....
....
....
....
....
....
....

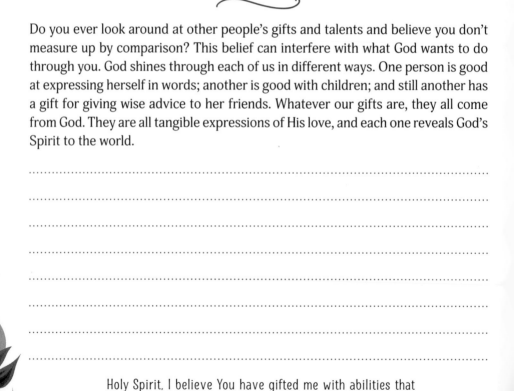

Holy Spirit, I believe You have gifted me with abilities that
demonstrate God's reality. Let no self-doubt or false modesty
interfere with me using these gifts to spread Your love.

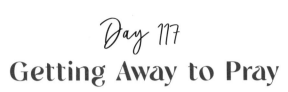
Day 117
Getting Away to Pray

While it was still night, way before dawn, he got up and went out to
a secluded spot and prayed. Simon and those with him went looking
for him. They found him and said, "Everybody's looking for you."

MARK 1:35-37 MSG

Sometimes we just need to get away to pray. We need to find sacred space where it's just us and God—space where we can let it out without worrying that anyone else will pop in. Even if we close the door behind us, there are moments when others in the house feel too close for the conversation we need to have with the Lord. We may not need to steal away every time we pray, but sometimes our hearts require it. Be kind to yourself and honor what you need. Do you need to get up early to take a walk and talk to God? Do you need to go on a drive and pray? Does the shower work? The back porch? The next time you're stirred to find a sacred space to connect with your Father, do it. It's a setup for a blessing.

Father in heaven, I get this! There are times I need to feel miles
away from anyone here so I can pour out my heart to You in
private. Help me be intentional to create that space when
I need it. In the name of Jesus I pray. Amen.

Day 118
Diligence

The desires of the diligent are fully satisfied.
PROVERBS 13:4 NIV

I have no choice in the matter. Perhaps you've said those words when you were faced with a difficult decision. If so, you might have felt trapped by that belief. The truth is you *do* have choices; you just may not be able to see them at first glance. You can ask questions, research your options, consider the pros and cons, and then make a reasonable choice based on the knowledge you have at the time. By your own diligence—following through, taking action, digging in—that boxed-in feeling may disappear, so that you enjoy new freedom. Believe this: God will bless you as you exercise diligence in your life!

....
....
....
....
....
....
....
....
....
....

God, when I feel like giving up, remind me that You bless
diligence. Give me the strength to keep looking until
I find the answers that are right for me.

Day 119
Quiet and Ready

If your heart is broken, you'll find God right there; if you're kicked in the gut, he'll help you catch your breath.
Psalm 34:18 MSG

I confess, sometimes when I'm in the middle of a problem, I'm not all that interested in hope. If my heart is broken, I may be crying too loudly (either figuratively or actually) to listen to what God is trying to say to me. When I'm angry about something, I sometimes want to hold on to that anger, listening to its voice instead of God's. And when I'm anxious, I often want to go over my worries again and again (and again) rather than surrendering them to God.

We need to get quiet enough to hear God's voice amid our disappointing moments and be ready to act on the hope He gives. It's that "quiet and ready" piece we sometimes have a hard time with. If we can step back from our emotions, disengaging ourselves from their racket and clamor, then we can ready our hearts to once again hear the still, small voice of hope.

....

....

....

....

....

....

....

....

Gracious God, thank You that You are always with me,
even when I'm overwhelmed by my emotions.
Teach me to listen for Your quiet voice.

Day 120
Glimpses

*I consider that our present sufferings are not worth
comparing with the glory that will be revealed in us.*
ROMANS 8:18 NIV

Today, amid whatever suffering you are experiencing (whether it's trivial or immense, physical or emotional, chronic or fleeting), ask God to give you a "knothole" to peek through, a tiny glimpse of the glory and splendor that He has in store for you.

And notice that in this letter to the Romans, Paul indicates that this glory will be revealed *in us*. God intends that each one of us, despite all our flaws and failures, our heartaches and physical limitations, will become shining beacons of hope.

....

....

....

....

....

....

....

....

....

....

....

God, it's hard for me to believe that I will ever shine with glory;
but my hope is You, not myself or my own abilities. When I
feel most discouraged with myself, please give me just
a glimpse of the person You intend me to be.

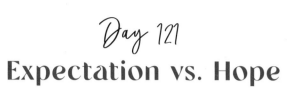

Day 121
Expectation vs. Hope

You can make many plans, but the LORD's purpose will prevail.
PROVERBS 19:21 NLT

Our expectations are not the same as hope. We might expect that the sun will shine tomorrow, only to have the clouds pour down rain from sunrise to sunset. At work, we may expect to get a substantial raise that never materializes. We may expect to impress people with our talent, only to find them uninterested in our abilities. Expectation makes plans. It believes it's in control and has the future all figured out. It thinks it knows exactly what tomorrow will look like. Meanwhile, hope realizes that it doesn't know what the future will be but it *does* know that the future is in God's hands. It is confident that no matter what happens, God's purposes are prevailing.

....

....

....

....

....

....

....

....

....

....

Remind me, Lord, that expectation and hope are not the same things. When I try to take control of the future with plans and expectations, remind me that You know better than I do and that I can trust Your love.

His Firsthand Experience

Now that we know what we have—Jesus, this great High Priest with ready access to God—let's not let it slip through our fingers. We don't have a priest who is out of touch with our reality. He's been through weakness and testing, experienced it all—all but the sin. So let's walk right up to him and get what he is so ready to give. Take the mercy, accept the help.

HEBREWS 4:14–16 MSG

What a blessing to realize everything we face in this life—every temptation or testing—was experienced by Jesus on earth. There is nothing we could talk to Him about that He doesn't have firsthand knowledge of. Some people say it's futile praying to the Lord because He's unable to relate to the challenges His creation may be up against, but that simply isn't fact. He is not out of touch with the reality we face as humans. To Him, it's not just book knowledge. Jesus lived it out on earth; He has real-life understanding. That means He recognizes our struggles and needs. He has compassion for the journey. And through prayer, we are the beneficiaries of His grace and wisdom as we take the next steps toward healing.

....
....
....
....
....
....
....

Father in heaven, what a privilege to serve a God who gets it.
Thank You for knowing exactly what I am facing because it grows
my confidence and faith in You! In the name of Jesus I pray. Amen.

Day 123
Unknown Blessings

"For I know the plans I have for you," declares the Lᴏʀᴅ, "plans to prosper you and not to harm you, plans to give you hope and a future."

JEREMIAH 29:11 NIV

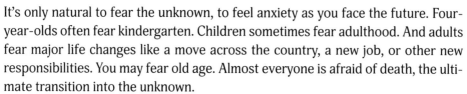

It's only natural to fear the unknown, to feel anxiety as you face the future. Four-year-olds often fear kindergarten. Children sometimes fear adulthood. And adults fear major life changes like a move across the country, a new job, or other new responsibilities. You may fear old age. Almost everyone is afraid of death, the ultimate transition into the unknown.

When you look back at your life, though, do you notice that when the change you dreaded actually arrived, you were ready for it? It probably brought you greater freedom, greater satisfaction, greater happiness than you had experienced before. The four-year-old is not ready for kindergarten—but the five-year-old usually is. The ten-year-old is not ready for the responsibilities of adulthood—but the twenty-two-year-old revels in them. And the new job or new home that filled you with anxiety brings with it new friends and new accomplishments that fulfill you in ways you never imagined. Old age has special rewards of its own—and death, that great unknown, will lead you into the presence of God.

You don't have to fear the unknown; instead, believe it holds more blessings than you have ever dreamed of!

....

....

....

....

Lord, I'm so glad You know what the future holds, even though I don't.
I believe that just as You have blessed me in the past, You will also
bless me in the future. You are not limited by what I can imagine
now. The unknown that lies ahead is rich with blessing.

Day 124
Shared Hope

Let the message about Christ, in all its richness, fill your lives.
Teach and counsel each other with all the wisdom he gives.
COLOSSIANS 3:16 NLT

Hope is not something we're meant to keep private, hugging it in the secrecy of our hearts, keeping it hidden from others. Instead, it's meant to fill our lives so full that it visibly spills over where others can see it. Hope is meant to be shared.

We all have moments when our hope and faith waver, when we can't see past our pain or sadness, our frustration or anger. Despair can often seem like a dark forest in which no light or path can be found. It can feel defeating to even try to find the way out. I've been in that dark forest, and so, I suspect, have you. Sometimes we need someone to show us the way back into the light—and other times it's our turn to be the one who says, "I've been in the place where you are standing now, but I'm not there anymore. Can I share my hope with you until you have some of your own again?"

....

....

....

....

....

....

....

....

Today, Lord, show me someone in need of some shared hope. And the next
time I'm feeling hopeless, please send someone along to share theirs
with me. Thank You that You reveal Your love through us.

Day 125
Hopeful Choices

The righteous choose their friends carefully,
but the way of the wicked leads them astray.
PROVERBS 12:26 NIV

There are things we can do to make a positive difference in our outlooks, and actions we can take that will increase our sense of hope. One of these things is choosing with whom we spend time. The right kind of friends will encourage us rather than drain our hope and energy.

We can also be careful about what we read and watch. If we continually stuff our minds full of doom and gloom, we may find our hope ebbing away. We can choose, instead, to read books and watch programs that renew our hope. This doesn't mean our friends always have to be cheery and good-natured, that every book we read must have a happy ending, or that every television program we watch is a Hallmark special. But when we leave a friend, finish reading a book, or turn off the television, our hope should be intact rather than swamped with despair or doubt. The choice is ours to make.

....
....
....
....
....
....
....

Help me, Lord God, to choose my friends wisely. Remind me
to be discriminating when it comes to what I read and
watch. Show me how to nurture my hope in You
rather than allowing it to be weakened.

Day 126
Love Is What Matters

Prophecy and speaking in unknown languages and special knowledge will become useless. But love will last forever!

1 CORINTHIANS 13:8 NLT

Sometimes we pride ourselves on our skills, talents, and achievements. On the other hand, we doubt ourselves if we feel we are not good enough to excel at anything. If we look at our lives and realize we've made no major contribution to the world (at least from our own perspectives), our self-esteem may falter.

Meanwhile, the Bible tells us that God is not as impressed by fame or fortune as He is by our ability to love. If we did nothing in life except allow His love to flow through us in countless tiny ways, blessing the lives of others, God would consider us to be successes. God gives us many abilities with which to serve Him, but it's love that truly lasts on into eternity.

....

....

....

....

....

....

....

....

....

Remind me, God, that love is my highest goal. Even if the world
never sees me as successful, may I always be a vehicle of
Your love, bringing hope to every person I meet.

The Truth about Asking

Just ask and it will be given to you; seek after it and you will find. Continue to knock and the door will be opened for you. All who ask receive. Those who seek, find what they seek. And he who knocks, will have the door opened.

MATTHEW 7:7–8 VOICE

Be careful not to be deceived when scripture tells you that whatever you ask for you will receive. It's important we remember that God will bless our requests when we ask in accordance with His will. If you're asking for the ability to forgive someone who has deeply wronged you, you'll get it. When you ask for His help to love someone who is difficult and hateful, you'll be blessed with compassion to do so. The Lord calls us to forgive and love, so it aligns with His will. But if you ask for the money to go on a lavish vacation in the Bahamas, chances are it won't appear. Why? Because God doesn't want us to store up treasure on earth. His plan is for us to crave eternal things instead. Every time you go to God in prayer with a need that reflects your faith, He is ready to bless.

Father in heaven, thank You for answering prayers. And thank You for answering with great discernment, knowing what is best for us in all circumstances. In the name of Jesus I pray. Amen.

Freedom from People-Pleasing

Fearing people is a dangerous trap, but trusting the LORD means safety.
PROVERBS 29:25 NLT

Your friend wants you to do one thing. Your husband suggests something else. Both their ideas are different from what your parents think you should do. You feel torn and confused by their differing opinions. You're afraid that if you do what one person would like, the others will be unhappy with you. You get that familiar pain in the pit of your stomach, the one that makes you doubt yourself and your ability to make a choice on your own. But God doesn't want people-pleasing to rule your life, and you don't have to be afraid of others' opinions. God can help you escape this trap. As you grow closer to Him, His opinion will matter more to you than the opinions of others. As you believe in His absolute love, you will finally be free to be yourself.

....
....
....
....
....
....
....
....
....
....

God, thank You that You just want me to be myself. You don't
want me to spend my life trying to please others. I believe
You will bless me as I learn to be true to myself.

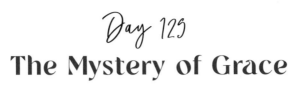

The Mystery of Grace

So we're not giving up. How could we! Even though on the outside it often looks like things are falling apart on us, on the inside, where God is making new life, not a day goes by without his unfolding grace.

2 Corinthians 4:16 MSG

"Appearances can be deceiving": it's a well-known saying, one we've probably heard repeated hundreds of times throughout our lifetimes. And yet we humans continue to judge reality by the messages we get from our five physical senses. We forget that our senses are merely portals through which we catch glimpses of God's creation; but reality is greater, deeper, and more mysterious than our senses can detect or our brains can ever fathom.

Hope is not something that depends on sight or hearing, touch or taste or smell; nor can we manufacture it by thinking hard. Instead, hope rises out from another dimension altogether. No matter what the external appearance is of our lives, the mystery of grace is always unfolding.

....

....

....

....

....

....

....

....

Remind me, loving Lord, not to judge Your plans for my life by appearances. Teach me to live with mystery. While my understanding is still incomplete, keep me rooted in hope, always anticipating Your work of unfolding grace.

Success

*"You will succeed in whatever you choose to do,
and light will shine on the road ahead of you."*
JOB 22:28 NLT

A recent sociological study found that men and women tend to have different beliefs about success. Women in the study highlighted the importance of a balance between work and relationships, whereas men focused more on material success. Both sexes, however, believed that success is something that has both external manifestations and internal, emotional rewards. However people define it, everyone longs to be successful!

The word *success* originally meant simply "the thing that comes next." Over the years, we've added to that meaning the sense that success has to be the thing we *wanted* to happen, the outcome we hoped for. But God does not necessarily define success the way we do. Whatever comes next, no matter what, His love transforms it, using circumstances to shape us into the complete and joyful people He created us to be. So if you've been feeling disappointed in your life or yourself, take a look at your beliefs about success. Do they line up with God's definition?

....
....
....
....
....
....
....
....

God, I believe You can use even the things I perceive as failures
as openings for Your creative love to flow out into the world.

Day 131
Believe in the World's Ultimate Freedom!

Creation waits in eager expectation for the children of God to be revealed. For the creation was subjected. . .in hope that the creation itself will be liberated from its bondage to decay and brought into the freedom and glory of the children of God.
ROMANS 8:19–21 NIV

Some days it's hard to feel very optimistic. As we listen to the evening news and hear story after story about natural disasters and human greed, it's difficult to believe God has a triumphant and joyful plan in store for our world. Instead, it looks more like everything is going to hell in a handbasket! God doesn't want us to be ostriches, hiding our heads in the sand, refusing to acknowledge what's going on in the world; there is real suffering and injustice out there, and we should not shut our eyes or pretend it doesn't matter. But God also wants us to believe that the future is full of wonderful things He has planned. All creation is holding its breath, waiting for God's wonderful love to fully reveal itself and set both the natural world and the human world free from their bondage to brokenness and pain.

Creator, I believe You have amazing, beautiful things in store for the world You made. Despite the violence, prejudice, suffering, and conflict that are so common, Your love is constantly at work. Use me to further Your work of love on this earth.

Day 132

Encourage the Stragglers and the Strugglers

Gently encourage the stragglers, and reach out for the exhausted, pulling them to their feet. Be patient with each person, attentive to individual needs. . . . Look for the best in each other, and always do your best to bring it out.

1 THESSALONIANS 5:14–15 MSG

If we see someone struggling in life (perhaps battling an addiction, sinking into despair, or overflowing with anger), our first impulse should not be to judge or condemn; instead, God asks that we reach out our hands to help and encourage. If you have a friend who loves to gossip, instead of complaining about her to other friends (which is itself gossip!), focus on what is good in her and do your best to strengthen that in her. Instead of always yelling at your children for their mistakes, catch them succeeding and let them know you noticed. Comment on your husband's strengths rather than constantly criticizing his failures. As we shift our attention to lifting others rather than dragging them down, the hope and love of God will help others thrive.

....

....

....

....

....

....

....

Help me, Lord, to catch myself when I start to criticize rather than
encourage, frown instead of smile, or turn away instead of
reaching out to help. Use me to bring hope to others.

Day 133
Praying All the Harder

Don't burn out; keep yourselves fueled and aflame. Be alert servants of the Master, cheerfully expectant. Don't quit in hard times; pray all the harder. Help needy Christians; be inventive in hospitality.

ROMANS 12:11–13 MSG

What does it mean to "pray all the harder"? Sometimes prayer is confusing, and since it's not something we want to get wrong, we worry whether we're messing up. We wonder if our lack of understanding is why God isn't answering in the ways we want. And so we feel insecure and unsure doing what we think is right. The Word tells us to pray always and about everything. It says prayer is both praise and a weapon. We're told it's an important way to build our relationship with the Lord. So maybe praying harder means that every time our struggles come to mind, we pray. Every time we are stirred up by fear or stress, we pray right then and there. Maybe the idea is to start a conversation as we wake up and let it string through our entire day. Wouldn't that be an open door for blessings!

....

....

....

....

....

....

....

....

Father in heaven, I would appreciate You telling me what it means to pray harder. I know Your love for me isn't performance based, but I want my life to please You. Bless our daily conversations. I am so grateful to be able to talk directly to You! In the name of Jesus I pray. Amen.

Day 134
God's Unfailing Love

But I trust in your unfailing love. I will rejoice because you have rescued me.
PSALM 13:5 NLT

Have you ever done that trust exercise where you're asked to fall backward into another person's arms? It's hard to believe the other person will actually catch you. The decision to let yourself drop is something you have to make up your mind to do, no matter what your emotions tell you, despite your fear. In the same way, you can commit yourself to God's unfailing love. As you make up your mind to trust Him, letting your life drop into His hands, you'll experience new blessings each time His arms keep you from falling. Your belief in God will no longer be something that lives only in your head; it will become the certainty that flows through each aspect of your life.

....

....

....

....

....

....

....

....

....

I am so glad, Lord, that You will never let me crash and break.
Give me the courage to be open to new blessings. Help me have
the strength to believe Your promises more and more.

The Focal Point of Your Life

I wait for the Lord, my whole being waits, and in his word I put my hope.
Psalm 130:5 NIV

We use the word hope so frivolously, so carelessly. "I hope the sun shines tomorrow," we say. Or "I hope you feel better soon." "I hope to go to Hawaii someday." "I hope I can lose weight this year." "I hope I get a raise." When the Bible talks about hope, however, it's neither referring to wishful thinking nor talking about any sort of ego-driven speculations about the future (such as "I hope to be rich one day" or "I hope I become a well-known musician"). Biblical hope is serious business, and it's always focused on God. It challenges us to wait patiently, even as we make up our minds to act. For the psalmist, hope was something that required the commitment of his entire being.

Hope in God isn't based on data or logic; if it were, then it wouldn't be hope! Instead, hope comes when we surrender to love and commit our entire being to trust. It springs up whenever we sharpen our focus on God.

....
....
....
....
....
....
....
....

Help me, Lord, to wait for You, trust You, and place all my hope
in You. May my entire being find its focal point in You.

Day 136
Worry

"So don't worry about these things, saying, 'What will we eat? What will we drink? What will we wear?' . . . Seek the Kingdom of God above all else, and live righteously, and he will give you everything you need."
MATTHEW 6:31, 33 NLT

One of the great destroyers of hope is worry. Women seem to be especially prone to it. We worry about our children, we worry about our spouses, and we worry about our parents. We also worry what people will think of us; we worry we may have offended someone; we worry about our weight and our appearance; we worry our houses aren't clean enough; we may even worry about those two tiny chin hairs that keep sprouting!

The best strategy for counteracting the worry habit is to pray first and allow God to manage all the things outside of our control. Each time our thoughts become tinged with anxiety, we can choose to talk to God instead. It takes effort—old habits are hard to break—but it is well worth it. Prayer will help us focus on God's kingdom as our priority. And prayer can replace our constant worry with a sense of hope.

....

....

....

....

....

....

....

....

Jesus, thank You that You never condemn me for my worries. I know that, instead, You long to take them from me so that I can be free to experience the joyful certainty of a hope that rests in You.

Day 137
Children

*"Let the little children come to me, and do not hinder them,
for the kingdom of God belongs to such as these."*
MARK 10:14 NIV

The children in our lives can be powerful messengers of hope. Usually, if they are growing up surrounded by love, they have not learned yet to dread the future. They experience each moment, each *now*, with their whole hearts. They know that there will always be things in life that make them cry, but at the same time, they have no problem believing that life will always be filled with fresh wonders and delights. As we spend time with them, we too can be infected with their joyous curiosity and hope. As Jesus pointed out here in the Gospel of Mark, children just naturally live in the kingdom of God.

Jesus also made clear that we have a responsibility to children to not stand in the way of their coming to Jesus. Adult anger, criticism, and lack of integrity can all squelch a child's hope. As adults, we must take our responsibility of pointing children to Jesus very seriously and show them the hope they have in Him.

Thank You, Jesus, for each child in my life. May I learn from
the joy, hope, and wonder they bring to each day—and may
I never do anything to hinder them from seeing You.

Day 138
I AM

*But Moses protested, "If I go to the people of Israel and tell them,
'The God of your ancestors has sent me to you,' they will ask me,
'What is his name?' Then what should I tell them?" God replied to Moses,
"I AM WHO I AM. Say this to the people of Israel: I AM has sent me to you."*
EXODUS 3:13–14 NLT

After God speaks to Moses from the burning bush, Moses asks God for His name. God's reply is simply: "I AM." This is not the sort of name that sits quietly on a shelf, requiring no attention, allowing us to take it for granted or forget about it. Basically, God said to Moses that He is Being itself—and not in some remote, abstract kind of way, but in a first-person, present-tense, relational sort of way.

Our personal relationships with this great I AM are the source of all our hope. We can trust that He is ever-present. He is right with us.

....
....
....
....
....
....
....
....
....

God, I cannot begin to fathom what Your name means. I can only
thank You for giving me Your attention, care, power, and
grace—for Your hope-giving presence in my life.

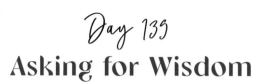

Day 139
Asking for Wisdom

Those people who are listening to Me, those people who hear what I say and live according to My teachings—you are like a wise man who built his house on a rock, on a firm foundation. When storms hit, rain pounded down and waters rose, levies broke and winds beat all the walls of that house. But the house did not fall because it was built upon rock.

MATTHEW 7:24–25 VOICE

Among the other requests you put before the Lord, let one of the most important be the ability to live with wisdom. We may be smart, but we don't have all the answers. We don't have all the solutions. And there will be plenty of times we simply don't know what to do next. That's why asking God to give us wisdom is so valuable. It's a blessing we have access to through asking. As we pray, we will begin to see the right path illuminate. We will have a deeper and sharper perspective on each situation. We will be able to discern the right way from the wrong way with more precision. And our eyes and ears will be better trained to see God's direction and to hear His voice leading us toward the next right step.

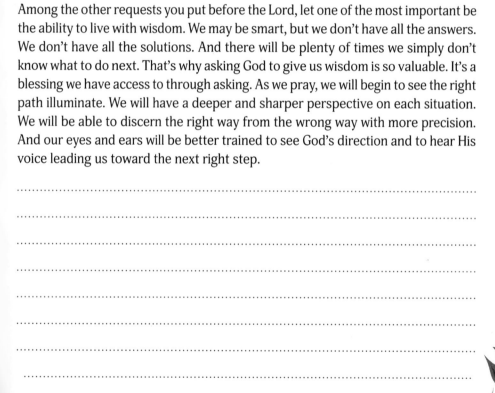

Father in heaven, please bless me with wisdom and discernment
to know the path You have for me. I want to do what is
right by You. In the name of Jesus I pray. Amen.

Day 140

The Fullness of Life

"I have come that they may have life, and have it to the full."
JOHN 10:10 NIV

Deep down, what do you really believe about life? The life that Jesus described to His followers is wide, deep, rich, and fulfilling. This is the life He wants you to believe in too, a life that is never restricted or narrow. God's love doesn't flow to you in a stingy trickle. Instead, God has blessings in store for you that will fill your life to the brim. Believe in His promises—and you will realize that blessings come to you each moment, day after day, year after year, an abundant, bountiful flood that fills every crack and crevice of your life and then overflows, spreading out from your life into the world around you.

....

....

....

....

....

....

....

....

....

....

....

Jesus, thank You for Your promise of a full and abundant life.
I believe in You, and I know You will keep Your promise.

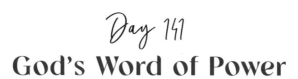

Day 149
God's Word of Power

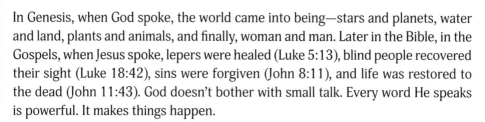

"It is the same with my word. I send it out, and it always produces fruit. It will accomplish all I want it to, and it will prosper everywhere I send it."
ISAIAH 55:11 NLT

In Genesis, when God spoke, the world came into being—stars and planets, water and land, plants and animals, and finally, woman and man. Later in the Bible, in the Gospels, when Jesus spoke, lepers were healed (Luke 5:13), blind people recovered their sight (Luke 18:42), sins were forgiven (John 8:11), and life was restored to the dead (John 11:43). God doesn't bother with small talk. Every word He speaks is powerful. It makes things happen.

What is God speaking today in your life? It may seem like a whisper so far. You may feel that you've misheard or that it's impossible God will bring anything new into your life. In other words, don't judge the future by the past; each day brings new hope, new possibilities, and the promise of a new blessing. Whatever God is saying to you today is just the beginning. His words are never empty.

Creator, speak Your words of healing and hope in my
heart and my life. Prosper and bless Your work in me.

Impossible Hope

"Blessed is she who has believed that the Lord would fulfill his promises to her!"
LUKE 1:45 NIV

Elizabeth, the wife of Zechariah and the cousin of Mary, had never been able to have a baby. For a woman of her culture, this was a particularly bitter disappointment. When she was well past the age of being able to get pregnant and had given up all hope of ever becoming a mother, the angel Gabriel came to her husband in the temple and told him that Elizabeth would bear a child. The angel's message came true, and Elizabeth gave birth to the child who would grow up to be John the Baptist. "Elizabeth's barrenness and advanced age—a double symbol of hopelessness," wrote Pastor Charles Swindoll, "became the means by which God would announce to the world that nothing is impossible for Him."

What "impossible" situations are in your life? Instead of allowing them to discourage you and rob you of hope, remember that these may be the very circumstances God wants to use in some surprising way!

....
....
....
....
....
....
....
....

Lord, You know all the problems that seem impossible to me to solve. Help me to give each one to You, trusting You to do what is best in each situation. I don't know what You will do, but my hope is in You.

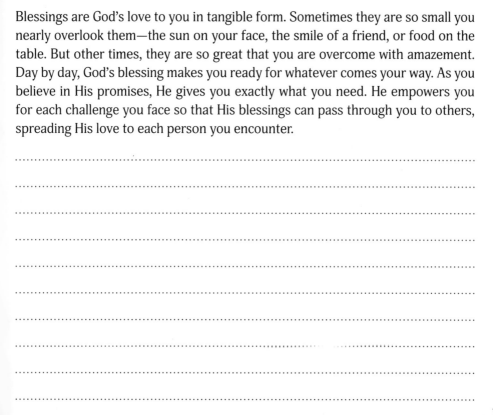

Day 143

The Empowerment of Blessing

God can pour on the blessings in astonishing ways so that you're ready for anything and everything, more than just ready to do what needs to be done.
2 CORINTHIANS 9:8 MSG

Blessings are God's love to you in tangible form. Sometimes they are so small you nearly overlook them—the sun on your face, the smile of a friend, or food on the table. But other times, they are so great that you are overcome with amazement. Day by day, God's blessing makes you ready for whatever comes your way. As you believe in His promises, He gives you exactly what you need. He empowers you for each challenge you face so that His blessings can pass through you to others, spreading His love to each person you encounter.

....
....
....
....
....
....
....
....
....
....

God, I believe You love me endlessly—and this means You are constantly blessing me. Remind me not to ignore the expressions of Your love that are everywhere I turn. Keep me sensitive to what You are doing in my life so that Your Spirit will fill me with the strength and love I need to serve You.

Day 144
Be a God-Loyal Woman

Prayerful answers come from God-loyal people; the wicked are sewers of abuse. G od keeps his distance from the wicked; he closely attends to the prayers of God-loyal people.

P roverbs 15:28–29 msg

Ask the Lord to help you become a God-loyal woman, trustworthy and steadfast. He is always looking throughout the earth for the faithful. God is looking for those who love Him enough to choose His ways over the temptations of the world. His hope is that we stay devoted day in and day out rather than allow our faith to be tossed around on the waves. Yes, the Lord is looking for committed believers.

So each time you pray, ask for strength to be loyal. Ask for discernment so you'll keep company with those on the same journey of faith as you. And then watch as God richly blesses you with a holy resolve to stay the course. Watch as He provides encouragement through other like-minded followers. Watch Him answer your prayers in meaningful and mighty ways as you stay focused on Him. Your dedication will spark His delight.

....

....

....

....

....

....

Father in heaven, don't be distant. Don't turn Your gaze from me.
Instead, let my devotion draw You closer. Hear my prayers and
know I love You! I'm committed to following Your will and ways,
so bless me with the determination I need to walk it out
every day. In the name of Jesus I pray. Amen.

Day 145
God's Long Arm

Surely the arm of the LORD is not too short to save.
ISAIAH 59:1 NIV

Have you ever noticed that when you have a big problem, God can seem further away than He usually does? That's because your need is taking up all your attention, looming large on the horizon, blocking your vision of God. All you can see is your huge problem filling your entire range of vision. When that happens, it's time to step back and get a new perspective. Scripture says that God's "arm" is long enough to reach past any problem. It is strong enough to reach down into your life to deal with the situation that seems so overwhelming to you. His mighty outstretched arm will reach down to you and meet you at your point of deepest need. Believe this: absolutely nothing is too hard for God—and He is never too far away to bless you!

....
....
....
....
....
....
....
....
....

Lord, when my problems loom so large that I can't see You, reach past my
troubled thoughts and show me Your presence. I believe Your arm is
long enough to reach me, no matter the circumstances of my life!

Day 146

Your Best Day Ever

"Arise, Jerusalem! Let your light shine for all to see.
For the glory of the Lord rises to shine on you."
Isaiah 60:1 NLT

A friend of mine has a habit of saying, "Best day ever!" whenever anyone asks her how her day is going. She says it started early in her marriage when she and her husband were stumbling around getting ready for work in the morning. When she asked her husband why he was always so cheerful, even in those pre-coffee moments, he said, "Happiness is a choice!" He convinced her that she too could choose hope and happiness each morning for the day that lay ahead. And now, every single day of her life—no matter how challenging—is her "best day ever."

We too can choose to live in hope and expectancy, anticipating each morning as our "best day ever." The light of God shines on us every day, every moment.

Glorious Lord, give me the strength and courage to choose
hope again and again, morning by morning and night by
night. May each day bring me closer to You.

The Door of Hope

"I know your deeds. See, I have placed before you an open door that no one can shut. I know that you have little strength, yet you have kept my word and have not denied my name."

<small>REVELATION 3:8 NIV</small>

In the book of Revelation, Jesus promises the church at Philadelphia that He has new opportunities in store for them. Notice that He doesn't condemn the church for being weak; instead, He praises them for their commitment to Him despite their weakness. We too can lay claim to Jesus' reassurance. Although we are often lacking in strength, Jesus has new doors for us to open, doors that will lead us to amazing vistas and thrilling adventures. He promises that nothing and no one can keep us from walking through those doors. As the apostle Paul knew, when we are at our weakest—and we stop trying to be in control of our own lives and surrender them to God—that is the very moment when God gives us the most strength (2 Corinthians 12:10).

When I find myself in a valley of trouble, all my strength gone, show me Your doorway to hope, Lord Jesus.

Day 148
Stress

When doubts filled my mind, your comfort gave me renewed hope and cheer.
PSALM 94:19 NLT

The Hebrew word translated here as *doubt* refers not to intellectual doubt about God but rather to that state of excited anxiety we've all experienced when our thoughts race, our stomachs churn, and our hearts beat hard.

In fact, what the psalmist is describing is what scientists today call the *fight-or-flight response*, when a sense of danger triggers our bodies to prepare to either run away or fight. That response is all well and good when we have to either avoid danger or struggle against it; but most of the time, particularly in our modern world, the dangers we face aren't the sort we can either flee or slug in the nose. Situations like unhappy bosses, troubled marriages, rebellious children, or financial worries create the same response as physical danger, but our bodies' reactions can build up into the destructive condition we call *stress*. No amount of willpower can stop these reactions—but we can find ways to manage our stress more effectively. One way is to seek God's comfort as quickly as possible through praying, reading scripture, or talking to a trusted friend. Although it's unlikely God will remove all stress from our lives, as we renew our hope in Him, we will discover that His joy goes much deeper than our anxiety and stress.

....

....

....

....

....

....

When I'm overwhelmed with stress, Lord,
renew my hope and comfort me.

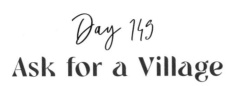

Day 149
Ask for a Village

Back in the city, they went to the room where they were staying—a second-floor room. This whole group devoted themselves to constant prayer with one accord: Peter, John, James, Andrew, Philip, Thomas, Bartholomew, Matthew, James (son of Alphaeus), Simon (the Zealot), Judas (son of James), a number of women including Mary (Jesus' mother), and some of Jesus' brothers.

ACTS 1:13–14 VOICE

This passage sets a precedent for the need for community prayer—men and women together lifting their requests to the Father is beautiful. There are some situations where it's more appropriate that we create our own sacred space and pray to God solo. There are other times when we gather a few close friends to come alongside us as reinforcements as we ask God to help remedy a tough circumstance. But there are also moments when a collective prayer with a trusted community is exactly what's needed. Who are the people you would trust to stand with you as you lift your voices to God? Do you have a small group or a church family? Maybe you have a circle of friends who support each other through life. If you don't, ask the Lord to bless you with a village of like-minded and loving people for this adventure called life.

....

....

....

....

....

....

....

*Father in heaven, please bless me with a community
of caring believers as we journey through this life
together. In the name of Jesus I pray. Amen.*

Victorious Love

Overwhelming victory is ours through Christ, who loved us.
ROMANS 8:37 NLT

Do you ever have days when victory seems elusive? When everything you do seems doomed to failure? Meanwhile, the world tells you that success is important, essential even. Countless books have been written on the topic, each one offering yet another secret formula for guaranteeing that success will be yours.

Believing that success is essential creates a false reality, however. The truth is, everyone experiences failures. Even the heroes of our faith experienced their share of failures. Abraham and Sarah, Elijah and David, Peter and Paul—all knew what it was like to make mistakes. God used even those failures, though, to bring them to the places where He wanted them to be.

"Failure should be our teacher, not our undertaker," motivational author Denis Waitley once said. "Failure is delay, not defeat. It is a temporary detour, not a dead end. Failure is something we can avoid only by saying nothing, doing nothing, and being nothing." Don't let the fear of failure paralyze you. Instead, believe that even in the midst of failure, you can still find victory in Christ.

....

....

....

....

....

....

....

Christ Jesus, thank You that even when I feel like I'm a failure,
You promise me I'm victorious through Your love. May this belief
replace the world's emphasis on external success.

Walking Forward

*Whoever catches a glimpse of the revealed counsel of God—
the free life!—even out of the corner of his eye, and sticks with
it. . .will find delight and affirmation in the action.*

JAMES 1:25 MSG

Nelson Mandela dedicated his life to dismantling racism. In the 1940s, when he was still a young man, he began fighting apartheid in South Africa, and his work continued for many decades. Imprisoned in 1964 for his activism, he was allowed only one thirty-minute visit with a single person each year and could send and receive only two letters a year. Mandela did not give up, even after twenty-seven years in prison. In 1990 he was finally released; in 1991 apartheid, at last, came to an end; and in 1994 Mandela was elected to be his nation's first Black president— and yet how easily he might have given up during his fifty-year struggle for justice!

But Mandela had caught a glimpse of the "free life" to which God calls us all, and he stuck with the hard work of changing the world. He credited perseverance as the reason he didn't succumb to his circumstances. He just kept walking forward and never gave up. We too must put one foot in front of the other and persevere toward hope and promise.

....

....

....

....

....

....

....

*Father, give me glimpses of Your plan for my life;
keep me always walking toward You.*

Day 152
Never Alone

Now may our Lord Jesus Christ himself and God our Father, who loved us and by his grace gave us eternal comfort and a wonderful hope, comfort you and strengthen you in every good thing you do and say
2 Thessalonians 2:16–17 NLT

Again and again, the Bible assures us that we are not on our own. As we read these verses, we, along with the church at Thessalonica, can lay claim to Paul's prayer for eternal comfort and a wonderful hope, coming to us directly from Jesus and the Father.

What's more, in each thing we do and say (provided we speak and act in love), God is there with us, strengthening us and encouraging us. No matter how discouraged or weak we may feel, we are not alone. We have a coworker and companion whose grace and power are big enough to handle anything we encounter. God's grace gives us the strength for anything we may face.

....

....

....

....

....

....

....

Dear holy companion, thank You that as we work together to build Your kingdom, I never have to face anything alone. Your power and love undergird my every action and every word, making up for any mistakes or weaknesses on my part. Whenever I falter today, remind me that my hope does not rely on my strength but on Yours.

Day 153
Asking God for the Big and Small

Whenever crowds came to Him, He had compassion for them because they were so deeply distraught, malaised, and heart-broken. They seemed to Him like lost sheep without a shepherd. Jesus understood what an awesome task was before Him, so He said to His disciples, "The harvest is plentiful but the workers are few. Ask the Lord of the harvest to send more workers into His harvest field."

MATTHEW 9:36–38 VOICE

Jesus knew they needed more people to help. In all His power, He could have sparked others to come forward. He could have stirred their spirits to join in the work. But maybe Jesus, instead, wanted to teach His disciples the power of prayer. Maybe He wanted to show them they could pray for things great and small. Maybe this request was part of their training, letting each see that their needs should be taken to the Father. Solutions weren't always up to them to figure out.

Let this be a reminder for you too. There's nothing too weighty or too insignificant to discuss with God. Be it relief from a headache or help choosing a paint color or the healing of an illness, talk to Him about your needs, because the Lord is interested! He is ready to bless.

....

....

....

....

....

....

....

Father in heaven, what a gift to know I can talk to You about everything. You're my confidant in all things! In the name of Jesus I pray. Amen.

Day 154
Prosperity

Whoever pursues righteousness and love finds life, prosperity and honor.
PROVERBS 21:21 NIV

We tend to believe that prosperity means material riches. According to Merriam-Webster.com, the definition of *prosperity* is "the condition of being successful or thriving, especially: economic well-being." Some Christians have even decided that God guarantees them this sort of prosperity. But when the Bible speaks of prosperity, it's referring to a different kind of blessing. The Hebrew word in this verse also refers to God's justice, salvation, and redemption. It has to do with being safe, healthy, and complete, with a sense of physical, emotional, and spiritual well-being. So, as Proverbs 21:21 promises, as you believe in God's righteousness and love, you will be blessed with well-being inside and out. You will thrive in ways that extend far beyond mere material riches.

....

....

....

....

....

....

....

....

....

....

Bless me with fullness of life, I pray, Lord. May I experience the
well-being You want me to have. Show me if any of my beliefs,
behaviors, or attitudes are blocking the flow of Your blessing.

Day 155
Joyful Expectancy

Waiting does not diminish us, any more than waiting diminishes a pregnant mother. We are enlarged in the waiting. We, of course, don't see what is enlarging us. But the longer we wait, the larger we become, and the more joyful our expectancy.
ROMANS 8:24–25 MSG

"Joyful expectancy" is a creative way to describe hope. Like a pregnancy, hope starts out as something small, undetectable to the naked eye. But then it grows, slowly and surely, even though it is still not fully revealed. The process can't be rushed. We must surrender to its demands, nurturing the new life that is waiting to be born. Sometimes we may feel weak and tired, overwhelmed by the immensity of what we have committed ourselves to; we may doubt our abilities to nurture this new life that is coming into the world. All we can do is be patient and trust God. Patient hope leads to new growth, new possibilities, and new revelations of God's love. These are the fruits of hope.

Patient Lord, enlarge me with hope. Empower my patience and strengthen my trust in You. Fill me with Your joyful expectancy.

Day 156
In the Here and Now

So I saw that there is nothing better for people than to be happy in their work.
That is our lot in life. And no one can bring us back to see what happens after we die.
ECCLESIASTES 3:22 NLT

What the ancient author of Ecclesiastes wrote in this verse is a truth we all must face: this life is the only one we know. We believe in the life to come in eternity with God, but we have never seen or experienced what that life will be like. We also cannot see what will happen in the future; we may never know what the results will ultimately be to many of the projects and causes we hold so dear. We face the future with hope, but at the same time, we must find joy and satisfaction in our work in the here and now. Hope is what allows us to surrender to God, allowing Him to hold what lies ahead in His hand while we do the best we can with the responsibilities He has given us today.

God of past, present, and future, give me the courage
and hope to work hard for You today, giving my best
effort to building Your kingdom while, at the same time,
I leave the future of my work in Your hands.

Day 157
Discipline and Learning

To learn, you must love discipline.
PROVERBS 12:1 NLT

Discipline. It's a word that has a range of beliefs attached to it, many of them negative. Sometimes it summons memories of disapproving grade-school teachers. But when the Bible talks about discipline, it isn't referring to scoldings and being sent to the principal's office. It's not talking about criticism and punishment. Instead, the Bible's discipline is always connected to learning. It has to do with developing the skills you need to live the full life God wants for you. The English word *discipline* also comes from similar root meanings: "instruction given, teaching, learning, knowledge."

Think about what it takes to learn a sport or to play an instrument. It requires the willingness to hear and learn, the commitment to practice, and the patience to keep going despite stumbles and setbacks. That's discipline! In the Bible, discipline is a good thing, something that makes you stronger, more skillful, more capable. So erase any leftover negative beliefs from childhood you have about discipline—and replace them with the joy and excitement that come from learning and growing with God.

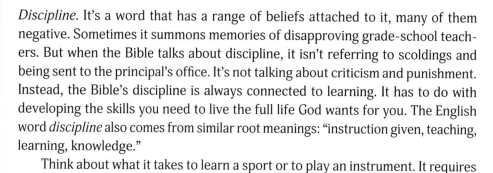

Heavenly teacher, I believe I have so much to learn from
You. May I be Your willing and disciplined student.

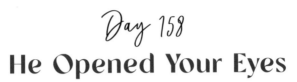

Day 158
He Opened Your Eyes

*"You claim to know nothing about him, but the fact is, he opened my eyes!
It's well known that God isn't at the beck and call of sinners, but listens
carefully to anyone who lives in reverence and does his will. That someone
opened the eyes of a man born blind has never been heard of—ever. If
this man didn't come from God, he wouldn't be able to do anything."*

JOHN 9:30–33 MSG

Rather than boast about all your accomplishments and the good things you've done for others, boast in the fact that God has opened your eyes to see Him. He's revealed Himself through the Word so you can know and understand Him better. What a blessing to realize the Lord made a way for you to talk directly to Him through prayer, anytime and anywhere.

So choose today to live your life in such a way that it honors Him. Know what God expects from those who love Him, and walk it out daily. Keep His commands, because they're the doorway to freedom. And keep your focus solely on God because He will help you navigate the mountaintop experiences as well as the deep, dark valleys. What a beautiful gift!

....
....
....
....
....
....
....

Father in heaven, thank You for choosing me as Your beloved. I'm blessed
because You see value in me. Help me live in reverence as I keep Your
ways because I see value in You! In the name of Jesus I pray. Amen.

Day 159

A Double Blessing

At the same time, don't be callous in your exercise of freedom, thoughtlessly stepping on the toes of those who aren't as free as you are. I try my best to be considerate of everyone's feelings in all these matters; I hope you will be, too.

1 Corinthians 10:32–33 msg

God has blessed you with freedom, and He wants you to claim this gift and make it your own. You no longer need to live trapped by self-doubt or false guilt. God wants you to believe Him when He says you are free.

At the same time, though, He wants you to be sensitive to others' feelings and beliefs. Not everyone is at the same place in their spiritual journeys, and some of the people around you may not have yet claimed the full freedom God wants for them. As you follow the Spirit's leading, you'll learn not to trip over other people's beliefs. You won't shove your way through conversations, insisting that your beliefs are the only correct ones. Instead, you will learn to be more aware of other people's reactions.

This doesn't mean you surrender your own spiritual freedom to others' narrow minds, legalistic opinions, and limited perspectives—but it does mean you'll let God-given empathy direct your words and actions. As you do so, you'll receive a double blessing: the rewards of both inner freedom and a life of active compassion.

....

....

....

....

....

....

God, I believe You have set me free. May I use the
freedom You have given me to bless others also.

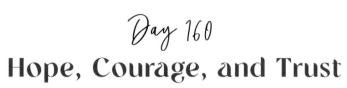

Day 160

Hope, Courage, and Trust

Trust in the Lord with all your heart and lean not on your own understanding; in all your ways submit to him, and he will make your paths straight.

PROVERBS 3:5–6 NIV

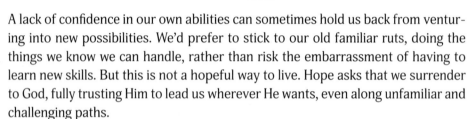

A lack of confidence in our own abilities can sometimes hold us back from venturing into new possibilities. We'd prefer to stick to our old familiar ruts, doing the things we know we can handle, rather than risk the embarrassment of having to learn new skills. But this is not a hopeful way to live. Hope asks that we surrender to God, fully trusting Him to lead us wherever He wants, even along unfamiliar and challenging paths.

Hope, courage, and trust in God go together. They are the stepping stones that lead us out of our ruts and into new experiences, new blessings. We cannot surrender to the waves if we do not lose sight of our familiar shore.

....
....
....
....
....
....
....
....
....
....

Lord of my life, my hope is in You. I trust You more
than I trust myself. Lead me wherever You want.

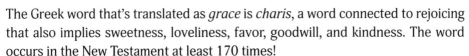

Day 161
Believe in God's Grace!

For the grace of God has been revealed, bringing salvation to all people.
TITUS 2:11 NLT

The Greek word that's translated as *grace* is *charis*, a word connected to rejoicing that also implies sweetness, loveliness, favor, goodwill, and kindness. The word occurs in the New Testament at least 170 times!

Our English versions have translated the same word in different ways, all of which help us get a fuller picture of what grace looks like. In some places, it has to do with gratitude and thanks. (This is why we "say grace" before a meal.) In other translations, it comes to us as "bounty," "liberality," or "generosity."

Sometimes it seems like a joyful, sweet *feeling* we experience; sometimes it appears to be more like an *act* of mercy and love; other times it appears to be a word that describes a *quality* of utter loveliness; and still others, it looks like something that is given, an undeserved *gift*.

The Greek word has one more shade of meaning that doesn't often come through in English: it has to do with God reaching toward us, a sense of God stretching across the distance between Himself and us, a divine act of leaning forward in eager love. Ultimately, grace takes many forms—but it is always something beautiful that God holds out to us in His outstretched arms.

....

....

....

....

....

....

....

God, I believe in the power of Your grace to fill my heart and life.

The Fuel of Hope

Be renewed in the spirit of your mind.
EPHESIANS 4:23 KJV

We all need to be regularly renewed. We are like cars that need to fill up regularly with gas; none of us can keep running on an empty tank. This means that when our supply of hope runs dry, we don't need to feel ashamed or think that God is displeased with us. Instead, we simply must go back to the source of our hope and ask for a new supply.

One way to do this is to spend some time focusing on the good things God has already given us. Each of us has our share of problems, but all of us are also blessed in countless ways. We must turn our attention away from our limitations and instead focus on our blessings!

....
....
....
....
....
....
....
....
....
....

When discouragement creeps into my thoughts and emotions, Lord God, remind me to turn to You for a new "tank" of hope. Don't let my trials and tribulations block the sight of all the joys my life still holds.

Simply Come Clean

If we claim that we're free of sin, we're only fooling ourselves. A claim like that is errant nonsense. On the other hand, if we admit our sins— simply come clean about them—he won't let us down; he'll be true to himself. He'll forgive our sins and purge us of all wrongdoing.

1 JOHN 1:8-9 MSG

Many of us would rather hide our shortcomings than reveal them. We don't like how it feels to point out what we've done wrong. . .so we don't—sometimes not even to God. It's not that we think we're sinless; we just don't want to shine a light on failure. But unlike others in our lives, the Lord isn't keeping score. There's no chart in heaven that tallies up the number of bad choices we've made. And no matter what, God's love for us will never diminish. You see, His desire for us to come clean about our sins and take responsibility is because doing that removes any barriers between us and God. That act of obedience triggers forgiveness and keeps communication unhindered. So go ahead and confess to the Lord, and let His blessings of peace and relief restore your anxious heart.

....

....

....

....

....

....

....

Father in heaven, I am coming clean about my sin and admitting the places I've fallen short of Your glory. Thank You for being a safe place to be honest. Thank You for forgiveness. In the name of Jesus I pray. Amen.

Belief in God's Love and Life

But each day the LORD pours his unfailing love upon me, and through
each night I sing his songs, praying to God who gives me life.

PSALM 42:8 NLT

Life itself is a blessing. The very blood that flows through your veins, the beat of your heart, the steady hum of your metabolism—all are blessings from God. God's constant and unconditional love pours into the cells of your body; it nourishes you through the food you eat; it surrounds you with the healing benefits of rest as you sleep each night. Like an unborn child who is constantly surrounded by her mother's care, you too live and move within the very being of God. As you become more and more convinced that you are so deeply loved, so intimately cared for, so immersed in blessing, you'll find yourself singing, even in the darkness.

....

....

....

....

....

....

....

....

....

....

I believe Your love surrounds me, God. I believe it flows through my own
body. I believe I can find Your love all around me. I believe in You!

Day 165
Repentance and Hope

"Produce fruit in keeping with repentance."
MATTHEW 3:8 NIV

We often think repentance has to do with guilt: examining our mistakes and expressing that we're sorry for them. In doing so, we often become discouraged and sad; we may feel shame and lose self-confidence. But this is not what God wants from us. Repentance is not about guilt so much as it is about hope. It's not wallowing in regret for the past but, instead, taking action to move forward. When we repent, we are filled with the hope of a future that brings us closer to Christ day by day. We gladly turn away from the things that pull us away from Him. Repentance is hope in action, leading us to a healthier, more abundant life in Christ.

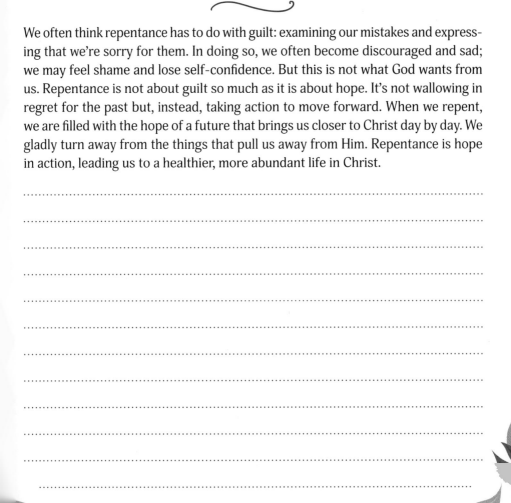

....
....
....
....
....
....
....
....
....
....
....
....

Christ Jesus, help me to follow You with hope and energy,
growing more like You as we travel through life together.

Daily Belief

In all your ways submit to him, and he will make your paths straight.
PROVERBS 3:6 NIV

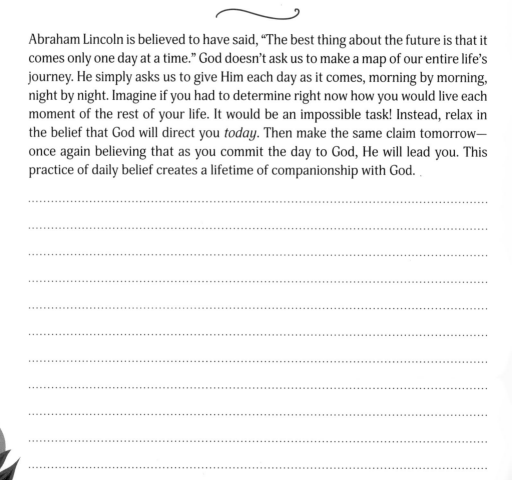

Abraham Lincoln is believed to have said, "The best thing about the future is that it comes only one day at a time." God doesn't ask us to make a map of our entire life's journey. He simply asks us to give Him each day as it comes, morning by morning, night by night. Imagine if you had to determine right now how you would live each moment of the rest of your life. It would be an impossible task! Instead, relax in the belief that God will direct you *today*. Then make the same claim tomorrow— once again believing that as you commit the day to God, He will lead you. This practice of daily belief creates a lifetime of companionship with God.

Lord, I thank You that You never ask me to have my life all mapped out ahead of time. I believe in Your promise of guidance. I give You this day to use as You want. Remind me to do the same thing again tomorrow!

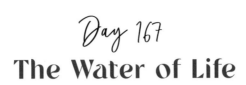

Day 167
The Water of Life

"Let anyone who is thirsty come to me and drink."
JOHN 7:37 NIV

If we believe in Christ intellectually, why don't we also believe in Him emotionally? Why do we settle for a life of frustration, irritation, and dejection? The source of all hope is freely available to us; there's no reason not to turn to Him for help and comfort.

In the next couple of verses after this one, John lets us know that Jesus was talking about "living water," and then he explains that Jesus was referring to the Spirit. Why might Jesus have used water as a metaphor for the Holy Spirit? Maybe because all life is dependent on water. Without water, our planet would be a barren rock. Without water, we would not be alive. And the Spirit is just as essential to life as water is. The Spirit is the giver of life, the one who refreshes our hearts and gives us hope. Why go thirsty when there is living water freely available?

....
....
....
....
....
....
....
....
....

Spirit of life, thank You that You are always ready and eager to satisfy my thirst for hope. Remind me that if my heart feels dry and barren, all I need to do is seek You out and You will restore my life.

Day 168
Don't Turn from God

*The one who turns his ear from hearing God's instruction will
find that even his prayers are detestable to God.*
PROVERBS 28:9 VOICE

Let this be a warning when we want to follow what our flesh wants. Let this be a verse that sounds the alarm bells in our minds when we're taking our eyes off God. The truth is, we can't have it both ways. We can't live for ourselves and expect the Lord to bless us. We can't choose the path away from Him and think He'll join us there. It's when we repent of our careless choices and dangerous decisions that God comes close again.

He is holy, and His desire is for us to walk in a right relationship with Him. It may be messy and imperfect. We may fail and falter on the regular. But God will see the condition of our hearts and know we are trying to be faithful. Be quick to turn back to the Lord and repent—He will be there with open arms, waiting for His beloved. And thank Him for embracing and blessing your return.

....

....

....

....

....

....

....

....

Father in heaven, help me cherish Your instruction and stay focused
on the path that leads to You. Bless me with Your presence, and
guide me in the right ways. I don't ever want to turn my ear
or eye from You. In the name of Jesus I pray, Amen.

Day 169

Are You Gullible?

The gullible believe anything they're told;
the prudent sift and weigh every word.
PROVERBS 14:15 MSG

Buy this diet product and you'll lose twenty pounds. Drink this soda and life will be more fun. Splash on this perfume and romance will be yours. Invest in this program and your savings will double. Apply this face cream and you'll look twenty years younger. Commercials have tremendous power to shape your beliefs. But the wise author of Proverbs 14:15 has good advice for you: don't fall victim to false promises. Before you believe something, ask questions, research your options, sift through the facts.

The Hebrew word that's been translated here as *believe* has these additional meanings: security, sureness, nourishment, stability, truth. Be careful where you look for these things; be careful what you choose to believe. Belief in God's promises will never let you down.

....

....

....

....

....

....

....

....

....

Remind me, Lord of truth, to be careful about what I believe.
May Your love be the standard against which I measure my beliefs.

Alone Time

*Before daybreak the next morning, Jesus got
up and went out to an isolated place to pray.*

MARK 1:35 NLT

Jesus lived a busy life, surrounded by people who were constantly clamoring for His attention and seeking His help. Sound familiar? All those people might have pushed Him back and forth until He lost His equilibrium. His disciples wanted Him to follow the crowds (Mark 1:37); the crowds wanted Him to take a political role as their king (John 6:15); and everywhere, people wanted Him to heal them (Matthew 8:16, 12:15, 15:30; Mark 6:56). Jesus knew the only way He could maintain His sense of purpose and hope was by regularly renewing His connection to His Father, and so He made the effort of spending time alone in prayer.

    If Jesus needed that, how much more do we! We are renewed with God's strength and energy when we spend time alone with Him in prayer. We need that energy to keep going and meet all the demands of our busy lives. Even more, we need time alone with God to keep our hope alive.

....
....
....
....
....
....
....

Jesus, when my busy life begins to drag me down, when I feel my
hope draining out of me while discouragement floods my heart,
remind me that what I need most is time alone with You.

Day 171
Belief and the Imagination

Now faith is confidence in what we hope for and assurance about what we do not see. . . . Without faith it is impossible to please God, because anyone who comes to him must believe that he exists and that he rewards those who earnestly seek him.

HEBREWS 11:1, 6 NIV

You believe in God, but sometimes your belief wavers. So how can you bolster your belief in God? Try using the power of your imagination. Children are good at make-believe, but as adults we've often forgotten this mental skill. While it's true that our imaginations can get us into trouble, an imagination that's guided by scripture and the Spirit is a gift from God.

Try this: As you scrub the kitchen floor, imagine that Jesus will walk across it. As you prepare a report at work, imagine that Jesus will review it. As you do the family laundry, imagine that Jesus will wear the clean clothes. Or as you go for a walk, picture Jesus walking beside you, keeping you company. At night, when you can't sleep, pretend you are being rocked in God's arms. This is no make-believe game. Our imagination allows us to catch a glimpse of spiritual realities our physical eyes are unable to see. It can strengthen our belief in God, transforming an intellectual idea that lives only in our minds into an emotional reality that gives shape and meaning to our everyday lives.

Use my imagination, Lord, to strengthen my belief in Your promises.

Day 172
ALL Your Hope

So prepare your minds for action and exercise self-control. Put all your hope in the gracious salvation that will come to you when Jesus Christ is revealed to the world.

1 Peter 1:13 NLT

Notice that little word *all* in this verse. Hope in Christ takes a full commitment of our entire selves. We don't hedge our bets by placing half our hope in Christ and half our hope in ourselves (or anything else), nor do we base our hope on statistical odds that might indicate to us what the future is likely to be.

In this epistle from Peter, he emphasizes that hope and action go together. However, we don't just run around in a frenzy, doing this, that, and the other thing in a desperate, last-ditch effort to save the world. Instead, before we act, we think things through. We prepare ourselves so that we're ready as soon as we hear God's voice telling us where to go.

....

....

....

....

....

....

....

....

....

....

Jesus, my hope is all in You. Prepare me to do Your work, and then show me what to do and say to help reveal You to the world.

Fragrant and Robust Prayers

O Eternal One, I call upon You. Come quickly! Listen to my voice as
I call upon You! Consider my prayer as an offering of incense that
rises before You; when I stand with my hands outstretched pleading
toward the heavens, consider it as an evening offering.

PSALM 141:1–2 VOICE

The psalmist wanted his prayers to be something good for God. He wanted his words to be fragrant and robust, rather than a burden. He wanted the Lord to receive them as an offering—a gift. He hoped his requests and thanksgiving were honoring so they would be noticed by God. And as his heartfelt words drifted up to the throne room, the psalmist's desire was for them to be well received.

Chances are you feel the same way. Even without giving it much thought, your sincere expectation is for God to be moved into action when you pray. Approach prayer with a wholehearted genuineness. Be honest and authentic as you talk to the Father. And be blessed simply because you are deeply loved by Him. God delights in who you are, and He stands ready to help His beloved.

....
....
....
....
....
....
....

Father in heaven, I want my prayers to put a smile on Your face.
Even when I fumble and have trouble expressing myself, I want my
words to touch Your heart. Bless me with Your delight as I open
my heart and share it with You. In the name of Jesus I pray. Amen.

Day 174
Guard My Mouth

Guard my mouth, O Eternal One; control what I say. Keep a careful watch on every word I speak. Don't allow my deepest desires to steer me toward doing what is wrong or associating with wicked people or joining in their wicked works or tasting any of their pleasures.

PSALM 141:3–4 VOICE

Every single one of us should take this scripture passage seriously. We know the words we speak can bring life or death to those we love. They can encourage or they can cut down. Our lips have the power to bless or curse. And we get to choose.

The problem is that too often we speak before we think. We let a statement fly out of our mouths in frustration without considering how it will affect those around us. Rather than take a breath before we share what's on our minds, we recklessly purge our thoughts and cause offense. But if we take this prayer seriously and start the day asking God to guard our mouths, He will bless us with the ability. Giving Him consent to control our tongues will help protect the ones we love. And we'll honor the Lord by following His command to love.

Father in heaven, help me bless others and honor You by watching
the words that come out of my mouth. I want to bless and not
curse. I want to encourage rather than dismantle. Give me
self-control. In the name of Jesus I pray. Amen.

Day 175
Fixing Your Gaze on God

My gaze is fixed upon You, Eternal One, my Lord; in You I find safety
and protection. Do not abandon me and leave me defenseless.

PSALM 141:8 VOICE

Every time you choose to fix your gaze on God rather than on the craziness around you, you will be blessed. When you stay steadied on Him, the fears of the day melt away. This means you focus more on His promise to keep you safe than on what worries you. You trust that God will rescue you from the mess, not let you sink in it. Rather than allow the unknowns to overwhelm you, you take the next right step God reveals through prayer. You wait in expectation for the blessing of His presence to overwhelm you instead of giving in to the stress and strife of the situation.

Fixing your gaze on the Lord requires His help, and it's an ability He will give you when you ask. Let Him be the one who protects you, knowing your prayers for His presence will keep you from being defenseless.

....
....
....
....
....
....
....
....

Father in heaven, bless me with the steadfastness to stay focused on You
in the difficult moments. Give me courage to ask You for help when
I need it. And keep me from taking control of my circumstances,
because I know I can't fix things on my own. I need You, Lord.
And I need You now. In the name of Jesus I pray. Amen.

A Wonderful Promise

*"Whatever you ask for in prayer, believe that you
have received it, and it will be yours."*

MARK 11:24 NIV

This is a wonderful promise Jesus made to us—but it's also hard to know what to do with it. How can we believe in something that's just not there? And if our belief is too weak, will God punish us by withholding the thing we're praying for? Is it the power of our belief that shapes God's ability to answer prayer? Should we try to "work up" more belief so we can get the thing we want?

Questions like these are natural ones, but they come from thinking with a human perspective rather than God's. Prayer is not about getting what we want; it's not meant to satisfy our egotistical and selfish desires. Instead, prayer is about spending time with God; it's about opening our hearts to His Spirit so that He can begin to shape our beliefs and desires. His power and ability to act do not depend on anything we can "work up," only on our surrender to His love.

....

....

....

....

....

....

....

....

Spirit of love, I believe in You. I believe You have the power to work in my life.
I ask that You shape my longings and give wisdom to my prayers. May
my prayers and the desires of my heart lead me ever closer to You.

Day 177
Seeds of Hope

"The Kingdom of Heaven is like a mustard seed planted in a field. It is the smallest of all seeds, but it becomes the largest of garden plants; it grows into a tree, and birds come and make nests in its branches."

MATTHEW 13:31–32 NLT

When we are discouraged, sometimes we long for some big, spectacular change to come along and turn our lives around. Often, though, that's not the way things work. Instead, we need to look for little seeds of hope in our lives—and then water them, nurture them, and wait patiently for them to grow.

Today, look for little hopeful things in your life. Is the sun shining? Are the birds singing? Did something make you laugh? Did a stranger smile at you? As Jesus reminds us in the Gospel of Matthew, even the tiniest seed can grow into a tree where birds can come and nest. What "tree" might be sprouting even now in your life?

....

....

....

....

....

....

....

....

Jesus, thank You for telling us stories that help us understand Your kingdom. Show me seeds of possibility in my life. Shift my focus away from all the big, discouraging things in my life so that I can pay attention to these little signs of hope.

Grace

"My grace is all you need."
2 CORINTHIANS 12:9 NLT

Hope isn't constantly looking behind it, worrying about the past and what could've been done differently. Hope rests in the knowledge that God's grace is all we need. The Greek word our Bibles translate as "grace" is *charis*, a word that has all these meanings wrapped up in it: favor, kindness, sweetness, joy, delight, generosity, pleasure. The word also contains an additional layer of meaning our English word is missing altogether: the image of God leaning toward us, extending Himself to give Himself away, reaching out to us.

When we begin to understand this full meaning of grace—and when we begin to believe it is real in our own lives—then hope will come more easily to our hearts. Because of grace, we have everything we need for today and all our tomorrows.

....

....

....

....

....

....

....

....

God of love, thank You for Your infinite grace that is always reaching out to give me everything I need. I don't know what shape Your grace will take in my life, but I'm willing to wait and see.

Day 179

Believe in Your Inner Beauty!

*What matters is not your outer appearance—the styling of your hair, the
jewelry you wear, the cut of your clothes—but your inner disposition.
Cultivate inner beauty, the gentle, gracious kind that God delights in.*

1 Peter 3:3–4 MSG

We want to be pretty. It's a longing that has been whispered into our hearts ever since we were little girls. Disney movies told us we had to look like a princess; Barbie dolls said we needed to be both skinny and curvy; and countless TV shows and commercials promised that pretty women are the ones who are most loved. As grown-up women, we often still believe that our appearance matters more than it does—that our hair, our clothes, our makeup are necessary ingredients to the persona we present to the world.

Although God delights in our physical beings and wants us to care for and respect our bodies, we can become overly worried about our appearance, fretting over whether we measure up to the demanding standards of that little girl who still lives in our hearts. We need to replace that old childish belief in the necessity of princess-perfect prettiness with a new and stronger belief in our spiritual value. As we allow God's Spirit to shine through us, our deepest, truest beauty will be revealed.

....

....

....

....

....

....

Spirit, I believe my true beauty comes from Your presence
in my heart. Shine through me so that others see You.

The Protection of God

*Protect me from the jaws of the trap my enemies have set for me
and from the snares of those who work evil. May the wicked be
caught in their own nets while I alone escape unharmed.*

PSALM 141:9-10 VOICE

Let this be a prayer you pray often, both for yourself and those you love. The Word tells us that in this life we will have trouble. We will battle against evil forces manifesting in our earthly enemies to trip us up. We'll face heartache and grief because of others. Just like everyone else, we will walk out seasons of deep discouragement. We will suffer loss, rejection, and betrayal. So when we fail to ask God for protection, we are left wide open to attacks. Let the Lord bless you with His shelter as you seek it through prayer. Watch as you reap the benefits of His presence. And while the difficulties will come, God will help keep your head above water. Traps may be set, but you will be blessed and protected.

....

....

....

....

....

....

....

....

Father in heaven, please bless me with Your protection from the snares I am able
to see and the ones I cannot. Don't allow the enemy to overwhelm me with
the negatives. I pray that I will, instead, stand strong in faith and in Your
strength, trusting Your presence to protect and save me. Bless me with
an escape route every time. In the name of Jesus I pray. Amen.

Day 181
The Prince of Peace

For to us a child is born, to us a son is given....
And he will be called...Prince of Peace.
ISAIAH 9:6 NIV

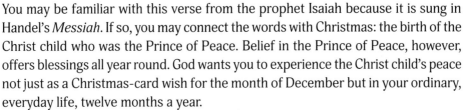

You may be familiar with this verse from the prophet Isaiah because it is sung in Handel's *Messiah*. If so, you may connect the words with Christmas: the birth of the Christ child who was the Prince of Peace. Belief in the Prince of Peace, however, offers blessings all year round. God wants you to experience the Christ child's peace not just as a Christmas-card wish for the month of December but in your ordinary, everyday life, twelve months a year.

The Hebrew word translated "peace" is *shalom*, a word with many shades of meaning that include completeness, prosperity, safety, contentment, health, rest, comfort, ease, and wholeness. If you believe in the Prince of peace, you can trust He will lead you along paths to comfort and contentment; He will work to make you whole and healthy, safe and sound. You can relax, even on your most stressful days, knowing you're relying on Christ's shalom at work in your heart and life.

....

....

....

....

....

....

....

Prince of peace, even in a world of conflict and tension,
I believe in Your shalom. Bring comfort, completeness,
safety, and wholeness to the world—and to my heart.

Nourished by Hope

You prepare a feast for me in the presence of my enemies.
PSALM 23:5 NLT

Fear is the great enemy of hope. Again and again, throughout the Bible, God says to us, "Fear not." This is the command God gives us more often than any other; in fact, some preachers say there are at least 365 Bible verses that say, "Fear not" (or words to that effect). But can we ever remove fear completely from our hearts and minds? According to psychologists, that would be an unrealistic, even unhealthy, expectation. Fear may often be our enemy, and yet it is also a normal part of human life.

But the psalmist tells us that God feeds us a feast even when our enemies are all around us. Note that the psalm doesn't say, "You destroy my enemies so that I can feast undisturbed." Instead, even when we are attacked by our old enemy fear, we can be nourished by hope.

....

....

....

....

....

....

....

....

....

*Dear God, when fear attacks my mind, shaking my confidence
in both myself and You, may I feast on Your hope.*

Tiredness

So take a new grip with your tired hands and strengthen your weak knees. Mark out a straight path for your feet so that those who are weak and lame will not fall but become strong.

HEBREWS 12:12–13 NLT

We all have times when we're just plain tired. Our weariness may come from a long stretch of sleepless nights (maybe because of a new baby, a new puppy, or just good old insomnia), a challenging week at work, or a lingering illness that has sapped our energy. Not only is tirednessa physical feeling, but also it affects our emotions, making us feel discouraged or tearful. In moments like that, hope is what gives us the incentive to keep going.

Notice also the advice the author of the book of Hebrews gives us in verse 13 (NLT): "straight path. . .so that those who are weak and lame will not fall but become strong." In other words, when you're tired is not the time to attempt a new challenge. If you do, you may cause harm to yourself. Instead, take an easier path and give yourself time to rest and heal.

....
....
....
....
....
....
....
....

Lord, when I am tired and weak, make my hope in You strong.
Lead me on paths that will restore my body and mind.

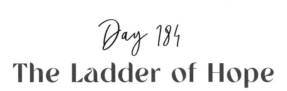

Day 184

The Ladder of Hope

He had a dream in which he saw a stairway resting on the earth, with its top reaching to heaven, and the angels of God were ascending and descending on it.

GENESIS 28:12 NIV

Because of a family conflict, Jacob was fleeing his family home. When he stopped for the night, he was so tired that he settled for a stone as a pillow. As he lay down to sleep, he must have been feeling discouraged and afraid. But right there in the middle of his troubles, God gave him a vision that brought new hope to him. He saw that this world was connected to the heavenly realm by a shining ladder, a ladder that the angels used to constantly go back and forth between earth and heaven.

We may never have a dream like Jacob's (and our dreams probably won't be remembered and retold for thousands of years!), but hope is a little like Jacob's ladder: it gives us a new vision of our world, allowing us to glimpse a deeper reality beyond our ordinary lives.

....

....

....

....

....

....

....

....

....

God of Jacob, may my hope in You inspire me
to build Your kingdom amid my everyday life.

Day 185
God Is Good All the Time

Sing songs to the tune of his glory, set glory to the rhythms of his praise.
Say of God, "We've never seen anything like him!" When your enemies see you
in action, they slink off like scolded dogs. The whole earth falls to its knees—
it worships you, sings to you, can't stop enjoying your name and fame.
PSALM 66:2–4 MSG

God is so good all the time. That means every good thing you experience or receive comes from Him. Maybe it was a restored marriage or a proposal. Maybe it was adoption papers or a plus sign on the pregnancy test. Maybe it was loan forgiveness or an unexpected invitation.

As believers, it's important to have our eyes wide open so we can watch for God's blessings in our lives. We need to keep our eyes trained on Him, waiting with expectation for tangible reminders of His love. And when we see a demonstration of His compassion or restoration, let us fall to our knees and glorify His name. Let us be filled with awe and wonder at the ways God chooses to bless the faithful.

....

....

....

....

....

....

....

Father in heaven, my heart is full of gratitude for the ways You show love through
blessings. I will acknowledge You through both private prayer and public
praise, giving You the glory for every good thing in my life. Thank You
for blessing me with abundance. In the name of Jesus I pray. Amen.

Day 186
Clothed in Belief

She is clothed with strength and dignity,
and she laughs without fear of the future.
PROVERBS 31:25 NLT

The woman in Proverbs 31 believed in God's promises. She clothed herself in them as though they were her finest robes. They gave her strength, dignity, beauty, and a sense of security. They allowed her to look into the unknown and smile with the same playful anticipation a child feels on Christmas Eve.

When the Proverbs 31 woman laughed at the future, she wasn't pretending that troubles and challenges didn't lie ahead. She knew that sooner or later she would face the loss of loved ones and that the day of her own death would one day arrive. But those realities did not shake her belief in God. She could joke at her fears for the future, not because she was hiding her head in the sand but because she was confident that God's love was the foundation of each thing she would experience, including death. When we share her belief, we too no longer have to fear the future; we can even face death with a smile of anticipation.

....
....
....
....
....
....
....

Lord of both life and death, I ask that You give me the strong belief of the woman in Proverbs 31. May that belief be the clothing I wear each day as I head out into the world so that I may look into the future and laugh with joy, knowing You have infinite blessings in store for me.

Day 187
Hope in Action

Dear friends, do you think. . .merely talking about faith indicate[s] that a person really has it? For instance, you come upon an old friend dressed in rags and half-starved and say, "Good morning, friend! Be clothed in Christ! Be filled with the Holy Spirit!" and walk off without providing so much as a coat or a cup of soup—where does that get you? Isn't it obvious that God-talk without God-acts is outrageous nonsense?

JAMES 2:14–17 MSG

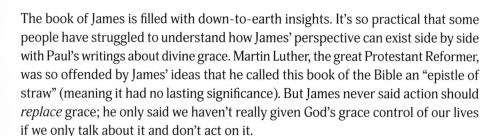

The book of James is filled with down-to-earth insights. It's so practical that some people have struggled to understand how James' perspective can exist side by side with Paul's writings about divine grace. Martin Luther, the great Protestant Reformer, was so offended by James' ideas that he called this book of the Bible an "epistle of straw" (meaning it had no lasting significance). But James never said action should *replace* grace; he only said we haven't really given God's grace control of our lives if we only talk about it and don't act on it.

The action grace inspires is what changes our world. It brings the light of hope to the darkness of sin and sadness.

....
....
....
....
....
....
....

God, help me to take action so that Your hope,
love, and grace will shine out into the world.

Everyday Hope

Our help is from the Lord, who made heaven and earth.
PSALM 124:8 NLT

According to the online Oxford dictionary, *hope* as a noun is "a feeling of expectation and desire for a certain thing to happen," and as a verb it means to "want something to happen." These meanings equate hope with wishing. When we say, "I hope the sun shines tomorrow," we're saying, "I *wish* the sun would shine tomorrow." But this is not at all the hope that the Bible describes.

Biblical hope relies on the Creator of the universe. It is not a wish but an open-ended certainty that no matter what happens, God will help us through. Even as committed followers of Christ, however, we often settle for the dictionary definition of hope, forgetting that there is another form of hope that is ours. We often wait until we're in trouble before we reach for hope in God. But we don't have to wait for something bad to happen to us. Hope is ours every day.

....
....
....
....
....
....
....
....

Remind me today, Creator, that hope shines from within
even the most ordinary circumstances (as well as the most
challenging ones). Teach me to daily live in Your hope.

Day 189
Hard-Earned Growth

God blesses those who patiently endure testing and temptation.
Afterward they will receive the crown of life that God has promised.
JAMES 1:12 NLT

Here it is again: the promise that hard times can lead to a richer life. This biblical truth has been reaffirmed by psychologists, who have noticed that, after a trauma, many people grow stronger in several ways:

- They become more empathetic and able to not only identify with others' pain but find practical ways to reach out and help.
- Their attention shifts away from material possessions and achievements, while relationships and spirituality become more important to them.
- They turn to their faith for help and grow stronger spiritually.
- They use their experiences to fuel their creativity, whether in art, writing, music, or some other form of creation.
- They realize that they are strong enough to survive future troubles, and they gain the courage for facing trials.

....
....
....
....
....
....
....

God of blessing, may my hope in You help me to grow even
during the hard times, giving me a richer, fuller life as
well as the potential to serve You in new ways.

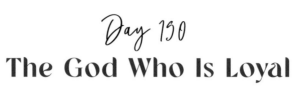

The God Who Is Loyal

*I called out to him with my mouth, my tongue shaped the sounds of music.
If I had been cozy with evil, the Lord would never have listened. But he most
surely did listen, he came on the double when he heard my prayer. Blessed
be God: he didn't turn a deaf ear, he stayed with me, loyal in his love.*

PSALM 66:17–20 MSG

There are countless words to describe God, but sometimes we struggle to find the right way to express who He is to us. For many, God is healer and restorer. He's the one who's mighty to save. He's the Prince of Peace and King of kings. God is Comforter. He is Redeemer. He's our source of all good things. God is the giver of strength and wisdom.

But one of the most beautiful words to describe Him is *loyal*. In His faithfulness, God stays with us. He fulfills every promise He's made. He doesn't turn a deaf ear to those who love Him and aim to live the life He's planned. When you pray, be sure to call out the attributes that mean the most to you. It may be different every day, based on your situation. But let God know who He is to you. Tell Him why His presence blesses you.

....

....

....

....

....

....

....

Father in heaven, thank You for being loyal. It's refreshing
to know I can always count on You to show up.
In the name of Jesus I pray. Amen.

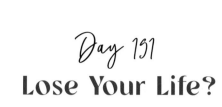

Day 199
Lose Your Life?

*"For whoever wants to save their life will lose it,
but whoever loses their life for me will save it."*
LUKE 9:24 NIV

Life is full of paradoxes. God seems to delight in turning our ideas inside out and backward; and again and again, we come across scriptures that seem hard to believe. This verse is a good example. It doesn't seem to make sense—and yet we can believe its truth. The more we try to cling to people and possessions, the emptier our lives end up being. The only way to possess our life is to surrender it absolutely into God's hands. As we let go of everything, God's grace gives everything back to us, transformed by His love.

....

....

....

....

....

....

....

....

....

Lord of paradox, I believe Your Word even when it's hard to understand.
Your love turns my reality inside out: when I lose my life, You give
it back to me; when I let go of my need to be in control, You
give me true freedom; and when I release my grasp on my
belongings, You bless me with everything I need.

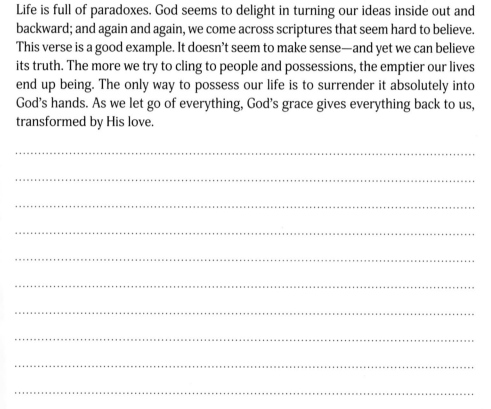

A Flame in the Darkness

"Because of God's tender mercy, the morning light from heaven is about to break upon us, to give light to those who sit in darkness and in the shadow of death, and to guide us to the path of peace."

LUKE 1:78–79 NLT

If it weren't for life's dark days, we would not need hope. Death is all too real; hatred and violence are facts of life we cannot turn away from. Hope in God's mercy brings light to even the darkest nights, a light that shows us the way to a better world, a world where God's peace rules, a world where shadows are dispelled, and where the Lord of love is on the throne. Hope is the voice of God's Spirit, promising us that all that was broken will one day be mended and all who are sick from sin will be healed through the power of divine grace.

....

....

....

....

....

....

....

....

....

....

Merciful God, when my life is dark, shed the light of Your hope into my heart and mind. Make my life a flame that carries Your hope out into the world so that others will see the path ahead that leads us to Your peace, Your wholeness, Your infinite love.

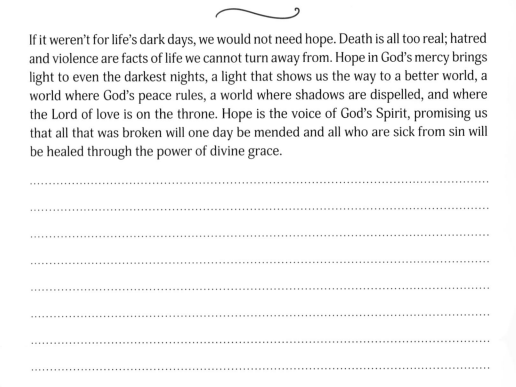

Day 193
Knowing God

I know whom I have believed, and am convinced that he is
able to guard what I have entrusted to him until that day.
2 TIMOTHY 1:12 NIV

An author once expressed hope as being the "unknown" in life. While this statement is true in many ways (hope not only accepts but welcomes the future, regardless of what it holds), in our case, as followers of Christ, we *do* know the source of our hope. The more we get to know Him and the deeper we grow in our relationship with Him, the surer and steadier our hope will be.

In the second half of this verse, Paul (who wrote this letter to Timothy) stresses another aspect of our hope in God: the surrender of our lives and everything they hold into God's hands. Hope in God holds nothing back. Notice that giving something to God isn't the same as throwing it away; instead, God guards each thing we give Him, keeping it far safer than we ever could.

....

....

....

....

....

....

....

....

....

Help me, Lord God, to get to know You more and more deeply. I know
I can trust You with everything I love, and so I give it all to You.

Believe in a God Who's Stronger Than Your Enemies!

*My times are in your hands; deliver me from the hands
of my enemies, from those who pursue me.*

PSALM 31:15 NIV

Do you ever believe that trouble is chasing you? No matter how fast you run or how you try to hide, it comes after you relentlessly, dogging your footsteps, breathing its hot breath down your neck, robbing you of peace. What's even worse is that it not only follows you; it waits for you down the road as well!

Maybe you need to stop running and stop hiding and, instead, let yourself drop into God's hands, believing He will hold both the present and your future safe. No matter what form your "enemies" take, He is stronger than they are!

....

....

....

....

....

....

....

....

....

Faithful Lord, I believe You hold my life in Your hands. I don't need
to worry about either present or future dangers because You
have everything under control. You will let no enemy—
whether spiritual or physical—defeat me.

Asking for Wisdom

If you don't have all the wisdom needed for this journey, then all you have to do is ask God for it; and God will grant all that you need. He gives lavishly and never scolds you for asking. The key is that your request be anchored by your single-minded commitment to God. Those who depend only on their own judgment are like those lost on the seas, carried away by any wave or picked up by any wind.

JAMES 1:5–6 VOICE

Of all the things you pray for on the regular, asking the Lord to bless you with wisdom should top your list. Always ask for His discernment to cover your decisions. While we may be wise and smart beyond our years, we all need the kind of knowledge only God can give. Sometimes we don't ask because of our pride. Sometimes it's because we forget that God is sovereign and all-knowing. But sometimes we don't ask because we're afraid our asking will anger Him. Let today's scripture remind you that a request for wisdom won't ever frustrate God. What's more, your dependence on Him will bless you with wisdom in abundance.

....
....
....
....
....
....
....
....

Father in heaven, what a blessing to know You give lavishly. Help me be fully committed to You and not my own judgment so I can benefit from Your wisdom in every situation. On my own, I'm helpless. But with You, I'm ready for anything. In the name of Jesus I pray. Amen.

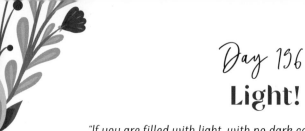

Day 156
Light!

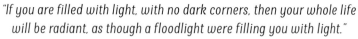

"If you are filled with light, with no dark corners, then your whole life will be radiant, as though a floodlight were filling you with light."
Luke 11:36 nlt

We like to believe we can hide parts of ourselves where no one will see them: out of sight, out of mind. We hide them from others; we hide them from ourselves; we even try to hide them from God. We somehow convince ourselves that what we refuse to look at doesn't exist. But those hidden things don't go away. No matter what we believe, they still have the power to hurt us and others. Meanwhile, God wants to shine His light into even our darkest, most private nooks and crannies. He wants us to step out into the floodlight of His love—and then believe that His love will make us shine.

....
....
....
....
....
....
....
....
....

God of light, I believe You can make me shine. I ask You
to reveal anything I've kept hidden, even from myself,
so that I can be radiant with Your love.

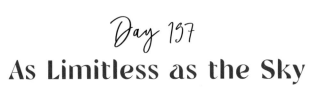

Day 197

As Limitless as the Sky

Now all glory to God, who is able, through his mighty power at work within us, to accomplish infinitely more than we might ask or think.

EPHESIANS 3:20 NLT

No goal we set ourselves, no task we attempt, and no dream we have for the future will ever be quite as big as what God actually has in mind for us. When we focus on what we can imagine for ourselves, we may think we are envisioning our maximum potential, when actually we may be putting limits on God.

The God who is all-powerful, all-knowing, and ever-present, the God of eternity and infinity, sets no boundary lines in our lives. He makes all things possible, and His creative power far exceeds our limited imaginations. He has big dreams for our lives—and God's dreams are always full of hope, power, and possibility.

Infinite God, may I always be open to Your dream for my life.
Remind me that You are as limitless as the sky. Help me to
trust Your power at work in my life. Fill me with Your hope.

Day 158
On Eagles' Wings

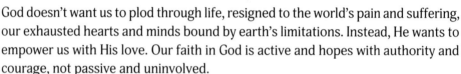

Those who hope in the LORD will renew their strength. They will soar on wings like eagles; they will run and not grow weary, they will walk and not be faint.
ISAIAH 40:31 NIV

God doesn't want us to plod through life, resigned to the world's pain and suffering, our exhausted hearts and minds bound by earth's limitations. Instead, He wants to empower us with His love. Our faith in God is active and hopes with authority and courage, not passive and uninvolved.

When, despite our weariness, we place our hope in God, He will not only give us the power to take one more step—He will make us *fly*! We will soar on eagles' wings, and we will shine with hope.

When I feel so tired that I can't go on, Lord Jesus,
remind me to lean on Your strength. Give me a
hope that blazes with Your love and Your peace.

Day 199

Everything Is under Control

Trust God from the bottom of your heart;
don't try to figure out everything on your own.
PROVERBS 3:5 MSG

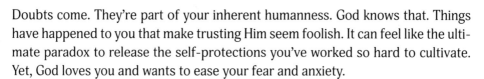

Doubts come. They're part of your inherent humanness. God knows that. Things have happened to you that make trusting Him seem foolish. It can feel like the ultimate paradox to release the self-protections you've worked so hard to cultivate. Yet, God loves you and wants to ease your fear and anxiety.

Picture this: unclenching the fist of your heart and releasing the problems you've tried relentlessly to figure out on your own, placing them each into God's outstretched hands. You don't have to go through life alone, always on guard. God waits patiently for you to believe He has everything under control.

....
....
....
....
....
....
....
....
....
....

God, I believe You are completely, totally, utterly trustworthy. I know
You hold my life in Your hands—and You will never let it drop.

Light in the Darkness

Even the darkness will not be dark to you; the night will shine like the day.
Psalm 139:12 NIV

Sojourner Truth was someone who knew all about darkness—and all about hope. Born into slavery, she often found her mother weeping for her siblings who had been sold. When Sojourner was nine years old, she was sold to a man who often beat her until she bled. She knew almost nothing about Christianity, but she told all her troubles to her friend "who lived in the sky."

One day, while talking to this friend, she realized someone was there with her, someone who had also been beaten. She expressed to her friend that she'd always felt His love but did not know His name. She heard Him respond that He was Jesus.

When Sojourner gained her freedom many years later, she used it to speak out for the rights of both women and black people. Her powerful voice, faith in God, and passion for justice captivated audiences. She stood for hope and light during a time of great darkness.

....

....

....

....

....

....

....

....

....

Friend Jesus, may my life shine bright with the
hope in You that empowered Sojourner Truth.

Be Vocal in Your Praises

Give thanks to the Eternal, and call out to Him. Teach the people His deeds. Sing to Him! Sing praises to Him! Talk about all His wonders. Brag about His holy name; let your heart rejoice in following the Eternal. Always follow the Eternal, His strength and His face.

1 Chronicles 16:8–11 voice

It's so important we are vocal in our praises to the Lord because it has a supernatural way of encouraging everyone. When we hear spoken words, we learn. Many of us are audible learners, so listening to accounts of God's greatness grows our faith, even if we're the ones speaking. When we brag about Him to others, it encourages them by offering hope in their situation. And it also glorifies and praises God when we recognize and acknowledge His mighty hand in our circumstances.

Ask God to give you opportunities to call attention to His goodness in front of others. Ask for open doors to talk to people about God's good deeds. Embrace every opportunity to sing His praises and talk about His wonders. We are blessed in sharing and others are blessed in hearing.

....

....

....

....

....

....

....

Father in heaven, let me be vocal in glorifying Your name because You're worthy of all praise! Open my eyes to see Your wonders and deeds, and open my mouth to share them with others who need hope in You. In the name of Jesus I pray. Amen.

Forgiveness and Hope

Peter came to him and asked, "Lord, how often should I forgive someone who sins against me? Seven times?" "No, not seven times," Jesus replied, "but seventy times seven!"

MATTHEW 18:21–22 NLT

At first glance, you might think that forgiveness and hope have very little to do with each other. A lack of forgiveness, however, can keep us tied to the past. It can make us bitter, and it can crush our sense of hope. We must remember that forgiveness is not forgetting or ignoring pain caused but is forgiving the one who did the hurting and walking in peace and hope for a better future.

We may feel as though forgiving someone frees that person from guilt, but as Jesus knew, forgiveness frees our own hearts. Refusing to forgive locks us into the past, but forgiving makes room for new possibilities. It gives God's Spirit space to bring divine healing into even the most painful memories so that we can hope again.

Jesus, give me the strength to release the past, including the individuals who have hurt me. Help me to give them to You so that there's more room in my heart for hope and joy and love.

Day 203

Trained by Trouble

No discipline seems pleasant at the time, but painful. Later on,
however, it produces a harvest of righteousness and
peace for those who have been trained by it.

HEBREWS 12:11 NIV

Sometimes life just seems to wear us down. We can usually cope with the endless mini crises that fill our lives, but eventually, sooner or later, we all reach a point where we start to believe we've had all we can take. Giving up seems like the only option. It may be some small event that tips us over from belief in God's promises to fear and doubt—or it may be a major life change, an illness or the death of a close friend or loved one. Whatever it is, it's the last straw. Life just doesn't make sense anymore.

God never wants you to feel unnecessary pain, and His heart aches for you when your belief in Him is shaken. But He also wants you to learn that He can use even the hard things in life to draw you closer to Him. He is training you to trust Him, absolutely and totally.

....

....

....

....

....

....

....

Train me, God, to trust You more. May my belief in You
remain firm, even in the midst of crisis and challenge.

Day 204

The Power of Love

*May you experience the love of Christ, though it is too great
to understand fully. Then you will be made complete with all
the fullness of life and power that comes from God.*

EPHESIANS 3:19 NLT

A popularly circulated quote, which has made its rounds on the internet, speaks of finding strength when we are loved and becoming courageous when we love someone else. There is certainly truth to that. Love, whether it's given or received, empowers us. It brings new life into our hearts and minds. It allows us to see new possibilities. It gives us hope.

"God is love," the Bible tells us (1 John 4:16), and I believe we find God's presence wherever we find real love. God loves us through other people. I think He even shows us His love through our dogs and cats, those furry faithful friends of ours. But most of all, He loves us through Jesus.

....
....
....
....
....
....
....
....
....

Thank You, Jesus, for revealing God's love to me. May Your love
work in my life and in my heart, making me strong, courageous,
and full of hope so that I can do Your work on earth.

Day 205
Hope That Stays Alert

"They waited for me as for showers and drank in my words as the spring rain."
JOB 29:23 NIV

In this verse, we are again reminded that hope often involves waiting. The author of Job directs our attention to the natural world, where the seasons of the year remind us that even the hardest phases of our lives give way to new life as God refreshes us with His Word.

This verse reminds us that hope not only lifts our hearts but also inspires us to be open to opportunities for God's grace to flow into our lives. While hope waits, it stays alert so that it will be ready to take advantage of all the possibilities and potential God brings to our lives—like the life-giving showers of springtime.

Keep my mind and heart alert, watching for whatever
work of grace You are about to do in my life, Lord God.

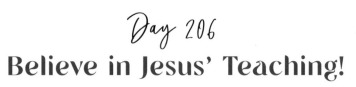

Day 206

Believe in Jesus' Teaching!

*"Let me teach you, because I am humble and gentle at
heart, and you will find rest for your souls."*
MATTHEW 11:29 NLT

Sometimes we keep trying to do life on our own—even though we don't know what we're doing, even though we're exhausted. Somehow we believe we have to just keep stumbling on; we believe we have no other options. And all the while, Jesus waits quietly, ready to show us the way. He yearns to lead us with His quiet, gentle strength, carrying our burdens for us. We don't have to try so hard. We can let go of the belief that we have to do it on our own—and simply rest our souls in His presence.

....
....
....
....
....
....
....
....
....
....
....

Jesus, I believe You have everything I need in life—love, wisdom, strength,
creativity. Thank You that You offer Yourself to me so humbly, so gently.

Day 207
Private Prayer

"But when you pray, go away by yourself, shut the door behind you, and pray to your Father in private. Then your Father, who sees everything, will reward you."

Matthew 6:6 NLT

The world is full of a variety of beliefs about prayer. A 2017 Barna research study found that prayer is not only the most common faith practice among American adults but also one of the most complex and multifaceted. The Bible speaks of numerous kinds of prayer (supplication, intercession, and worship, for example) and uses a range of ideas to describe the practice, telling us that prayer takes many shapes and forms. There's the corporate kind of prayer, where we lift our hearts to God as part of a congregation. There's also the far less elaborate kind of prayer that's said quickly and on the run, the whispered cry for help or a song of praise in the midst of life's busyness. But verses like this one tell us we need to make some time in our lives for the prayer that comes out of solitude—when, in the privacy of some quiet place, we come into God's presence all alone. Fortunately, the Barna study found that this is the form of prayer that 95 percent of Americans believe in most, with only 5 percent indicating they most believe in corporate prayer or prayer with at least one other person. God promises to bless this belief!

....

....

....

....

....

....

I believe, Lord, that prayer and solitude are necessary parts of my life. I believe that You hear my prayers and that You will use prayer to bring Your love and blessing into my life.

When You Choose to Be Present

Don't run from tests and hardships, brothers and sisters. As difficult as they are, you will ultimately find joy in them; if you embrace them, your faith will blossom under pressure and teach you true patience as you endure. And true patience brought on by endurance will equip you to complete the long journey and cross the finish line—mature, complete, and wanting nothing.

JAMES 1:2–4 VOICE

If you're struggling in marriage, stand strong and press into God. If a company merger means the loss of your job, don't waver as you trust. If you receive papers revealing an unexpected court date, be bold. If grief from your parent's medical diagnosis overwhelms you, cling to God.

Friend, when you choose not to run away in fear, even when everything in you wants to, some amazing blessings will come to pass. Not only will standing fast cause your faith to blossom, teaching you true patience, but it will also build your endurance muscle for hardship. It will mature your belief like nothing else. And it will enable you to cross the finish line with passion and purpose, knowing you stayed present with God through it all.

....

....

....

....

....

....

Father in heaven, help me embrace the hardships that come my way.
I know You'll use them to benefit me and glorify You. Let me be
present and awake as I press into You for strength and grow
deeper in my faith. In the name of Jesus I pray. Amen.

Day 209
World-Changing Love

Do everything with love.
1 CORINTHIANS 16:14 NLT

What do you believe about love? If you're like most people, you have conflicting beliefs. Our world isn't too clear on what the definition of love actually is. Sometimes our beliefs limit the power love has to change the world, especially if we think love is only an emotion. The Bible teaches us that love is more than a feeling; it needs to become real through action. We grow in love as we act in love. Some days the emotion may overwhelm us; other days we may feel nothing at all. But if we express our love while making meals, driving the car, talking to our friends and families, or doing our work, God's love will flow through us to those around us. Our belief in the power of love will grow wider and deeper.

....
....
....
....
....
....
....
....
....
....

God of love, I believe Your love is the most powerful thing in the world.
I ask that You remind me to never limit Your love with beliefs that
diminish its power and reality. May everything I do and say be
an expression of Your miraculous, world-changing love.

Adventuresome Hope

Hezekiah put his whole trust in the GOD of Israel. . . . And GOD,
for his part, held fast to him through all his adventures.
2 KINGS 18:5–6 MSG

A life of hope is also a life of adventure. This doesn't mean we'll necessarily travel down the Nile, climb Mount Everest, or explore the pyramids. Adventures also have the potential to happen every day amid ordinary life. Adventure leaps into the unknown. It is eager to learn new things, and it requires the willingness to commit to an uncertain outcome with an open heart.

Obviously, an adventuresome spirit and a hopeful spirit have a lot in common! Adventure is open to thinking big; it doesn't place limits on life. It embraces challenges with confidence. It knows that adversity and discomfort can give way to exhilaration and triumph. A sense of adventure brings energy and passion to our days. It makes life interesting!

Thank You, God, that life with You is filled with adventure.
And thank You that through all my adventures,
You hold me tight just as You did Hezekiah.

Day 211

Wake Up!

*Then Jacob awoke from his sleep and said, "Surely the
Lord is in this place, and I wasn't even aware of it!"*
GENESIS 28:16 NLT

Sometimes we find ourselves walking through our lives like sleepwalkers. We're meeting our daily responsibilities, going to work, and caring for our homes and families, but we're on autopilot. It's as though something inside us has frozen and we have no sense of God's presence with us. Feelings like this happen to us all; they're a normal aspect of human experience.

Thankfully, God will send something along to wake us up from our stupor—and then, like Jacob, we'll say, "Oh, God was here with me all along! I just didn't know." God's reality in our lives does not depend on our emotional perceptions.

....

....

....

....

....

....

....

....

....

....

Wake me up, Lord, so that I can once more
experience the hope of Your presence in my life.

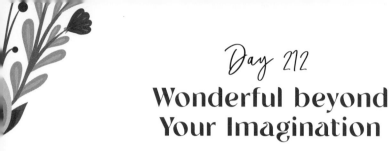

Wonderful beyond Your Imagination

May he give you the desire of your heart and make all your plans succeed.
PSALM 20:4 NIV

There's a belief that's been going around for a while that has various names. Some people call it "the secret"; others refer to it as "the power of positive thinking" or "the law of attraction." There's even a Christian version that's sometimes known as "the prosperity gospel." This belief says that if we picture what we want in life, we will "attract" that thing; focusing on our hopes and wishes will turn them into a reality. And while there's some truth to the belief that focusing on the positive can shape our lives positively, there's no magic we can accomplish simply by the power of our thoughts. Just because we *want* something to happen doesn't mean it will, no matter how hard we pray or wish or hope. But when we truly commit everything we do to God, praying only for His love to be given free rein in our lives, then we may be surprised by what comes about. It may not be what we imagined—but it will be wonderful, and it will fulfill the deepest desires of our hearts.

....

....

....

....

....

....

....

*Lord, I believe You want to give me the desires of my heart. I give You
all my plans, all my hopes and wishes. I trust You to know more than
I do about how my yearning heart will be most satisfied.*

Day 213

How to Be Happy in Trials

Happy is the person who can hold up under the trials of life. At the right time, he'll know God's sweet approval and will be crowned with life. As God has promised, the crown awaits all who love Him.

JAMES 1:12 VOICE

Remember a time you faced huge obstacles and God gave you the ability to overcome them? Remember how good it felt knowing your difficult circumstances didn't have power to take you down because you chose to trust the Lord for strength? Don't forget the power He gives to cope. Too often we give up or give in rather than stand strong. We try to weather the storm in our human strength instead of relying on the Lord to bolster our confidence. And rather than feel a sense of accomplishment, we feel defeated. When you include God in the trials you're facing, asking for help to navigate through them, your joy won't be lost. Your steadfast faith will be met with the Lord's approval. And you'll be blessed for choosing to trust Him every step of the way, happy to be deeply loved by God.

....
....
....
....
....
....
....
....

Father in heaven, remind me not to handle the hardships of life on my own.
It only leads to defeat and depression. Help me anchor my trust in You
as You bless me with a sense of joy and happiness, regardless
of my circumstances. In the name of Jesus I pray. Amen.

Day 214
Vision

Where there is no vision, the people perish.
PROVERBS 29:18 KJV

The long-ago author of Proverbs knew that we needed to be able to see past our present circumstances in order to keep going. Without those glimpses of a better tomorrow, we would give up. George Washington Carver, the early-twentieth-century scientist and inventor, echoed the wisdom from Proverbs when he said that there is no hope without vision.

Born into slavery and denied the education white children received, Carver committed his life to Jesus when he was a young boy, and his faith never let him down. His certainty that God loved him gave him the confidence he needed to pursue education and then use his education to help others. He believed that God would reveal great things to him if he simply put His trust in the Lord. This was the vision that gave him hope in the endless possibilities God created. And this is the same vision that will fill our own lives with joyful hope.

....

....

....

....

....

....

....

....

*God of vision and love, may I keep my eyes on You, waiting for
You to reveal to me new possibilities, new reasons to hope.*

Day 215
God's Plans

*"For I know the plans I have for you," declares the L*ORD*, "plans to prosper you and not to harm you, plans to give you hope and a future."*
JEREMIAH 29:11 NIV

Do you ever get the feeling that God is just waiting to bop you on the head with some new problem? Your life is so full of pain that you're scared to hope for anything better; you don't want to be disappointed again. Pastor John Piper spoke of times like these when we may feel tempted to quit and not move forward because the future seems bleak. He encouraged his readers to focus on God and pray without ceasing in order to renew the hope that God will bring you through those difficult seasons. God has plans for you—plans to bless you, not to hurt you. No matter how bad things may look right now, there is hope. Nothing is impossible with God.

....
....
....
....
....
....
....
....
....

Lord, when I'm tempted to give up, when I can't see any way forward, remind me that You always come to the rescue. Help me to wait and pray and hope, knowing that You are planning even now to bless me.

God's Presence

"If you seek him, you will find him."
1 Chronicles 28:9 NLT

What do you believe about prayer? Do you know if your beliefs line up with scripture? The Bible doesn't say you have to pray in a particular way in order to find God. It doesn't tell you to follow an elaborate prayer discipline or practice specific techniques. Certain disciplines can be helpful to your spiritual life, but when it comes right down to it, the Bible makes clear that prayer is very simple: all you have to do is look for God—and whether you sense His presence with you or not, you can be confident He is with you. The very act of turning toward God, believing in His potential and power, is the most basic and effective form of prayer. The moment you cry out to God, "Help!" you acknowledge that your own strength is not enough, that you're willing to let go of your control of your life and believe in God's love and power. God doesn't need a special signal from you to get His attention. He's always there, ready to listen, ready to help.

....

....

....

....

....

....

....

....

God of power and love, I believe You are always with me, always waiting to bless me, and always willing to help me, no matter what my need is. Thank You for Your constant presence in my life.

Day 217
Hopeful Love

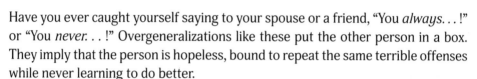

Love never gives up, never loses faith, is always hopeful,
and endures through every circumstance.
1 Corinthians 13:7 nlt

Have you ever caught yourself saying to your spouse or a friend, "You *always. . .*!" or "You *never. . .*!" Overgeneralizations like these put the other person in a box. They imply that the person is hopeless, bound to repeat the same terrible offenses while never learning to do better.

When you say something is hopeless, you are saying there's no room for God to work in the other person's life. True love, the sort of love described in 1 Corinthians 13, is not so easily discouraged. It keeps believing the best of the other person. It endures the challenges of hurt feelings and irritation. That doesn't mean, of course, that we should put up with abuse; God wants us to protect ourselves and set healthy boundaries. But when we're talking about the ordinary selfish or careless failures, of which we're all guilty, love keeps plugging along. It has faith in the other person. It never gives up hope.

Forgive me, Lord, for the times when frustration or hurt has
made me impatient with a loved one. Remind me that I too
am far from perfect. Thank You that Your love never
gives up on me. Teach me to love more like You.

Day 218

The Domino Effect

"Remember that you were slaves in Egypt and that the Lord your God brought you out of there with a mighty hand and an outstretched arm."
DEUTERONOMY 5:15 NIV

When we feel discouraged with our lives today, remembering what God has done in the past can give us new hope for the future. As we look back from today's perspective, we can see all the ways God was there with us, even in our lowest moments, and how He used those moments to lead us into the promise of new adventures and greater growth.

Then, as we face today's trials with greater hope, we will impart our future selves with still more memories of God's power in our lives.

....
....
....
....
....
....
....
....
....
....
....

Lord God, give me eyes to see Your presence in my past so that I have renewed hope today, creating a legacy of hope for tomorrow.

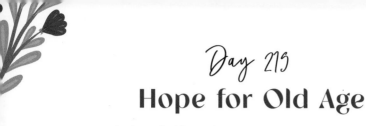

Day 213
Hope for Old Age

*For his sake I have discarded everything else, counting
it all as garbage, so that I could gain Christ.*
PHILIPPIANS 3:8 NLT

Have you ever noticed there are two kinds of old people? One is bitter and crotchety while the other has a wise serenity. Since we're all going to be old people one day (if we're not already!), we might try to understand why old age can take such different routes.

I wonder if the ability to hope isn't the explanation as well as the ability to let go. Old age asks us all to let go of so many things—physical strength, professional roles, the sense of our own importance, often eyesight or hearing, sexual attractiveness, and sometimes even mental acuity and memory. The spiritual discipline of old age may be the biggest challenge we'll all face. Yet, if we freely surrender to Christ everything age takes from us, we may find we have more room in our hearts for the eternal hope that is ours.

....

....

....

....

....

....

....

As I age, Lord Jesus, help me not to cling to the memory
of who I once was but instead be filled with the joyful
anticipation of who I am becoming in You.

Day 220
Joyful Song

The Lord is my strength and my shield; my heart trusts in him, and he helps me. My heart leaps for joy, and with my song I praise him.

PSALM 28:7 NIV

God proves Himself to us over and over again—and yet over and over, we doubt His power. We need to learn from experience. When doubts assail us, making it hard for us to believe in the promises God has given us, we need to look back at our lives and remind ourselves of what He has done for us in the past. The God whose love and strength rescued us yesterday and the day before will certainly rescue us again today. As we celebrate the blessings we received in the past, we gain confidence and faith for today and tomorrow. Our lives will be blessed with joy.

You are my strength, Lord. I believe You will always be there to help me and protect me. May my belief in You fill my life with joyful song.

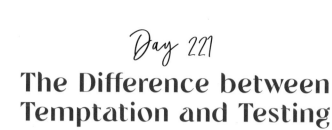

Day 221
The Difference between Temptation and Testing

No one who is tempted should ever be confused and say that God is testing him. The One who created us is free from evil and can't be tempted, so He doesn't tempt anyone.

JAMES 1:13 VOICE

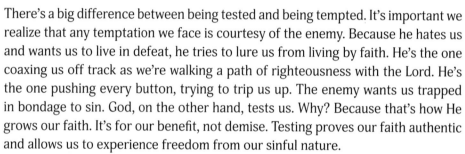

There's a big difference between being tested and being tempted. It's important we realize that any temptation we face is courtesy of the enemy. Because he hates us and wants us to live in defeat, he tries to lure us from living by faith. He's the one coaxing us off track as we're walking a path of righteousness with the Lord. He's the one pushing every button, trying to trip us up. The enemy wants us trapped in bondage to sin. God, on the other hand, tests us. Why? Because that's how He grows our faith. It's for our benefit, not demise. Testing proves our faith authentic and allows us to experience freedom from our sinful nature.

How can you know the difference between the two? Well, shame is a by-product when you give in to temptation, but a sense of encouragement comes from choosing God's help through a testing. The end goal of temptation is sin; the end goal of testing is faith. Ask God to bless you with discernment to know the difference.

....

....

....

....

....

....

Father in heaven, bless me with insight to know if I'm being tempted or tested. And give me what I need to stand strong regardless. In the name of Jesus I pray. Amen.

Day 222
Belief in Yourself

To acquire wisdom is to love yourself; people who cherish understanding will prosper.
PROVERBS 19:8 NLT

The author of Proverbs 19:8 has wise advice for you. His voice comes to you across the millennia, assuring you that wisdom and understanding go hand in hand with self-respect. God wants you to have healthy self-love. In fact, false beliefs about your own unworthiness can actually get in the way of God's blessings. The kind of self-love the Bible talks about isn't arrogant or egotistical; it doesn't have anything to do with selfishness. Instead, if you believe in your own worth, you will find you are more able to be of use in God's kingdom. If you are patient with yourself, you are likely to be more tolerant of others as well. And if you have learned to forgive yourself, you will find you can more easily forgive someone else.

So believe in yourself. Know that God loves you and has a purpose for your life. Use your abilities joyfully to serve God and those around you. Let go of any false beliefs about yourself that are interfering with God's blessing, and replace them with the sure knowledge that you are worthy of respect and care.

....
....
....
....
....
....
....

Wise Lord, I believe You created me to be a strong woman, beautiful inside and out. My God-given identity deserves my care and respect. Banish the lies I've believed about myself, I pray, and replace them with Your love.

Day 223
Joyful Hope

I will be filled with joy because of you. I will sing praises to your name, O Most High.
PSALM 9:2 NLT

Sometimes it seems as though we can't possibly be happy when so much in our lives is uncertain. We don't know how we're going to find enough money for all the financial demands that lie ahead. We don't know what the future holds for our children. We don't know if we'll be able to spiritually, physically, and emotionally rise above the challenges of growing older. We don't know the answers to our world's enormous problems (like racism, poverty, and war). Amid so many questions that make us feel vulnerable and anxious, how can we even dare to be happy?

We can trust that when God is the source of our hope, we can live without knowing all the answers. A life of hope is also a life of joy.

God, You are the source of my life and my only true satisfaction. Even when I feel anxious about the future, please fill me with Your hope. May Your joy live in my heart, and may I share it with everyone I encounter.

Day 224
You're Never Alone!

O Lord, you know all about this. Do not stay silent.
Do not abandon me now, O Lord.
PSALM 35:22 NLT

Have you ever seen a child suddenly look up from playing, realize she's all alone, and then run to find her mother? Meanwhile, her mother was watching her all along. You may have had that experience with God: you looked around at your life and believed He had abandoned you, when all along His loving eye was on you.

Sometimes solitude is a good thing, but other times it's just plain lonely. When loneliness turns into isolation, remember that God is always lovingly watching you. He sees what is happening in your life, and He will never abandon you to deal with it alone. Believe in His constant and watchful love—and you will experience the blessings He longs to give you.

....
....
....
....
....
....
....
....
....
....

I believe You are always with me, Lord, watching everything that happens
in my life. Nothing is hidden from You, and Your love knows no limits.

Day 225
Resting in God

"Only in returning to me and resting in me will you be saved."
Isaiah 30:15 NLT

We'd like to believe we can save ourselves from the messes we get ourselves into. We want to believe that we can rely on our own abilities and strengths, that we are competent and independent people. But sooner or later, that belief comes crashing down around our heads. Some days we try everything we can think of to save ourselves; but no matter how hard we try, we fail again and again. We fall on our faces and embarrass ourselves. We hurt the people around us. We make mistakes, and nothing whatsoever seems to go right.

When that happens, it's time to take a break and reconsider the faulty premise that's underlying our efforts. Belief in our abilities is healthy, but we also need to remember that our abilities and strengths are limited. Only God's love and creative power have no limits. Belief in His promises allows us to step back and stop trying so hard. Then we can rest in God's arms, knowing He will save us.

....

....

....

....

....

....

....

....

....

God, I believe Your love is my salvation. Remind me not to rely
on my own efforts when, instead, I need to rest in Your arms.

Transformation

"You'll be transformed. You'll be a new person!"
1 Samuel 10:6 msg

Have you ever read *Hinds Feet on High Places*? It's an allegory about the spiritual life written in the 1950s by Hannah Hurnard. In the story, Much Afraid travels from the Valley of Humiliation to the high places of the shepherd. Fear and shame have made her unable to hope, but the shepherd introduces her to a new image of herself. At first, she believes it's impossible that she will ever be able to surmount her various disabilities and scars. But the shepherd says to her that He loves to do preposterous wonders like transforming things.

Jesus loves to do amazing, transformative things in our lives. He turns around impossible situations, and He gives butterfly wings to even the most earthbound caterpillars. What "preposterous" thing might He be waiting to do in your life?

....

....

....

....

....

....

....

....

....

Shepherd, thank You that You believe in me. You see past my flaws to the person I was created to be. Day by day, You are transforming me, freeing me from all the old scar tissue that has held me back for so long.

Day 227

All Good Things Come from God

So, my very dear friends, don't get thrown off course. Every desirable and beneficial gift comes out of heaven. The gifts are rivers of light cascading down from the Father of Light. There is nothing deceitful in God, nothing two-faced, nothing fickle. He brought us to life using the true Word, showing us off as the crown of all his creatures.

JAMES 1:16–18 MSG

Let's never forget that everything good comes from God. Every single blessing we receive is a direct result of His love and care. Whatever is desirable, whatever is beneficial—those things are gifts from heaven. Sometimes we think it's because of our hard work, a stroke of luck, clean living, or something random that sparks His goodness in our lives. But it's important not only that we recognize His hand in it but also that we give God the glory for it.

Today, talk to the Lord about the ways you've seen His compassion in your life. Acknowledge the blessings and thank Him.

....

....

....

....

....

....

Father in heaven, give me spiritual eyes to see all the ways You have intersected with my life. Let me recognize it when Your hand is at work in my situation. As I think back to how You've blessed me, I'm overwhelmed with a sense of gratitude. Thank You for caring about the details and giving me hope and healing in such beautiful and meaningful ways. In the name of Jesus I pray. Amen.

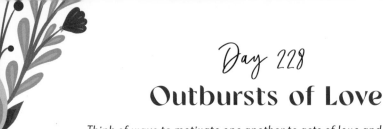

Outbursts of Love

Think of ways to motivate one another to acts of love and good works.
HEBREWS 10:24 NLT

What are the beliefs that define the beginning of your day? Do you believe God has something amazing in store for you in the next twelve hours—or do you believe the day ahead will be dreary and boring? Your beliefs about the day will shape what you experience, and they may also shape the experiences of those around you. Our beliefs are contagious!

Now, imagine you're sitting in the bleachers watching one of your favorite young people play a sport. You leap up and cheer for her; you make sure she knows you're there, shouting out encouragement. Hearing your voice, she jumps higher, runs faster. Your excitement spurs her on. That's the same sort of excitement that comes to life when you believe God is waiting to bless you each day. That excitement will spread to those around you, encouraging them as well. And as your beliefs change, pay attention. You may notice love and kindness bursting out into the world in surprising ways!

....

....

....

....

....

....

....

I believe You have something marvelous in store for me today,
Lord. Keep my eyes open to see Your blessings, and may the
excitement and anticipation I feel today spread to those
I meet. May Your love burst out from me!

Day 225
Gratitude

"It never occurred to them to say, 'Where's God, the God who got us out of Egypt, who took care of us through thick and thin, those rough-and-tumble wilderness years of parched deserts and death valleys.'"

JEREMIAH 2:6 MSG

During the prophet Jeremiah's time, God's people had begun doing whatever they wanted. They had put their faith in the things of this world, relying on material things to keep them safe and happy. Poor people were being oppressed, while the rich ran endlessly after the next new thing to satisfy their empty hearts. They had forgotten all that God had done for them in the past, and now they had lost their vision of the tomorrow God had planned for them.

Have you lost sight of God's hope? Maybe it's time you looked back at your life and spent some time thanking God for everything He has done. Gratitude can restore your hope.

....
....
....
....
....
....
....
....
....

Lord of love, when I start to feel hopeless, remind me to thank You for all You have already done in my life.

Metaphors

"But as I told you, you have seen me and still you do not believe."
JOHN 6:36 NIV

In these verses, Jesus is speaking with metaphors, as He so often did, comparing Himself to food and water. Our English teachers may have told us not to mix metaphors, but Jesus knew God is too large to be confined to a single analogy. If we said, "God is like a rock and nothing else," we would limit God to the qualities that a rock has—solidness and permanence, for example—but there is far more to God than that.

God nourishes us like food, gives us life like water, sheds light into our lives like the sun, understands us like a friend, adores us like a faithful husband, protects us like a fortress, cares for us like a mother, spreads out through reality like a tree, and unifies us the way a vine connects its branches.

The Bible shows us a God who comes to us in things as ordinary as wind and bread, birds and beasts. Notice that all these metaphors are drawn from the physical world. If we open our eyes and ears, we'll perceive God reflected everywhere.

....
....
....
....
....
....
....
....
....

Lord, may every glass of water, every bite of food,
every breath I take enlarge my hope in You.

Day 231
Draw Near to God

Come near to God and he will come near to you.
JAMES 4:8 NIV

When we're feeling swamped with discouragement and emotional weariness, it's always a good idea to look at our lives and see when the last time was that we shut everything else out and focused on God. If He seems far away, there's a pretty good chance we have forgotten to seek Him out. Of course, God hasn't gone anywhere; He's as close to us as ever, surrounding us with His love, but the stress and busyness of daily life can dull our spiritual perception.

When you find yourself in that state, try setting aside a quiet morning, afternoon, or evening (a time when you're not as likely to be interrupted) to spend alone with God. Go for a walk with Him. Read the Bible. Read a book that brings new insight into your spiritual life. Listen to music. Journal. And pray. Take time to catch up with God (and with yourself).

Thank You, heavenly friend, that You are always with me, even when I can't feel Your presence. May I remember that feelings of hopelessness are only reminders that I need to spend more time with You.

God's Ever-Present Love

So I decided there is nothing better than to enjoy food and drink and to find satisfaction in work. Then I realized that these pleasures are from the hand of God.

ECCLESIASTES 2:24 NLT

The author of Ecclesiastes had given up on finding any deeper, more eternal meaning in his life, so he decided to be a hedonist. Hedonists are people who believe life's only meaning lies in physical pleasures. But despite their belief, they can't escape God's love. Our food, our drink, the satisfaction we take in our work, our intimate relationships with our spouses, and all the physical pleasures of our lives are not separate from God. Instead, they are expressions of His love and blessing. It's a little like the old children's book *The Runaway Bunny*: no matter where the little bunny went, he found his mother already there; he discovered her love already embedded in each of his so-called escapes from her presence.

Bitterness and hurt can make us decide to turn away from belief in God—but no matter what we believe about Him, His love for us remains unchanged. As the psalmist discovered, "I can never escape from your Spirit! I can never get away from your presence!" (Psalm 139:7 NLT). But why would we want to?

Spirit of love, I believe You will never leave me. Even if I deny Your reality, Your loving presence is always with me.

Day 233

Landscaped by God's Word

Post this at all the intersections, dear friends: Lead with your ears, follow up with your tongue, and let anger straggle along in the rear. God's righteousness doesn't grow from human anger. So throw all spoiled virtue and cancerous evil in the garbage. In simple humility, let our gardener, God, landscape you with the Word, making a salvation-garden of your life.

JAMES 1:19–21 MSG

No doubt about it, walking out today's passage of scripture requires intentional time in prayer and a big dose of God's help. We simply cannot make this happen on our own. Sure, we may have a good week of listening first and speaking second. We may have a season when anger stays in check. Our desire and ability to live in a right relationship with God may be on track for a while. But if we want to be a blessing to those around us and live the way the Lord intended consistently, we need to humble ourselves and allow Him to landscape our lives through His Word. We need to understand God's commands for living and loving well and allow those truths to flourish in our lives.

....
....
....
....
....
....
....

Father in heaven, help me be the kind of woman You created me to be.
As You bless me with that ability, let me also be a blessing to others.
Let my life choices affirm and encourage those around me. Even
more, let them glorify You. In the name of Jesus I pray. Amen.

Guilt and Shame

Once you were far away from God, but now you have been brought near to him through the blood of Christ.

EPHESIANS 2:13 NLT

Do you ever believe the wrong choices you've made have separated you from God? Does your sense of guilt or shame create a barrier that prevents you from believing in the power of God's promises?

Psychologists say that guilt can be a healthy emotion, one that drives us to make positive changes in our lives. Shame, on the other hand, is toxic. Instead of pushing us to become better people, it over and over tells us the lie that we are bad, worthless, and ugly. So take a look at your beliefs about the mistakes you have made. Do you believe they are so great you can never be redeemed, never claim your birthright as a child of God? Or do you believe Jesus has the power to heal you? Are you confident that the creative force of God's love can help you grow into the person you were always meant to be?

....

....

....

....

....

....

....

....

Jesus, I believe Your life and death make all the difference in my own life. I can bring my guilt to You, and You will wash me and heal me. Remove any shame from my heart, I pray, so that I can believe the truth of Your love for me.

Day 235
It's a Brand-New Day

Great is his faithfulness; his mercies begin afresh each morning.
LAMENTATIONS 3:23 NLT

We have all had those mornings where simply getting out of bed seemed to be a courageous feat. Some days getting up to face a new day is a joyful moment; our courage and hope are high, and we feel confident that the day ahead will be a wonderful one. Other mornings, though, we have to work hard to muster up the courage and hope we need to face another day. Maybe yesterday wasn't so great, and we fear another day that's just as bad (or maybe even worse). Maybe we really messed up things yesterday, and today we must face the consequences of our actions. Still, no matter what yesterday was like, here's the good thing about God: He gives us a new beginning every morning. No matter how bad yesterday was, we can have hope today. God's faithfulness and mercy are always ready to start fresh.

....
....
....
....
....
....
....
....
....
....

God of mercy, thank You that each day is a brand-new, hopeful opportunity
to serve You, to get to know You better, and to rejoice in Your love.

Day 236
Let Your Faith Be Active

Anyone who sets himself up as "religious" by talking a good game is self-deceived. This kind of religion is hot air and only hot air. Real religion, the kind that passes muster before God the Father, is this: Reach out to the homeless and loveless in their plight, and guard against corruption from the godless world.
JAMES 1:26–27 MSG

Faith is active, not passive. It manifests through the words you speak and the way you live your life. It's revealed through your compassion for others and your selfless acts when it matters most. And when you activate it, it means you're choosing to guard your heart from the kind of corruption that comes from the world. When your faith is active, it means it's operational and will hold up under the weight of oppression. If, instead, you're all talk without substance, you will fold when things heat up.

Ask God to bless you with authentic faith—the kind that proves your belief. Pray that He will help you trust Him when it's hard and choose His way when it goes against the world's way. Let God help you follow Him with intention every day.

....
....
....
....
....
....
....

Father in heaven, I don't want to be a wimpy Christian. I don't want
to be a woman who just talks a good game. Please bless me
with real, true faith that can stand up through the ups and
downs of life. In the name of Jesus I pray. Amen.

Day 237
God Alone

We have put our hope in the living God, who is the Savior of all people.
1 TIMOTHY 4:10 NIV

We live immersed in a culture that has a different definition of hope than the one we find in the Bible, so our ideas about hope can easily get warped out of shape. Instead of the hope that is the close sibling of trust, which believes God has good things in store for us but allows God to decide what shape those things will take, we start to put demands on our hope. We want to dictate to God the exact things our future should hold. Our focus shifts from God to all the good things this life has to offer. We want to be able to control the form His blessings will take, and when things turn out differently from what we'd "hoped," we may feel angry or betrayed. Instead, focus all of your hope on God alone, for He never fails.

May my hope be in You alone, God. Help me to be open to whatever You send into my life. I know You will reveal Yourself to me through both joy and sorrow.

Day 238
The Happy Endings Love Brings

"Love one another. In the same way I loved you, you love one another. This is how everyone will recognize that you are my disciples—when they see the love you have for each other."

JOHN 13:35 MSG

Relationships built on love create hope. Friendship creates a space where two people mutually encourage each other, and so should marriage. Divine love also flows through the relationships between parents and children, allowing both sides of the equation to open new possibilities in the world. As we reach out past our close friends and family, seeking to spread love across a wider area, finding practical ways to help and serve, we bring hope to people who are suffering—and our own hearts are encouraged.

We live in a world that was created for community by the triune God. The good news of the restored relationship between God and man also allows for better relationships with others here on earth. That is the kind of hope the Bible gives us—and it is the kind of happy-ending story we are called to tell in our lives and in the world around us.

....

....

....

....

....

....

....

Today, Father, may I work with You to build
the hope of happy endings in others' lives.

Day 239

Held Steady

*"You'll be built solid, grounded in righteousness,
far from any trouble—nothing to fear!"*

Isaiah 54:14 MSG

Belief in God's promises leads to a grace-filled life. One of the meanings of *grace* is "effortless beauty of movement." A person with this kind of grace doesn't trip over her own feet; she's not clumsy or awkward. Instead, she moves easily, fluidly, and steadily. From a spiritual perspective, most of us stumble quite a bit. . .and yet we don't give up. We know that God holds our hands and that He will keep us steady, even when we would otherwise fall flat on our faces.

Balance isn't something we can achieve ourselves. Just when we think we have it all together, life has a tendency to come crashing down around our ears. But even in the midst of life's most chaotic moments, God keeps us balanced in His love. Like a building that's built to sway in an earthquake without falling down, as we believe in His promises, He will keep us grounded.

....

....

....

....

....

....

....

....

....

Lord of endless love, I believe You will keep me steady, even when my
life seems to be falling apart at the seams. I trust in Your promises.

Day 240
When We Need God the Most

Open your ears, God, to my prayer; don't pretend you don't hear me knocking. Come close and whisper your answer. I really need you. I shudder at the mean voice, quail before the evil eye, as they pile on the guilt, stockpile angry slander.

PSALM 55:1–3 MSG

Chances are we've all felt the way the psalmist felt. We've all been victims of someone who is mean-spirited and verbally inconsiderate. Every single one of us has felt shaken by the presence of evil in our circumstances. Many of us are very familiar with guilt and shame. And experiencing the wrath of people and hearing their upsetting lies being spread about us may even be a regular and relatable truth in our lives.

Rather than hide from God or take matters into his own hands, the psalmist cried out to God. Even when it seemed He wasn't listening, the pleas continued in earnest. Sometimes what we need the very most is God. His presence is the only thing that will calm us. So be quick to reach for Him when life feels too heavy and hurtful. God will bless you with relief.

....

....

....

....

....

....

....

....

Father in heaven, open Your ears and hear me. Come close because I need You. My heart is overwhelmed, and You're the only one who can save me. Please bring relief and hope. My trust is in You! In the name of Jesus I pray. Amen.

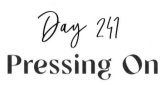

Day 241
Pressing On

I don't mean to say that I have already achieved these things or that I have already reached perfection. But I press on.
PHILIPPIANS 3:12 NLT

Jonas Salk, the man who developed one of the first successful polio vaccines, once spoke of hope being found in the dreams of those with the courage to turn them into their realities. Dr. Salk began to work on his vaccine in 1947, but it took eight long years before it was released to the public. During that time, he must have had many setbacks, days when his own mistakes and wrong turns might have tempted him to despair. And yet, he pressed on.

None of us is perfect; we all get confused sometimes. Sometimes we even fall flat on our faces. Hope, however, is what keeps researchers like Salk working to find cures for deadly illnesses. Hope is also what kept the apostle Paul going as he spoke and wrote about Christ despite his own failures and flaws. And hope is what can also get you and me back up on our feet when we stumble so that we can press on toward the plan Christ has for our lives.

Dear Jesus, You know I'm far from perfect—but my hope is in You.

Self-Doubt

Moses pleaded with the Lord, "O Lord, I'm not very good with words. . . . I get tongue-tied, and my words get tangled."
EXODUS 4:10 NLT

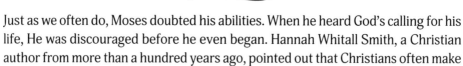

Just as we often do, Moses doubted his abilities. When he heard God's calling for his life, He was discouraged before he even began. Hannah Whitall Smith, a Christian author from more than a hundred years ago, pointed out that Christians often make the mistake of confusing self-doubt with pious humility.

When Moses voiced his discouragement to God, God didn't try to encourage Moses by saying, "Come on now, your speech problems aren't all that bad." Instead, God said in verses 11 and 12 (NLT), "Who makes a person's mouth? Who decides whether people speak or do not speak. . .? Is it not I, the LORD? Now go! I will be with you as you speak, and I will instruct you in what to say."

No matter what discouragement we face, we know that, just as God promised Moses, He promises to be with us every step of the way and provide the abilities and opportunities we need to fulfill His plan.

....
....
....
....
....
....
....
....

Faithful Lord, when I feel discouraged with myself,
remind me that You are with me. My hope is in You.

Blind Hope

Now faith is confidence in what we hope for
and assurance about what we do not see.

HEBREWS 11:1 NIV

Manifestation is one of the ideas that's become popular lately (though it's been around since the nineteenth century). It's a belief that whatever can be imagined and held in the mind's eye is achievable. Simply by focusing on a clear mental picture of what we want in life, we will pull whatever it is toward us, making it a reality in our lives.

It's easy to confuse this with the biblical understanding of hope, but once again, we're reminded that our hope and certainty are based only on faith in Christ. We cannot see or even imagine what God has in store for us—but we are certain we can trust Him. We don't need to know the future or remember the dates of the past. When we walk in grace, peace, and biblical hope, we know that God's plan is what will come to fruition in our lives.

....

....

....

....

....

....

....

....

Remind me, Christ, to let go of my own ideas about the future and instead trust
Your creativity and grace to bring something better than I could ever imagine.

Day 244
Soak It In!

A good person basks in the delight of GOD.
PROVERBS 12:2 MSG

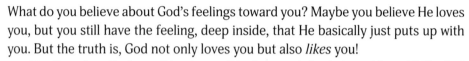

What do you believe about God's feelings toward you? Maybe you believe He loves you, but you still have the feeling, deep inside, that He basically just puts up with you. But the truth is, God not only loves you but also *likes* you!

Don't you love it when a friend says, "I had so much fun being with you"? You feel warm inside knowing that someone you like likes you back, that someone who gives you pleasure also gets pleasure from being with you. The Bible says God delights in you in a similar way. He loves to spend time with you. You make Him happy. Believe it or not—you are God's delight! Don't be afraid to bask in that knowledge, soaking it in like a cat soaking in the warmth by a fire.

....
....
....
....
....
....
....
....
....
....

Thank You, Lord, that You both love me and like me.
When I begin to doubt that, remind me to spend
more time with You, soaking in Your delight.

Day 245

He Is Our Strength and Knight

I love you, GOD—you make me strong. GOD is bedrock under my feet, the castle in which I live, my rescuing knight. My God—the high crag where I run for dear life, hiding behind the boulders, safe in the granite hideout. I sing to GOD, the Praise-Lofty, and find myself safe and saved.

PSALM 18:1–3 MSG

Let us never forget it's God who makes us strong. He is why we can be confident in the battles we face. He's why we can feel brave to stand up for what's right. God is why we can be fearless to take the next step out of our comfort zone. When the battle is ours, He infuses us supernaturally, giving us muscle to power through because in our own strength we can only be strong for so long.

But there are other times when God is our Knight, rescuing us at just the right moment and finishing the fight on our behalf. We're to stay safe in His shadow as He does the heavy lifting. The next time the heat is on, ask God if He is going to make you strong for the battle or battle for you. Friend, you're blessed either way.

....

....

....

....

....

....

....

....

Father in heaven, You have all the answers. . .and they're perfect. I'm grateful You bring victory either way, be it with Your own hands or using Your strength through me. In the name of Jesus I pray. Amen.

Day 246
Don't Believe the Perfection Lie!

The LORD directs our steps, so why try to understand everything along the way?
PROVERBS 20:24 NLT

As women, many of us were taught that "good enough" means perfection. We absorbed the idea that we need to make everyone happy all the time, and we need to do it *perfectly*. Of course, none of us can live up to that standard. That doesn't stop us from trying, but we end up feeling frustrated, ashamed, confused, overwhelmed, and exhausted.

Perfectionism and the need to please are based on false beliefs. When you replace them with the beliefs that God is moving in your life, that He is in control, and that His strength and love are working through you, you can begin to relax. God knows your desire to love others, to serve, and to make wise choices. He hears your prayers for help and strength. Now believe His promises. Lean back and take a deep breath. The Creator of the universe is directing your steps—and He knows what He's doing!

....

....

....

....

....

....

....

....

Creator God, I believe You are working in my life. Even when I
don't understand what's happening, I believe You have a
plan and a purpose You are bringing to fulfillment.

Day 247
God Won't Give Up

I am certain that God, who began the good work within you,
will continue his work until it is finally finished.
PHILIPPIANS 1:6 NLT

We human beings are easily discouraged. God has done so many wonderful things for us in the past, and yet, sometimes our hearts tell us that there's nothing left to hope for. We act as though the God who was able to get us through every challenge we've experienced so far has now somehow become too weak or too distant or too uncaring to help us. We're tempted to throw up our hands in despair and give up.

The apostle Paul knew, though, without any doubts at all, that the God who has been working in our lives ever since we were born will never stop working. With that assurance, we can pray for courage even when we are in despair. God is not limited by our thoughts and feelings, and He will give us the strength we need to keep going.

God of yesterday, today, and tomorrow, thank You that You never
give up on me. I know I can find in You everything I need to
follow You, even when everything I see seems hopeless.

Day 248
Pile Your Troubles on God

*Pile your troubles on God's shoulders—he'll carry your load,
he'll help you out. He'll never let good people topple into ruin.*
Psalm 55:22 msg

How much better we'd feel if we would just pile all our troubles on God's shoulders! Have you ever wondered why we try to carry it all ourselves? When you think about it, it's such a blessing to serve a God who will graciously carry the burden for us. He is a God who will bring help when we're feeling overwhelmed. It's a beautiful benefit that comes with a life of faith.

Friend, what troubles do you need to offload onto God today? Did you get some bad news? Maybe the bill was higher than you expected? Are you struggling in a relationship and at a loss as to the next step? Is someone you love battling a terminal illness? Maybe it's just been one of those years. Right now, ask the Lord to take this heavy weight off your shoulders. Thank Him for the promise and blessing of relief. And thank Him that He'll never let those who love Him sink under troubles.

Father in heaven, help me. I am so overcome with what's going on in my
life, and it's left me feeling hopeless. I need the kind of liberation
only You can bring. I need to feel Your presence bringing peace
to my weary heart. In the name of Jesus I pray. Amen

Day 249
A Private Audience with God

The hangman's noose was tight at my throat; devil waters rushed over me. Hell's ropes cinched me tight; death traps barred every exit. A hostile world! I call to G<small>OD</small>, I cry to God to help me. From his palace he hears my call; my cry brings me right into his presence—a private audience!

<small>P</small>SALM 18:4–6 <small>MSG</small>

With all that's going on in the world, it's hard to imagine that God has time to bring us into a private audience with Him. We may wonder why He would desire to single us out and give us one-on-one attention. But our heavenly Father is jealous for time with us. He delights in who He made us to be. So when we feel threatened, God's heart is to save us. He's the one who can gently untangle fear and insecurity. It's the Lord who will silence hostility and loosen the knots that strangle our joy and peace. Every time we cry out for His help, our voices are heard, and God brings us right into His presence. We're blessed because we are His, and the Lord never tires of caring for His children. Let prayer be an automatic response when you're overwhelmed by life.

....

....

....

....

....

....

....

Father in heaven, thank You for always making time for me. Thank You for making me feel special and important. I'm grateful for the blessing of Your presence in my life. In the name of Jesus I pray. Amen.

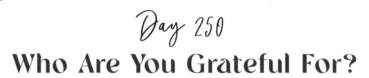

Who Are You Grateful For?

Our prayers for you are always spilling over into thanksgivings.
We can't quit thanking God our Father and Jesus our Messiah for you!
Colossians 1:3 msg

When you're praying, do you thank God for the people He's put in your life? Do you list off by name the ones you're especially grateful for? If not, maybe it's time to start. Chances are you pray for the struggles they're facing. You probably ask God to guide them as they pursue answers. When they're feeling hopeless, you most certainly ask for a strengthening of faith. But do you express thanks for who they are in your life?

Friend, count each person of importance as a rich blessing from the Lord. Daily, show appreciation for your husband if you're married. Thank Him for your parents. If you're a mom, let Him know how grateful you are for your children. Recognize the value of your coworkers, boss, pastor, group leader, or neighbors. Never quit thanking God for your community!

....
....
....
....
....
....
....

Father in heaven, I can see how You've strategically surrounded me with amazing people. Thank You for knowing the right ones to put in my life. I confess there have been times I've taken them for granted and treated them unkindly. I'm so sorry. Help me remember how blessed I am to be loved by them, and help me love them in return. In the name of Jesus I pray. Amen.

Day 251
Belief and Gratitude

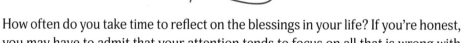

*God is able to bless you abundantly, so that in all things at all times,
having all that you need, you will abound in every good work.*

2 Corinthians 9:8 niv

How often do you take time to reflect on the blessings in your life? If you're honest, you may have to admit that your attention tends to focus on all that is wrong with your life instead of all that is right. But to be truly healthy and happy, you need to have a grateful heart. Gratitude bolsters your belief in God.

In a recent study, two psychologists tested the value of "counting our blessings." They asked three groups of students to respond to a weekly questionnaire for ten weeks. The first group listed five things they were grateful for each week, the second group listed five problems they'd had in the past week, and the third group simply wrote down five "events or circumstances" from the past week. Know what the psychologists discovered? At the end of the ten weeks, the students in the "gratitude group" were not only emotionally happier but also physically healthier. They reported that they had more energy for exercise, they got more sleep, and they felt more rested when they got up.

In other words, we are blessed by counting our blessings! Gratitude cuts through our misperceptions about ourselves and our lives, and it reveals the truth of God's presence.

....

....

....

....

*God of blessing, I believe You fill my life with good things every day.
Remove the beliefs I carry that say life is impossible, difficult, and
gloomy. Remind me that gratitude helps me see Your truth—
and in seeing and believing, I am still more blessed.*

The Power of Praise

When they had sung a hymn, they went out to the Mount of Olives.
MARK 14:26 NIV

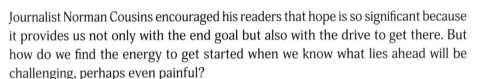

Journalist Norman Cousins encouraged his readers that hope is so significant because it provides us not only with the end goal but also with the drive to get there. But how do we find the energy to get started when we know what lies ahead will be challenging, perhaps even painful?

Jesus knew the answer to that question. When He was soon to face His death on the cross, He took time to sing a hymn with His friends. He knew that praising God in song can strengthen our hearts and give us the hope we need to walk into the future, even when it's hard to face. We see this same truth revealed in the Old Testament too, when Judah's army was led by singers praising God before a battle. (See 2 Chronicles 20.)

Praise shifts our focus away from difficult circumstances and allows us to see God more clearly. With our hearts fixed on God, we will have the hope we need to set off on our journey of faith, no matter what lies ahead.

....

....

....

....

....

....

....

God, when my heart fails me as I face something painful up ahead, remind
me to praise You in song. Lift my heart with Your joy so that I have the
courage I need to get started, knowing that the road, no matter
how rough and full of shadows, will lead me home to You.

Day 253
Ocean of Hate and Enemy Chaos

*But me he caught—reached all the way from sky to sea; he pulled me out
of that ocean of hate, that enemy chaos, the void in which I was drowning.
They hit me when I was down, but G*OD *stuck by me. He stood me up on
a wide-open field; I stood there saved—surprised to be loved!*

PSALM 18:16–19 MSG

When you're struggling with mean-spirited criticism, pray for God to intervene. When you're feeling judged by those who should love and cherish you instead, share the depth of your heartache with Him. In those times when friends betray your trust, cry out to the Lord. And then wait with expectation for Him to reach down from heaven and pull you from the ocean of hate and enemy chaos.

God is mighty to save, and you can count on Him to bring liberation to the weariest of souls. Chances are He's already blessed you by pulling you from the pit countless times before. And chances are you stood there in awe each time, surprised that God showed up once again.

....

....

....

....

....

....

....

Father in heaven, thank You for being mighty to save. Thank You for knowing
just what I need, right when I need it. I'm blessed by Your relentless love and
willingness to rescue me when I'm drowning. Thank You for the constant
compassion You show me. In the name of Jesus I pray. Amen.

Day 254

Dead-End Alleys
and Dark Dungeons

*God rescued us from dead-end alleys and dark dungeons. He's set us up
in the kingdom of the Son he loves so much, the Son who got us out of the
pit we were in, got rid of the sins we were doomed to keep repeating.*

COLOSSIANS 1:13–14 MSG

One of the most valuable and kind blessings we receive from God is being rescued from dead-end alleys and dark dungeons. This is not literal but symbolic of where we often find ourselves in life. It may be a battle with an addiction. It may be a dangerous path of temptation we're walking down. It may be a bout of depression or hopelessness. Maybe it's a secret life we're living that no one else knows about. It might even be a mess that our current choices will cause if we don't make a change. There is no one who can pull us from the pit better than the Lord.

So no matter where you are right now or where you're headed, grab on to the Savior. He's your greatest hope and worthy of your trust. And when you cry out for help, God will be there for you.

....

....

....

....

....

....

....

Father in heaven, help me. I'm trapped in the pit of despair and need
help. Open my eyes to truth and bring relief. Save me from this
mess. And let me experience the power of Your presence in
my situation. In the name of Jesus I pray. Amen.

Day 255

Kindness

Those who are kind benefit themselves.
PROVERBS 11:17 NIV

We live in a society that all too often believes in a dog-eat-dog reality. The person who pushes hardest gets ahead, and my needs are always more important than yours. But the Bible asks us to examine those beliefs and realize they're not in line with God's rule of love. The world God created is interconnected at so many levels that I can't hurt you without hurting myself—and when I'm kind to you, my own soul is nourished.

If I'm harsh with myself, constantly criticizing myself, I'll find it harder to be kind to you. The lies I believe about myself will hold me back from reaching out to you in love. Kindness is an attitude that's built on belief in God's love. As we demonstrate our belief through acts of kindness, both to ourselves and to others, we flourish and grow. We are nourished. We are blessed.

....

....

....

....

....

....

....

....

God, I believe Your rule of love is at the heart of all
creation. May I demonstrate Your love by being kind
to myself as well as to those around me.

Day 256
Daily Miracles

*"That is why I tell you not to worry about everyday life—whether
you have enough food and drink, or enough clothes to wear.
Isn't life more than food, and your body more than clothing?"*

MATTHEW 6:25 NLT

With our eyes fixed on what we *don't* have, we often overlook the blessings we have already received. We believe we need more and more and more in order to be happy; meanwhile, God has blessed us in so many ways we often ignore.

Think about it. Your body functions day after day in amazing ways you probably take for granted—your eyes taking in sights, your fingers feeling textures and temperatures, your ears hearing, your nose smelling, your mouth tasting. Inside your body, your heart beats steadily, moment after moment; your digestive processes do their work to break down food and provide nourishment to your cells; and the neurons in your brain and spinal cord fire endlessly, allowing you to think and move. Every cell of your body is busy with the life God gave you. When you look at the world around you with your spiritual eyes open wide, you'll also notice an abundance of daily miracles—from the love of friends and family to the smile of a stranger.

So why do we worry so much about material things when we live in such a vast sea of daily blessing?

....

....

....

....

....

....

Generous Lord, I surrender to You my belief that I need
more of everything in order to be happy. I believe You
bless me daily with everything I need to live and thrive.

Day 257
The Giver of Gifts

Remember the wonders he has done.
1 Chronicles 16:12 niv

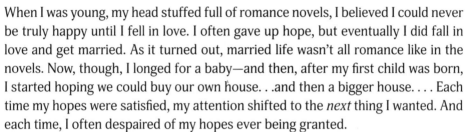

When I was young, my head stuffed full of romance novels, I believed I could never be truly happy until I fell in love. I often gave up hope, but eventually I did fall in love and get married. As it turned out, married life wasn't all romance like in the novels. Now, though, I longed for a baby—and then, after my first child was born, I started hoping we could buy our own house. . .and then a bigger house. . . . Each time my hopes were satisfied, my attention shifted to the *next* thing I wanted. And each time, I often despaired of my hopes ever being granted.

More than two thousand years ago, the Greek philosopher Epicurus was familiar with this dilemma. He encouraged his followers to recognize that what they currently have is something they at one time could only hope to have! When we feel hopeless, longing for something that still lies ahead, we need to remember what God has already given us. As we fully enjoy the wonder of His gifts today, we will find our hope in the future restored. Who knows what God will do next?

....

....

....

....

....

....

....

....

Lord, I know You have many more gifts to give me in the future, but teach
my greedy heart to be happy with what You have already given me.

Each Word a Gift

Say only what helps, each word a gift.
EPHESIANS 4:29 MSG

Our words have tremendous power. That's something the Bible tells us again and again. In fact, it talks more about the danger of careless words than it does about any other kind of sin. And yet, it's so easy to forget to be careful with our speech, so tempting to make excuses for gossip, cross words, and criticism. Even when we avoid those pitfalls, our words may be empty of any real meaning, or they may spread pessimism and negativity.

What if we selected our words as carefully as if they were gifts intended for a person we love? What if every single word's goal was to be of positive help? It sounds impossible, doesn't it? But new habits are built one step (one word) at a time—and God will do His part.

....
....
....
....
....
....
....
....
....
....

Lord of possibility, teach me to consider my words in a new way,
and help me to form habits of speech that give life and hope.

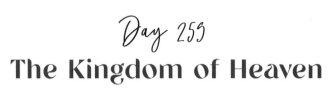

Day 259
The Kingdom of Heaven

"Your kingdom come, your will be done, on earth as it is in heaven."
MATTHEW 6:10 NIV

These words are so familiar that their meaning may escape us. We say them from habit, without stopping to consider what they ask of us. We are to work and pray that God's kingdom be tangible, as much here in our fallen world as it is in heaven.

Jesus described His Father's kingdom in many ways. It is like scattered seed, He said (Matthew 13:1–9); a wheat field (Matthew 13:14–30); a mustard seed (Matthew 13:31–32); leaven in bread dough (Matthew 13:33); a treasure, a pearl (Matthew 13:44–46); a net (Matthew 13:47–50); and a wedding feast (Matthew 22:2). In other words, God's kingdom is something that starts out small and grows into something larger. It exists within our current reality, hidden like buried treasure, sprinkled like seeds, bubbling like yeast. It is inclusive, as impartial in its vast sweep as a fisherman's net and as openhearted as a generous host. And it is our job to serve that kingdom.

Hope is the energy that keeps us working for God's kingdom no matter how dark the world may seem.

....

....

....

....

....

....

....

Spirit, guide me and teach me so that I can
work with You to build the kingdom of heaven.

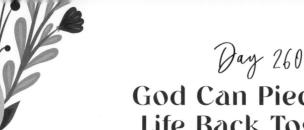

Day 260
God Can Piece Your Life Back Together

God made my life complete when I placed all the pieces before him. When I got my act together, he gave me a fresh start. Now I'm alert to God's ways; I don't take God for granted. Every day I review the ways he works; I try not to miss a trick. I feel put back together, and I'm watching my step. God rewrote the text of my life when I opened the book of my heart to his eyes.

PSALM 18:20–24 MSG

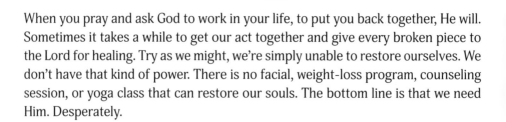

When you pray and ask God to work in your life, to put you back together, He will. Sometimes it takes a while to get our act together and give every broken piece to the Lord for healing. Try as we might, we're simply unable to restore ourselves. We don't have that kind of power. There is no facial, weight-loss program, counseling session, or yoga class that can restore our souls. The bottom line is that we need Him. Desperately.

Ask God to bless you with the spiritual eyes to see His work. Ask for the memory to recall His goodness in the past. And be in awe of the ways He pours into your life here and now.

....

....

....

....

....

....

....

Father in heaven, help me be alert to Your ways and never take them for granted. I know I'm deeply loved and cared for. I see your love manifest in beautiful ways. In the name of Jesus I pray. Amen.

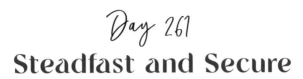

Day 261
Steadfast and Secure

They will have no fear of bad news; their hearts are steadfast,
trusting in the LORD. Their hearts are secure, they will have no fear.
PSALM 112:7–8 NIV

If you're like most people, you fear bad news. You dread the sound of the phone ringing in the middle of the night. You may tense up when you hear an ambulance's siren—you worry for your loved ones' safety, and your heart pounds, and adrenaline flows through your body. It's hard to control these natural reactions. Our bodies automatically respond to the threat of danger.

But the psalmist tells us that the secret to coping with life's bad news is the steadfast and secure heart that comes from believing in the Lord's promises. God can keep your mind and body from being swept away in a tide of fear and adrenaline. Prayer is the anchor that can hold you steady, tying you to God, who is unshakable. Whenever you feel the slightest nibble of anxiety, immediately turn your thoughts to God. Don't waste time worrying, letting your fear build up in your heart, mind, and body. Instead, make prayer your constant habit. Keep the anchor of your life safe and secure in the sea of God's love.

....

....

....

....

....

....

....

I believe, God, that You can hold me steady, no matter what happens.
When fears and anxiety fill my mind, remind me to turn to
You, knowing that Your love keeps my life secure.

Hope in the Darkness

The light shines in the darkness, and the darkness can never extinguish it.
JOHN 1:5 NLT

The world is a wondrous place—but it is also filled with terrible things: hatred and war, cruelty and intolerance, suffering and death. We can't pretend those things don't exist, and the Bible never asks us to. Instead, the Bible assures us that God's light never stops shining, even in the darkest corners of our world.

To paraphrase South African theologian Desmond Tutu, there is hope when you can look into darkness and still find a source of light. Tutu had seen hope in the long night of his nation's apartheid, and that hope had burst into brilliant light when apartheid finally came to an end. This is the sort of hope that only Christ can give us, a shining hope that helps us see the Spirit's presence and potential even in the world's darkness.

Christ Jesus, when everything around me seems dark, shine the light of Your hope into my heart. May my life be a lens for that light, sending hope out from my heart into the world.

Day 263

Approaching God with Reverence

When Jesus was on the earth, a man of flesh and blood, He offered up prayers and pleas, groans and tears to the One who could save Him from death. He was heard because He approached God with reverence. Although He was a Son, Jesus learned obedience through the things He suffered.

HEBREWS 5:7–8 VOICE

Don't miss today's revelation, because it may be the key to unlocking your prayers that seem to bounce off the ceiling. Have you been asking God to heal a marriage? Have you asked for wisdom in a big decision? Maybe you've been praying for financial relief or physical healing? If it feels like God isn't hearing you, maybe you need to look at how you're approaching the throne. Are you being flippant? Are you just repeating the same old words without the emotion behind them? Are you being demanding? When Jesus approached His Father, He did so with reverence. He came with respect and devotion. Scripture says that because of this position, He was heard.

If you're struggling with your prayer life, take inventory of your heart. See if anything in you needs to change. Then get ready for the blessing.

....

....

....

....

....

....

Father in heaven, I don't ever want to be disrespectful in prayer, so please forgive me for the times I've been irreverent. Help me remember my position in relation to Yours. And bless me as Your will in my life is done. In the name of Jesus I pray. Amen.

Light Bringer

*Each one of us needs to look after the good of the people
around us, asking ourselves, "How can I help?"*
ROMANS 15:2 MSG

As a child, Helen Keller lived in a dark and silent world. Only the persistence and kindness of her teacher were able to bring her out into the world of other human beings where, despite her total blindness and deafness, she became a famous author, speaker, and political activist. She knew that it was hope that took her from darkness into her purpose.

In the interconnected kingdom of heaven, we all need to look after each other—and when we lend a helping hand to another, our own world is lit with renewed hope. We can be like Helen's teacher, Annie Sullivan, who leaped for joy when Helen finally began to understand what was being taught, which opened a new world of possibilities for her. When we look after another person and give them hope, we see the miraculous possibilities in them and in ourselves.

....
....
....
....
....
....
....
....

Lord, I ask that You give me the courage, persistence, and love to bring
hope to others' lives. In every relationship and encounter with
others, may my attitude always be "How can I help?" Use me,
I pray, to bring Your light into even the darkest lives

Day 265

Negative Emotions

I will never forget this awful time, as I grieve over my loss.
Yet I still dare to hope when I remember this: The faithful love
of the LORD never ends! His mercies never cease.

LAMENTATIONS 3:20–22 NLT

If you ever feel as though God condemns you for having negative feelings about your life, read the book of Lamentations. This book in the Old Testament was written in response to the destruction of Jerusalem some six hundred years before Christ. It's full of the emotional ups and downs that come with human life. It records a pattern that most of us will find familiar: we are sunk in despair. . .then we climb up out of our depression and feel more optimistic. . .but something trips us up, and we sink back into our dark hole. . .and then we repeat the entire cycle. Lamentations acknowledges that there is good reason for despair and discouragement—truly terrible things happen in our lives and in the world around us—and yet, because of God's faithful love, we can still find the courage to hope, even amid our human emotions.

....

....

....

....

....

....

....

....

Lord, when negative emotions swamp me,
may I nevertheless cling to my hope in You.

Spring Is in the Air

The flowers are springing up, the season of singing birds has come, and the cooing of turtledoves fills the air.
SONG OF SOLOMON 2:12 NLT

We all have times in our lives when it seems winter will never end. Whether it's emotionally, spiritually, financially, or physically (or all four), life seems bleak and cold. We feel as though Narnia's White Witch has cursed our life, making it always winter. But just as Aslan brought spring to Narnia, so God will always bring new life to our hearts and circumstances.

We can expect that God will bring His promises to pass because it is what He reveals to us in His Word. We will not always be in a dry season but will soon see the rain of His blessing and favor in the form of answered prayers. Don't give up hope. Winter always comes to an end.

....
....
....
....
....
....
....
....
....

Lord God, give me hope even when things seem hopeless. Fill me
with excitement and expectation as I wait for what You will do
next in my life. Even as I shiver in the cold, may the first
breezes of Your springtime warm my heart.

Day 267

The Source of Nourishment

The eyes of all look to you in hope; you give them their food as they need it.
PSALM 145:15 NLT

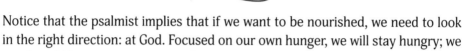

Notice that the psalmist implies that if we want to be nourished, we need to look in the right direction: at God. Focused on our own hunger, we will stay hungry; we need to shift our attention away from our emotions and the situations that have caused them and look instead at the source who can meet our needs.

We would not stare into an empty fridge or pantry just starving ourselves; we would go to the grocery store to stock our shelves and feed ourselves. In the same way, we must look to the Lord for our daily bread. Hope turns our hearts and minds in the right direction, toward the one who will always meet our needs.

....

....

....

....

....

....

....

....

....

....

When my heart feels empty, Lord, and my soul cries
out for nourishment, remind me that You alone
can supply me with what I need.

Day 268

Believe in Christ's Gift!

For by grace are ye saved through faith;
and that not of yourselves: it is the gift of God.

EPHESIANS 2:8 KJV

We live in a world that believes you can't get something for nothing. Everything comes back to "You scratch my back, I'll scratch yours." We learned that principle when we were very young—in the school cafeteria, maybe, when some little boy or girl said, "You give me your apple, and I'll give you my cookie." When we grew up, we understood that we wouldn't get far in life (or make any money) if we didn't work hard. We may have also learned that we have to earn others' respect and kindness with our own good behavior.

We tend to carry this understanding into our relationship with God. We believe we have to earn His favor, that He will only give to us if we give to Him. So we try to "be good." We follow all the rules. It's never good enough, of course. No matter how hard we try, we can never make ourselves good. But it doesn't matter! God turns our human rules upside down. He gives to us when we do absolutely nothing. He gives to us when we don't deserve anything. He gives to us no matter what.

....

....

....

....

....

....

Jesus, I believe I don't need to do anything to earn Your love.
Thank You for the gift of Your life. Teach me to trust You
more so that Your love can move through me and out into
the world, unhindered by my doubts or disbelief.

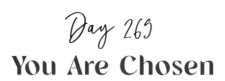

Day 265
You Are Chosen

I don't call you servants any longer; servants don't know what the master is doing, but I have told you everything the Father has said to Me. I call you friends. You did not choose Me. I chose you, and I orchestrated all of this so that you would be sent out and bear great and perpetual fruit. As you do this, anything you ask the Father in My name will be done.

JOHN 15:15–16 VOICE

Friend, you are chosen. It may be hard to grasp the truth that the one who created the heavens and the earth and everything in them knows you by name. Since God thought you up, it means He has full knowledge of who you are. He knows the complexity of your emotions. He knows what keeps you up at night and the little things that bring joy. He knows your tendency to be annoying to those around you as well as all the ways you bless others. And when God made you, He also placed in you a great calling to bear fruit in His name.

So learn to embrace who you're made to be. Thank Him for blessing you with being known and chosen. God is so good.

....

....

....

....

....

....

....

Father in heaven, it's humbling to think You have a divine plan for
my life. What a blessing that You would even want someone
like me, knowing my flaws and imperfections. My heart
is full! In the name of Jesus I pray. Amen.

Asking God to Floodlight Your Life

Suddenly, God, you floodlight my life; I'm blazing with glory,
God's glory! I smash the bands of marauders, I vault the highest
fences. What a God! His road stretches straight and smooth. Every
God-direction is road-tested. Everyone who runs toward him makes it.

PSALM 18:28–30 MSG

When life feels gloomy, look to God to floodlight your way because His light brings clarity and understanding. God has a supernatural way of brightening the darkness that brings fear and insecurity, helping us find our footing so we can stand strong. His light reveals what is true and dismisses any confusion that clouds our discernment. And it invigorates our spirits so we can confidently trust His leading. With Him, we're victorious! Let it be a blessing to know the power of God in your life. His ways are without fault and His Word is authentic. You can trust Him to keep you protected and on the right path.

So no matter what, choose to follow God. And at every crossroads you come to, ask for direction.

....

....

....

....

....

Father in heaven, sometimes the right path and the wrong path
look the same. I get confused and struggle to know what's best.
But I am blessed by Your perfect and powerful light that reveals
the path You have chosen for me. Open my eyes to see it and
walk it. I trust You! In the name of Jesus I pray. Amen.

Day 271
Facing the Day

*She gets up before dawn to prepare breakfast for
her household and plan the day's work.*
PROVERBS 31:15 NLT

If you're like most women, you've got a lot to do. Each of your roles shouts for attention. Some days you wonder, *How can I do it all?* There just aren't enough hours in a day—which means you *can't* do it all. No one can. No matter how strong and capable you are, you have physical, emotional, spiritual, and intellectual limitations.

Whenever you encounter a new challenge in your life—whether you're a newlywed, a new employee, a first-time mother, a start-up business owner, or heading back to school—you are bound to encounter huge learning curves. You'll need to make adjustments. You may need to wake up early in order to get the spiritual and physical nourishment you need, as well as to prepare your heart and mind for the day. Having a plan for the day will help you be more efficient. Believe in yourself. Believe God will help you through the day ahead. And then head confidently into your day, your head high.

....

....

....

....

....

....

....

God, when self-doubts begin to overwhelm me, I believe You have the answers
I need. Remind me to take extra time to be with You so that I can have
the spiritual strength and confidence I need to face each day.

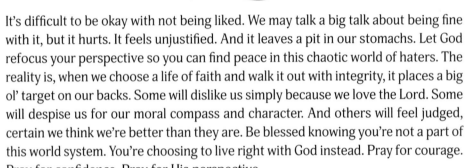

Day 272

The Need for God's Perspective

If you find that the world despises you, remember that before it despised you, it first despised Me. If you were a product of the world order, then it would love you. But you are not a product of the world because I have taken you out of it, and it despises you for that very reason.

JOHN 15:18–19 VOICE

It's difficult to be okay with not being liked. We may talk a big talk about being fine with it, but it hurts. It feels unjustified. And it leaves a pit in our stomachs. Let God refocus your perspective so you can find peace in this chaotic world of haters. The reality is, when we choose a life of faith and walk it out with integrity, it places a big ol' target on our backs. Some will dislike us simply because we love the Lord. Some will despise us for our moral compass and character. And others will feel judged, certain we think we're better than they are. Be blessed knowing you're not a part of this world system. You're choosing to live right with God instead. Pray for courage. Pray for confidence. Pray for His perspective.

Father in heaven, help me recognize that hatred from the world is often an indicator I'm standing strong in my faith. Bring peace to my heart as I meditate on Your truth and find strength to continue choosing Your ways. In the name of Jesus I pray. Amen.

Day 273
Choose Hope

Rejoice always, pray continually, give thanks in all circumstances.
1 Thessalonians 5:16–18 NIV

How does God expect us to *always* rejoice, pray, and give Him thanks? We've read in other portions of scripture that God understands our negative emotions, and we know that even Jesus experienced sorrow, anger, and fear. So how can we make sense of verses like these?

First, we don't have to be smiling and whistling a cheery tune all the time. (We'd be annoying to those around us if we did!) The Greek word translated as *rejoice* contains wider meanings than simple happiness; it also means "to thrive," and to experience and be conscious of God's grace. It's also the same word used in Romans 12:12, which instructs us to "rejoice *in hope*."

In other words, even amid sorrow and anxiety, we can continue to hope as we also continue to be aware of God's grace. When we make ongoing prayer and gratitude the habitual background of our thought lives, rejoicing in hope becomes possible.

Jesus, I choose hope. Show me how to rejoice in that hope,
giving thanks and praying, even when I'm sad or worried.

The Blessing of the Holy Spirit

I will send a great Helper to you from the Father, one known as the Spirit of truth. He comes from the Father and will point to the truth as it concerns Me.

JOHN 15:26 VOICE

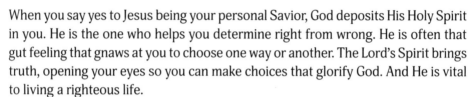

When you say yes to Jesus being your personal Savior, God deposits His Holy Spirit in you. He is the one who helps you determine right from wrong. He is often that gut feeling that gnaws at you to choose one way or another. The Lord's Spirit brings truth, opening your eyes so you can make choices that glorify God. And He is vital to living a righteous life.

Take a moment to thank God for the blessing of the Holy Spirit. Thank Him for the power He infuses into you, which helps guide you to handle tough and challenging circumstances. Tell God how you hear His Spirit best, how you recognize Him moving your heart to stand strong.

One of the most beautiful benefits we receive as His followers is the constant companionship and direction the Holy Spirit provides. Don't ever take His presence for granted. It's an unmatched blessing in the life of every believer.

....

....

....

....

....

....

....

Father in heaven, hear my praises of gratitude rise into the heavens.
Your Holy Spirit is deeply valued in my everyday life, and I'm beyond
blessed to have 24-7 access to hearing Your voice of discernment
in my own spirit. In the name of Jesus I pray. Amen.

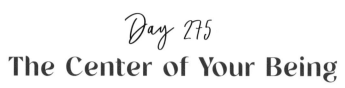

Day 275
The Center of Your Being

Above all else, guard your heart, for everything you do flows from it.
PROVERBS 4:23 NIV

The Hebrew word translated as "heart" in this verse doesn't refer to the physical organ in your chest, nor does it have as much to do with your emotions as it does your thoughts and mind. The Hebrew word—*leb*—includes these meanings: "center of your being, mind, attention, inner life, thoughts, will, knowledge, understanding." Your beliefs, your thoughts, your mental habits—all impact both your emotions and your actions.

Psychologists have learned that as we intentionally shape our thoughts and beliefs, we can change our lives. Ancient scholars were also wise enough to understand that when we protect our minds—the things we pay attention to, the thoughts we allow to occupy us, and the beliefs we harbor—we are actually caring for our entire being, body, mind, and soul.

Guarding our inner lives also has an effect on our actions that will impact the world around us. This means we are to be careful about the ideas and thoughts we allow into our heads. We don't mindlessly absorb beliefs from the internet and TV. We practice wise self-care so that we can be our best selves.

....
....
....
....
....
....

Lord of my life, I believe You want only the best for me. Make me
more aware of the thoughts and beliefs I've been allowing to grow
inside me. Help me exercise care and diligence as I guard my
heart against anything that denies You and Your love.

Day 276
Only God

Yes, my soul, find rest in God; my hope comes from him.
. . . He is my fortress, I will not be shaken.
PSALM 62:5–6 NIV

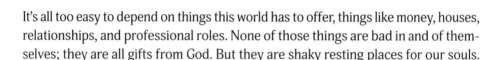

It's all too easy to depend on things this world has to offer, things like money, houses, relationships, and professional roles. None of those things are bad in and of themselves; they are all gifts from God. But they are shaky resting places for our souls.

Hope is where our souls can truly rest. First, however, we must figure out where our hope is found! Ask yourself: *Where am I resting my soul? What gives me hope? What holds me steady and keeps me safe? Am I living inside the fortress of my hope in God—or am I only admiring it from a distance?*

....

....

....

....

....

....

....

....

....

....

Lord, I know You are the source of all hope. Nothing else in life
is strong enough to hold me safe and secure. When I ask
myself what gives me hope, it's You and only You.

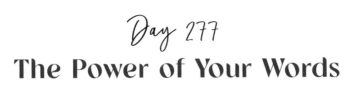

Day 277
The Power of Your Words

"Take this most seriously: A yes on earth is yes in heaven; a no on earth is no in heaven. What you say to one another is eternal."
MATTHEW 18:18 MSG

What a great reminder that our words matter. They mean something both here and in heaven. It's crucial we remember the power they hold not only in our lives but also in the lives of others. We can either bless others with our words or use them to curse. They can be a powerful way to encourage, or they can deflate someone. What we say can bring hope or dash it. It can usher in peace and confidence or crush it.

So be thoughtful, but more importantly, ask God to tame your tongue. When you ask, He will give you wisdom and discernment so you are careful. He will help you be quick to listen and slow to speak so your words are measured. The world is hard enough as it is. Life kicks us in the teeth enough on its own. Let's not be women who add to the pain of others, but instead, let's be women who use words to point to God in heaven. Let the Lord bless what you say so it's helpful and encouraging to those who need it the most. (And sometimes that includes yourself.)

Father in heaven, let my words bring forth life.
In the name of Jesus I pray. Amen.

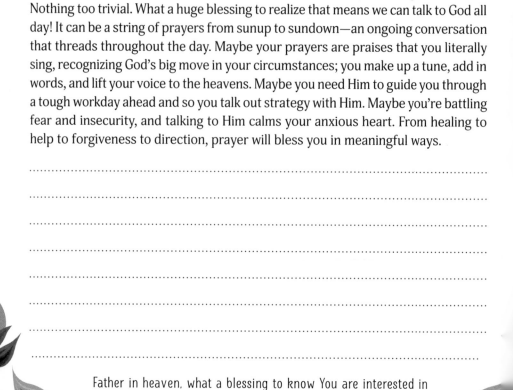

Day 278
What Can We Not Pray About?

Are you hurting? Pray. Do you feel great? Sing. Are you sick? Call the church leaders together to pray and anoint you with oil in the name of the Master. Believing-prayer will heal you, and Jesus will put you on your feet. And if you've sinned, you'll be forgiven—healed inside and out.

JAMES 5:13–15 MSG

What can we not pray about? When we dig into God's Word, we realize He wants us to pray in every way about all things. Nothing is too big. Nothing is too small. Nothing too trivial. What a huge blessing to realize that means we can talk to God all day! It can be a string of prayers from sunup to sundown—an ongoing conversation that threads throughout the day. Maybe your prayers are praises that you literally sing, recognizing God's big move in your circumstances; you make up a tune, add in words, and lift your voice to the heavens. Maybe you need Him to guide you through a tough workday ahead and so you talk out strategy with Him. Maybe you're battling fear and insecurity, and talking to Him calms your anxious heart. From healing to help to forgiveness to direction, prayer will bless you in meaningful ways.

Father in heaven, what a blessing to know You are interested in every part of my life. There is literally nothing I cannot pray about. Amazing. In the name of Jesus I pray. Amen.

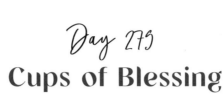

Day 275
Cups of Blessing

You serve me a six-course dinner right in front of my enemies.
You revive my drooping head; my cup brims with blessing.

PSALM 23:5 MSG

At the end of a long day, do you ever feel weak and ravenous with hunger? You've gone too long without eating, and now your body demands food. You may find yourself snapping at your family; when your blood sugar is low, it's hard to be your best self!

We often do the same thing to our spirits, depriving them of the spiritual nourishment they need—and then we wonder why life seems so overwhelming. We can't be our best selves without spiritual nourishment any more than we can without physical nourishment. But dinner is on the table, and God is waiting to revive us with platefuls of grace and cups brimming with blessings.

So today, no matter what enemies you are facing—discouragement, doubt, criticism, failure—believe in God's nourishing love. He has what you need to give you fresh energy and stamina.

....
....
....
....
....
....
....
....

Lord, I believe You have the nourishment I need to be strong, steady, and kind, no matter what challenges I face. When I've gone too long without a spiritual "meal," remind me I need to take time to sit down with You.

Gardeners of Hope

*Do not exasperate your children; instead, bring them up
in the training and instruction of the Lord.*
EPHESIANS 6:4 NIV

God calls us to not only have hope in our hearts but also to teach hope to the children in our lives—and this verse from Paul's letter to the church at Ephesus reminds us that we don't give children hope if we are constantly nagging and scolding them.

The Greek word translated as "instruction" in this version of the Bible had to do with calling attention to something. In other words, our words and actions around children need to help them notice what God is doing in the world. If we're going through a hard time in our lives, we need to be careful not to vent our emotions on our children or allow our negativity to infect their outlooks. We must protect their hearts and minds by cultivating hope and love within them so that they love the instruction of the Lord and don't feel burdened by it.

....
....
....
....
....
....
....
....

Help me, Lord, to plant seeds of hope in the life of each child in
my life, and then show me how to nurture and water those
seeds so that they grow up strong and healthy.

Thoughts

We take captive every thought to make it obedient to Christ.
2 CORINTHIANS 10:5 NIV

Psychologists tell us that thoughts have a significant impact on our lives. If our thoughts focus on self-judgment, negativity, and anticipating the worst, those thoughts have the power to shape our behaviors and even our physical health. But our thoughts tell lies, and when we believe those lies, they rob us of the hope we have in Christ. What's more, our negative thoughts can cause us emotional, spiritual, and physical harm.

But when negative thoughts pop up (as they always do), we don't have to automatically surrender to them. We can choose to talk back to them. As Paul wrote in his letter to the Corinthians, we can take our thoughts captive and make them obedient to Christ's message of hope and love.

So, remember—your thoughts are powerful, but you don't have to let them run your life. You can take control by putting your hope in Christ.

....

....

....

....

....

....

....

....

....

Teach me, Jesus, to give You control over my thought life.
Fill me, I pray, with thoughts of Your love and hope.

Day 282
Stand Firm in God's Love

You, however, should stand firm in the love of God, constructing a life within the holy faith, praying the Spirit's prayer, as you wait eagerly for the mercy of our Lord Jesus the Anointed, which leads to eternal life.

JUDE 1: 20–21 VOICE

Friend, you are so deeply loved by God. Scripture tells us to stand firm in that powerful and beautiful truth, never doubting that the Father sees our significance. Be alert to the outside influences trying to dilute that truth, and don't let anyone talk you out of believing it. Whenever—and for whatever reason—you begin to doubt, pray. Tell God how you're feeling. Let Him know why you're struggling to believe a perfect God could love an imperfect person. Share how past hurts influence your unbelief. And then ask Him to reveal His love in tangible and recognizable ways that will connect with your heart.

Being honest about your worries and fears deepens your relationship with God. When you surrender your control and pride and cry out to Him for help, your prayers will be answered.

....

....

....

....

....

....

Father in heaven, I confess there are times I worry You don't love me.
It's hard to stand firm when I feel so unworthy. Bless me with the
secure knowledge that there is nothing I can do to make You love
me any more or any less than You do right now. Strengthen
my belief. In the name of Jesus I pray. Amen.

Day 283

God's Power vs. the World's

Better to be patient than powerful; better to have self-control than to conquer a city.
PROVERBS 16:32 NLT

Our world values visible power. We believe that things like prestige and skill, wealth and influence are what make us important. But God looks at things differently. From His perspective, the quiet, easily overlooked quality of patience is far more valuable than any worldly power. Patience makes room for others' needs and brokenness. Patience creates a space in our lives for God's love to stream through us to those around us.

So ask yourself: *What do I believe about power? Do I believe that money, reputation, and talent will give me power? Or do I believe that nothing is more powerful than love?* The kind of power that relies on the world's values tends to be impatient; it's in a hurry to earn more, do more, consume more, and it's easily irritated when anyone or anything slows it down. Meanwhile, the power of love is gentle, willing to wait, ready to go without.

....
....
....
....
....
....
....
....

Lord of love, I believe Your power is greater than anything the world can offer. Remind me not to absorb the world's beliefs. Give me the patience and self-control I need to practice love in all my interactions.

Day 284
Make Up Your Mind!

But Daniel was determined not to defile himself by eating the food and wine given to them by the king.
DANIEL 1:8 NLT

Like you and me, Daniel lived in a society that did not honor God. He did not hide himself away from that society but was actively engaged in its politics—and at the same time, he did not allow anything to weaken his relationship with God. He did not consume the things this broken society considered nourishment. Instead, he received his sustenance from God, and as a result, God used Daniel to reveal Himself.

We can learn from Daniel's example. God wants us to bring His hope to our broken world just as Daniel did to his; but we can't do that if we've "consumed" too much of our society's thoughts and attitudes. Mother Teresa once spoke of lamps only burning if you consistently filled them with the oil they needed, and the same is true of our hearts. If we want to shine with hope, we need to feed ourselves with prayer and time spent with God. We can't keep hope lit with only our society's empty promises.

....

....

....

....

....

....

....

Faithful God, thank You that I can count on You, just as Daniel
did so long ago. And like Daniel, I've made up my mind:
only You can truly satisfy my longings. Only You can keep
the fire of hope burning brightly in my heart.

Day 285

Having a Healthy Sense of Value

So be content with who you are, and don't put on airs. God's strong hand is on you; he'll promote you at the right time. Live carefree before God; he is most careful with you.

1 PETER 5:6–7 MSG

Can we agree it's hard to be content with who we are? We may feel fine in the safety of our own homes, but when we turn on the TV, peruse social media, or subscribe to society's trends, we begin to doubt ourselves. We feel unworthy or unlovable, and it affects intimacy in our relationships, confidence in parenting, bravery in speaking up for truth, and courage to advocate for ourselves. We may even act haughty, trying to cover up the deep disappointment with certain parts of our lives.

Listen, friend, God wants you to trust Him enough to be confident. When He created you, it was a process of careful planning. You are exactly as He designed. Ask the Lord to bless you with a healthy sense of value—to see yourself the way He sees you. Let Him align your self-esteem with His truth.

....

....

....

....

....

....

....

....

Father in heaven, I'm struggling to embrace how You've made me. I look around at others and it makes me feel inferior. Give me Your perspective of who I am. Help me trust Your creation. And let me accept my perfect imperfections and move on. In the name of Jesus I pray. Amen.

Day 286
The Blessings of Tests and Trials

And I will put this one-third through the fire—refine them all as silver is refined, test them all as gold is tested. They will invoke My name, trust in My promises, and I will answer them. I will announce, "These are My people"; and they will confess, "The Eternal is our God."

ZECHARIAH 13:9 VOICE

So often, it's the fires of life that God uses to refine us. When faced with trouble, we'll run either to God or away from Him. When we cling to God in those difficult moments, we are refined and made more like Jesus. We may not understand how He can use heartache to purify and perfect us, but He does. God promises to restore us, and chances are we've all seen Him use hardship for good in our lives or someone else's. What did these situations produce? A closer connection with the Lord. Few things can create intimacy better than navigating a fire together. Those are defining moments that bond us to each other. If you see them from a divine perspective, you'll recognize the blessings that come from tests and trials.

....

....

....

....

....

....

....

....

Father in heaven, thank You for loving me enough to use everything in my life to make me more like Your Son. I'm in awe of how You use all things together to bring about good. In the name of Jesus I pray. Amen.

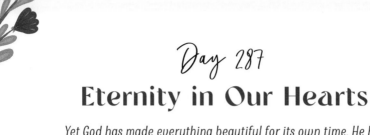

Day 287
Eternity in Our Hearts

*Yet God has made everything beautiful for its own time. He has
planted eternity in the human heart, but even so, people cannot
see the whole scope of God's work from beginning to end.*
ECCLESIASTES 3:11 NLT

Something inside the human heart insists that this life cannot be all there is. We all long for a world that lasts longer than our short lives. Over the thousands of years that humanity has been around, we've come up with lots of ideas about what eternity is like, but the truth is, we just don't know. But not knowing doesn't mean it doesn't exist.

The deep-seated feeling we have is not a lie: Christ promised us a home with Him in eternity. Our longing for deeper purpose and meaning than this life can offer leads us to the one who is the source of our hope.

....
....
....
....
....
....
....
....
....
....

Source of all hope, thank You that You have a
world of endless good in store for me. Amen.

Work for the Lord

Whatever you do, work at it with all your heart,
as working for the Lord, not for human masters.
COLOSSIANS 3:23 NIV

In J. R. R. Tolkien's great fantasy, *The Lord of the Rings*, the two hobbits Frodo and Sam have traveled together through many dangers, and now, as they near the end of their journey, they stand staring out at a dark land full of smoke and ruin where nothing grows. Sam points out all the things that make it seem impossible for them to keep going, but Frodo responds that even when he doesn't see or feel hope that he must do all that is in his power to do to make the best of it.

That is the attitude Paul is recommending in this verse from his letter to the Colossians. Even when we see no reason to hope, we keep working. We keep taking one faithful step after another. We look past the darkness and danger and work for God and His kingdom. And when, like Frodo and Sam, we refuse to give up, we too, with God's help, will ultimately do the work that has been entrusted to us.

....
....
....
....
....
....
....
....

Remind me, faithful God, that my work is not for myself or
for any human, but only for You—and that even when
my hope fails me, Your power never does.

Make This Your One Purpose

As for me, the last thing I would ever do is to stop praying for you. That
would be a sin against the Eternal One on my part. I will always try to
teach you to live and act in a way that is good and proper in His eyes.
Make this your one purpose: to revere Him and serve Him faithfully with
complete devotion because He has done great things for you.

1 Samuel 12:23–24 voice

Let your one purpose in life be to respect, worship, and serve God. Do so faithfully. Be committed to it every day. Live in a way that will please the Lord, making sure your words and actions reflect your loyalty to Him.

But let's be honest. This isn't easy to walk out. It takes sacrifice and focus, as well as daily prayer asking for strength. So, why do it? Life is hard enough, right? Why make it harder? We must pray for a change of mind to realize that making this our one purpose isn't a jail sentence but rather an opportunity to reveal our gratitude. We can show appreciation for the blessings we've experienced at God's hands by focusing on following His will and ways.

....

....

....

....

....

....

....

Father in heaven, thank You for not expecting perfection from me and for
knowing it's not possible even if I tried. May my one purpose be to glorify
You in how I choose to live my life. In the name of Jesus I pray. Amen.

Walls

The rich think of their wealth as a strong defense;
they imagine it to be a high wall of safety.
PROVERBS 18:11 NLT

Many of us believe that enough money will make us safe from the world's dangers. In reality, though, the walls that money builds can't keep out heartbreak and sorrow—but they can come between our hearts and God.

What walls have you built between you and Jesus? Try making a list of each barrier you sense between you and the Lord of love. Your list may be long—or it may have only one item, but that one item may have created a wall that stands tall and impenetrable. Once you have your list, take it in prayer to Jesus. His love can knock down any wall, no matter how tall.

You may want to prayerfully burn your list to symbolize your belief in the reality of Christ's power. Or you might want to discuss the "walls" with a trusted friend or spiritual adviser; sometimes we believe more easily in God's grace when it's spoken to us with a human voice. Whatever action you choose to take, you can be confident that no wall can separate you from the love of God!

....

....

....

....

....

....

....

Jesus, I believe Your love is stronger than any of the walls
I've erected in my mind. Knock down the false beliefs
that come between Your heart and mine.

Day 291
Hope That Takes Action

Act on what you hear!
JAMES 1:22 MSG

Again and again, the Bible describes a practical hope, not a pie-in-the-sky, wish-on-a-star fantasy, but a real-life goal that requires our engagement and action with the world around us. True hope is acting in faith according to God's Word and what He's calling us to do.

Bible scholars aren't positive who wrote the book of James—he may have been the brother of the apostle John, or he may have been Jesus' half-brother—but clearly, this long-ago author understood that spiritual hope takes concrete action in the real world. He challenges us to give our bodies as well as our souls to God. "Don't just offer thoughts and prayers," he says, in effect. "Get out there and do something practical."

Show me, Lord, the possibilities You have in mind for my life
and for the world around me—and then give me the
courage and strength I need to take action.

Day 232
Prompted to Pray for Others

Every time I think of you—and I think of you often!—I thank God for your lives of free and open access to God, given by Jesus. There's no end to what has happened in you—it's beyond speech, beyond knowledge. The evidence of Christ has been clearly verified in your lives.

1 CORINTHIANS 1:4–6 MSG

When God brings people to mind, bless them right then and there by lifting their names up in prayer. Trust that if the Lord put them on your heart, it's for a good reason. If you are constantly thinking of someone and the battle she's traversing, just take her to God's throne room. The truth is, God knows exactly what she's fighting, so you don't have to have all the details. It's not necessary to know exactly what help she needs. It doesn't require a phone call for more information. There's no reason to ignore the prompting because you aren't sure what's going on. Just be obedient and ask God to meet the pressing needs. Ask Him to give peace and wisdom. Pray for her faith to increase as she relies on the Lord. And then, thank God for the privilege to approach Him on her behalf.

Father in heaven, help me notice Your prompting and immediately pray for the ones You place on my heart. Let my heart be ready and willing to respond to Your nudge. In the name of Jesus I pray. Amen.

Day 293

Choosing a Righteous Life

Walk away from the evil things in the world—just leave them behind, and do what is right, and always seek peace and pursue it. For the Lord watches over the righteous, and His ears are attuned to their prayers. But His face is set against His enemies; He will punish evildoers.

1 PETER 3:11–12 VOICE

To be righteous means to be right with God. It means you are actively pursuing the Lord every day and living in ways that glorify Him. When met with a decision, you choose the right path rather than the easy one. Instead of being satisfied by the things of the world, you walk away and leave them behind. And when things get tough, you surrender control as you wait for the Lord to rectify the situation.

Scripture says that living righteously guarantees God's ears will be attuned to your prayers. He is always listening for your voice to rise into the heavens. Friend, there are beautiful blessings that come from choosing His way over the world's way. Ask Him to help you choose well.

....
....
....
....
....
....
....

Father in heaven, my heart's desire is to live a life that not only glorifies You but also makes me more like Your Son. I know purposeful living will be blessed by You. So help me walk away from the evil in the world and embrace all the Christian life offers. In the name of Jesus I pray. Amen.

Blessings Attached

Finally, all of you, be like-minded and show sympathy, love, compassion, and humility to and for each other—not paying back evil with evil or insult with insult, but repaying the bad with a blessing. It was this you were called to do, so that you might inherit a blessing.

1 PETER 3:8–9 VOICE

Ask God to help you be the kind of woman who is full of compassion and love for others, even when they seem undeserving. Ask Him to birth humility in you so you're selfless rather than selfish. Pray for a heavenly perspective so you don't live with a vengeful ideology but, instead, treat those around you with kindness regardless of how they treat you. This is who you were created to be.

When you ask God for His help to walk this out, you will receive it. The reality is, we all need His strength and vision. What's more, there's a blessing attached to living with this intentionality. It could be a long life, strong community bonds, a fulfilling marriage, good health, or something else altogether. And while we don't follow God's will and ways simply for the benefits and blessings, we can certainly appreciate them nonetheless.

....

....

....

....

....

....

....

Father in heaven, I want to live in such a way that I bless You and those around me. Give me the ability to live out today's scripture in my everyday life. In the name of Jesus I pray. Amen.

Believing in What We Can't See

Now faith is confidence in what we hope for and
assurance about what we do not see.

HEBREWS 11:1 NIV

"Seeing is believing." This little saying has been around since at least the seventeenth century. But the Bible asks us to believe in what we *can't* see. This goes against our human nature. It's hard to believe in something when we've never seen it, and like children, we hate to wait for the physical evidence of God's blessings. We get impatient, and we forget that God sees from a perspective outside time. He plans to give us everything we need at exactly the right moment. While we wait on His timing, we need to cultivate a grateful heart for both the things that we have and the things we are still waiting for. Gratitude will help us believe.

In the Hebrew scriptures, the Lord commanded the Israelites to count their harvest, beginning the day after the Sabbath during Passover (Leviticus 23:15). For nearly two thousand years, the Jewish people had no homeland, and they had no harvest to count—and yet they continued to obey this commandment. They counted a harvest that from the world's perspective simply didn't exist. But they counted it as an act of faith, a visible demonstration of their belief in God's promises. By comparison, how strong is *your* belief?

....

....

....

....

....

....

God, I do believe in You. I believe in Your promises. And yet some days I need to pray along with the man who came to Jesus, "I do believe, but help me overcome my unbelief" (Mark 9:24 NLT).

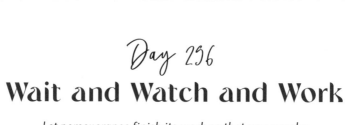

Day 236
Wait and Watch and Work

Let perseverance finish its work so that you may be
mature and complete, not lacking anything.

JAMES 1:4 NIV

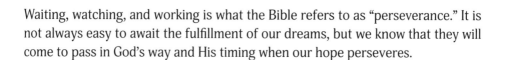

Waiting, watching, and working is what the Bible refers to as "perseverance." It is not always easy to await the fulfillment of our dreams, but we know that they will come to pass in God's way and His timing when our hope perseveres.

It's the visible demonstration of our invisible hope in God. Even though we may not be able to see more than one step ahead, we take that next step—and then we do it again and again and again, one step at a time. As we put our hope into action, we begin to change inside. God uses our perseverance to transform our hearts. And then, one day, we look around and realize the dawn has come.

....
....
....
....
....
....
....
....
....
....

God of hope, give me strength to keep going even when I can't see
where You're leading me. May I do Your work as I wait and watch
for You. May my perseverance help me to grow in You.

We Need God in Every Season

GOD, my shepherd! I don't need a thing. You have bedded me down in lush meadows, you find me quiet pools to drink from. True to your word, you let me catch my breath and send me in the right direction.

PSALM 23:1–3 MSG

So often we find ourselves clinging to God in the tough seasons of life. We hold on to Him with all we've got because we are scared and worried and unsure of the future. In our insecurity, we draw so close because we recognize He is our only hope. Many times our faith is never stronger than when we are in a messy situation. It's the times we aren't desperate and don't need anything that we struggle to stay connected. We're in a good place with our relationships. Our health and finances are stellar, and our work and home life are rockin' it. That's when we forget our constant need for God.

Be careful, friend. Be mindful that the lush meadows and quiet pools are an oasis. Be present with God in these times too. These are blessed moments to catch our breath and regroup before we continue on. And our relationship with God is just as valuable in these times as in the battle.

....

....

....

....

....

....

....

Father in heaven, thank You for reminding me to stay
present with You. You bless me in every season of
life. In the name of Jesus I pray. Amen.

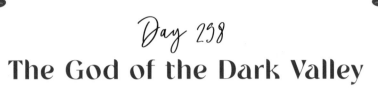

The God of the Dark Valley

Even when the way goes through Death Valley, I'm not afraid when you walk at my side. Your trusty shepherd's crook makes me feel secure.

Psalm 23:4 msg

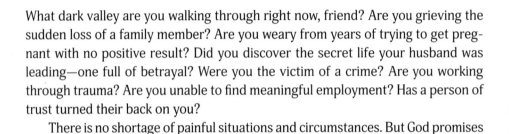

What dark valley are you walking through right now, friend? Are you grieving the sudden loss of a family member? Are you weary from years of trying to get pregnant with no positive result? Did you discover the secret life your husband was leading—one full of betrayal? Were you the victim of a crime? Are you working through trauma? Are you unable to find meaningful employment? Has a person of trust turned their back on you?

There is no shortage of painful situations and circumstances. But God promises to walk through each valley with us. He will be right there, guiding us through every step. The Lord is our shepherd, and He knows the way back to the light. So grab hold of God's mighty hand and feel safe in His protection. Ask Him to calm your anxiety and fear so you can walk in faith. You will be blessed as you trust His lead.

....

....

....

....

....

....

....

....

Father in heaven, in those dark-valley moments, remind me I can take Your hand whenever I need it. I know You will lead me through each valley unscathed. Give me confidence and courage to ask You for help rather than try to go it alone. In the name of Jesus I pray. Amen.

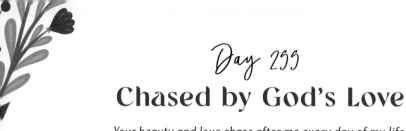

Day 299
Chased by God's Love

Your beauty and love chase after me every day of my life.
I'm back home in the house of God for the rest of my life.
PSALM 23:6 MSG

God's love is chasing after you right now. Even when you turn your back on the Lord, He pursues with passion. When you reach for the offerings of the world for comfort instead of God, He is still persistent to follow you. Your anger doesn't stop Him. The blame game you often play with Him doesn't negate His pursuit. Any momentary lapse of reason that may drive you from God never tempts Him to walk away. You are deeply loved, constantly cared for, and forever valued by Him.

As you allow that truth to sink in, open your heart to receive everything He has for you. Stop running and embrace the love God wants to pour out. He is the one who will calm your anxious heart and help you find your footing once again. So choose today to grab on to His steadfast compassion and grace. Everything about God is a blessing.

....
....
....
....
....
....
....

Father in heaven, forgive me for the times I've closed my heart to You.
In my pain, I often shut myself off from others as protection. I am
beginning to understand the love You have for me, and I want
to embrace it with gusto. Let me accept it with gratitude.
I need You. In the name of Jesus I pray. Amen.

Day 300

God Is Never Late

He caught Peter and imprisoned him, assigning four squads of soldiers to guard him. He planned to bring him to trial publicly after the Passover holiday. During Peter's imprisonment, the church prayed constantly and intensely to God for his safety. Their prayers were not answered, until the night before Peter's execution.

Acts 12:4–6 voice

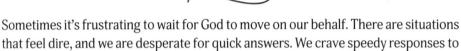

Sometimes it's frustrating to wait for God to move on our behalf. There are situations that feel dire, and we are desperate for quick answers. We crave speedy responses to the prayers we pray—but to no avail. Feeling unheard can lead to deep frustration. We can't understand why God doesn't intervene, especially because we live our lives for Him. He could change everything with the snap of His holy fingers. We wonder why God waits as we watch our circumstances deteriorate. It can feel hopeless.

It's important to remember that His ways are not our ways and that we can't understand why He works as He does. Honestly, we may never know the why. But the truth remains that God is never late; His timing is perfect. We will be blessed when we choose to trust Him no matter what.

....

....

....

....

....

....

....

Father in heaven, settle my heart. I've been trying to figure You out, but my job is to activate my faith so I can rest knowing You're in charge. I know Your heart for me is good. In the name of Jesus I pray. Amen.

Day 307

Wise Boundaries

"I, Wisdom, live together with good judgment. . . . I was there when [the Lord] set the limits of the seas, so they would not spread beyond their boundaries."
PROVERBS 8:12, 29 NLT

In Proverbs, Wisdom is personified as a woman. When God designed the world, Lady Wisdom watched with joy as He drew distinct boundaries around the oceans and seas to protect the rest of His creation from drowning. Wisdom understood that boundaries are necessary; they are there for our protection.

But many of us as women have a hard time with boundary setting. We feel guilty saying no, so we say yes until we're pushed past our strength and out of our comfort zones. We believe that boundaries are the same as walls, barriers that interfere with relationships, when in reality, boundaries foster healthy relationships as they guard our own well-being.

No one has the right to step over your boundary lines and take advantage of you. God wants you to believe that boundaries are a part of His plan for your life.

....
....
....
....
....
....
....
....

Loving Lord, remind me to follow Lady Wisdom's example and take delight in the boundaries of protection You have created for my life. I believe Your wisdom will lead me into healthier relationships at home, at work, and in my community.

Keep Hoping

Even when there was no reason for hope, Abraham kept hoping.
Romans 4:18 NLT

Abraham and Sarah had had a long life together, but they had never had children. When Sarah was far too old to give birth to a child, Abraham would have been sensible to give up all hope of having a family. But he didn't. He was not some starry-eyed fanatic, living in an unreal world of wishes and make-believe. He and his wife lived down-to-earth lives filled with the practical challenges and limitations of desert life two thousand years before the time of Christ. He understood the facts—that his wife was too old to get pregnant—but he also believed God's promise to him.

Our situations today may also be filled with the disappointments of real life. We must face those disappointments, not wish them away. But all the while, our hope is in the Lord.

....

....

....

....

....

....

....

....

....

....

God of Sarah and Abraham, thank You that You always
keep Your promises. May my hope in You hold firm,
no matter what the current circumstances may be.

The End of the Rope

"You're blessed when you're at the end of your rope.
With less of you there is more of God and his rule."

MATTHEW 5:3 MSG

In our human strength, we work to fix things ourselves. We are doers by nature, amen? We sweat over the details as we try to make sense of them. We try to control and manipulate so we can get the outcome we want the most. We walk around stressed out, wringing our hands as we worry. Then we throw our hands in the air in anger, realizing our limitations are real, and it's frustrating. We're at the end of our rope and hanging on for dear life.

There is something so beautiful about coming to the end of ourselves. It means we've arrived at the revelation that we don't have what it takes apart from God. Are you there today? If so, scripture says this is a good place to be because less of you means more of Him! So rather than beat yourself up for not being enough, see the blessing of God having more room to work in your life. Sometimes the best thing we can do is get out of the way.

....

....

....

....

....

....

....

....

Father in heaven, thank You that I don't have to figure it all out
on my own. Help me step aside and let You bring the hope
and help I need. In the name of Jesus I pray. Amen.

Day 304
Life-Giving Words

The soothing tongue is a tree of life, but a perverse tongue crushes the spirit.
PROVERBS 15:4 NIV

We've all heard the old saying "Sticks and stones may break my bones, but words will never hurt me." But do we believe it's true? The Bible says, no, it's not—and modern-day research shows that vicious teasing and persistent shaming and bullying lead to low self-esteem, depression, and even suicidal thoughts. On the flip side, encouraging, kind words not only heal and uplift but also cause a ripple effect, spreading out from seemingly unimportant conversations to bless situations and people we may never know of. Just as a well-watered tree produces nourishing fruit, we nurture others when we listen, reflect, and empower them with our words. That "fruit" will then go out into the world to bless others and grow new trees.

So believe in the positive power of your words!

....
....
....
....
....
....
....
....
....
....

Kind Lord, I believe You want my words to always reflect Your kindness.
Guide my conversations, I pray, with Your Spirit of love.

Day 305
The Invisible One

[Moses] kept right on going because he kept his eyes on the one who is invisible.
HEBREWS 11:27 NLT

You believe in God—but have you allowed your vision of Him to fade? In this life, you can't see God with your eyes, of course. Meanwhile, the physical world is right there in front of your nose: your family relationships, your household responsibilities, your job, your friends, your church—as well as the bills that keep arriving in the mail, the car that needs repairs, the furnace that is acting up, the roof that needs replacing, the child who is struggling at school, the arguments with your spouse that have been escalating lately, the tension between you and your mother.... The list is endless, and all these things can very easily become more real to you than God is. Your belief in Him becomes an intellectual thing only, rather than an emotional and spiritual confidence that keeps you grounded through all life's challenges. Moses had plenty of those challenges as well, but he was able to keep going because his belief in the invisible one was firm and steady.

God of Moses, I do believe in You—but sometimes it's hard to see past the demands of the world around me. Give me sharper spiritual vision. May my belief in You give me the energy I need to keep going, no matter the challenges I face.

Day 306
Blessed When You Trust

*"But blessed is the man who trusts me, G*od*, the woman who sticks with G*od*. They're like trees replanted in Eden, putting down roots near the rivers— never a worry through the hottest of summers, never dropping a leaf, serene and calm through droughts, bearing fresh fruit every season."*

JEREMIAH 17:7–8 MSG

Think about how wonderful it feels to jump in a pool after a day in the blazing-hot sun. When you're dripping with sweat from a day of yard work, a cold shower can rejuvenate your body and mind. How refreshing it is to put your feet in a cool stream after a strenuous hike—it has the power to recharge you! And dumping a bottle of water over your head after a long run can renew your energy.

Each time you place your trust in God to meet you in scary and exhausting circumstances, your faith will be invigorated and energized in the same way. It will revive you so you can continue. You'll be strengthened through His Spirit to stand strong. And when your situation heats up, your faith will let you cool down. God will bless you with peace.

....
....
....
....
....
....
....

Father in heaven, I'm sticking with You. No matter what, I'm placing my trust in You to restore my weary heart. Let my faith grow and mature because I can't do this life without You! In the name of Jesus I pray. Amen.

Day 307
Clearing the Air

The speech of a good person clears the air.
PROVERBS 10:32 MSG

Do you ever have a hard time speaking the truth? For many of us, the truth is hardest when we're afraid it will hurt people's feelings or make them not like us. We believe the old lie that, as women, we have to please everyone and make them happy always. Even though we've come a long way as women, these old beliefs can still hold us back from the full stature God wants for us.

Knowing when and how to speak the truth can be confusing, but one way you can discover how to speak wisely is to examine Jesus' communication style. What did He say to friends? To enemies? How did He initiate conversations? Jesus paid attention to each individual. He listened carefully to what people had to say. He didn't push Himself on anyone—but at the same time, He wasn't afraid to speak the truth. His straightforward responses led to greater clarity in the interaction. Not everyone was happy with what He had to say, but that never stopped Him from speaking the truth in love.

....
....
....
....
....
....
....

Jesus, I believe Your interactions are the model I need to follow. May I no longer be held back by my need to please or my fear of offending. Remind me that love and truth go hand in hand—and that both have the power to clear away confusion and misunderstanding.

Denial vs. Hope

If your heart is broken, you'll find God right there.
PSALM 34:18 MSG

Sometimes the toughest line for us to draw is the one between hope and denial. At some point, we may look at a particular situation and realize that, regardless of all we'd longed for, it just isn't going to change. The chronic disease isn't going to be miraculously healed. The other person in a struggling relationship has given up, and we can't change their mind. The dream job we'd hoped for isn't going to be ours. The child we'd hoped would achieve great things is perfectly happy to drift through life. Disappointments like this can break our hearts.

But in situations like these, we need to realize that hope is not the same as denying reality. Instead, we can allow God to bring us to the point of true acceptance and surrender. As we shift perspectives, letting go of the only options we were willing to consider, a range of new possibilities we hadn't previously considered may suddenly become available.

Lord, remind me that when You promise to do the impossible,
You may have an entirely different plan than I have in mind.
Make me open to whatever You want to do.

Day 309

Tuned to the Good,
the True, and the Beautiful

*You can show others the goodness of God, for he called you
out of the darkness into his wonderful light.*

1 PETER 2:9 NLT

Peter knew what it was like to be called out of the darkness into the light. When he first became Jesus' disciple, he was impulsive, quick-tempered, and weak. And yet Jesus saw past Peter's flaws to a new identity—the true identity to which God was calling Peter. Jesus even gave him a new name; now he would no longer go by the name Simon, as he had before, but by Peter, which meant "rock." Despite all of Peter's mistakes, this name reflected his true nature. It revealed the hope Jesus had in him.

God calls us to follow Jesus' example when we interact with others. As we see them as Christ sees them, with the eyes of hope, we make room for their real selves to emerge. We can speak life over someone even if they aren't yet walking in that identity. Simply having someone speak God's identity over them may be just what they need to begin living it out.

....

....

....

....

....

....

....

*Give me Your vision, Jesus, when I look at others in my life. Tune
my awareness to all that is true, good, and beautiful in them.*

Confidence to Be Content

"You're blessed when you're content with just who you are—no more, no less. That's the moment you find yourselves proud owners of everything that can't be bought."
MATTHEW 5:5 MSG

Finding a way to feel good about who you are is a worthy yet difficult pursuit because the world works against us. The world sets standards that are unreachable and unstable—changing as quickly as the direction of the wind. We're often left chasing an idea of acceptance that continues to elude us.

Friend, we can't win this battle alone. But when we pray for God to give us His eyes so we can see ourselves the way He does, it changes everything. Start asking for the gift of grace so you can learn to accept your flaws and imperfection. Ask for a heart of acceptance. Let God fill you with His perspective so the trends of the world don't become an idol in your heart. And when you find divinely inspired confidence to be content with how God made you, it's worthy of a celebration. It's a blessing from above.

Father in heaven, I confess there are so many times I struggle to like myself.
When I look at what society values, it trips me up. Help me care more
about what You say is important. Keep my eyes focused on Your will
more than the world's ways. In the name of Jesus I pray. Amen.

Day 311
Patient Persistence

*Patient persistence pierces through indifference;
gentle speech breaks down rigid defenses.*
PROVERBS 25:15 MSG

When we're in the middle of an argument, we often become fixated on winning. We turn conflicts into power struggles, and we want to come out the victor. By sheer force, if necessary, we want to shape other people to our will. We believe that winning will make us the better person.

But that's not the way God treats us. His grace is gentle and patient, rather than loud and forceful. He calls us to believe that love and gentleness matter more than winning any argument. He asks us to follow His example—and let His quiet grace speak through us, in His timing rather than ours. As we believe in His power and unconditional love, we can let go of our own need to be right.

....

....

....

....

....

....

....

....

....

....

I believe, Lord, that Your love needs to be the priority I set for my life. Help me be persistent and patient—rather than irritable and pushy, insisting on my own opinion. Teach me to be gentle rather than harsh.

Day 312

Dreams

"I, the Lord, reveal myself to them in visions, I speak to them in dreams."
NUMBERS 12:6 NIV

Do you have dreams for the future? If you do, are they wispy figments of your imagination, fantasies to while away the boredom of sleepless nights or a long car ride? Do you dismiss them as "castles in the air," with no foundation in reality? Or do you take your dreams seriously?

The Bible goes so far as to say that God speaks to us through our dreams. We often dismiss verses like that as referring to the sort of mystical visions that only the old-time saints had; but the next time you find yourself daydreaming about the future, listen for God's voice. What might He be calling to you through your dreams?

....

....

....

....

....

....

....

....

....

....

God of dreams, remind me that You are always speaking to me in countless
ways I often overlook. Teach me to listen for Your voice so that You can lift
me up above the clouds and give me a glimpse of Your vision for my
life. Give me hope for the future that has its foundation in You.

Day 313

Guarding the Word of God

*Jesus commented, "Even more blessed are those who
hear God's Word and guard it with their lives!"*

LUKE 11:28 MSG

God's Word is special and important. It's a living document that has power and truth in its pages. And it offers guidance and direction for every area of life. Too often, though, we take matters into our own hands. We trust in our own strength and wisdom. We lean on our own understanding. We decide we know what's best. But we're called blessed when we hear and read God's Word and take it to heart. Letting it sink into the marrow of our bones allows us to embrace the authority it gives us through the name of Jesus. Scripture says we must guard it with our lives! We do this by meditating on certain scriptures that empower us to stand strong. We may set aside time each day to watch sermons online or dig into a Bible study. Some may memorize verses weekly. And we can ask God to bring His Word to life in us, letting us see scripture in action as we navigate difficult situations. Regardless of the how, the reality is, we'll be blessed when we make God's Word a priority.

....

....

....

....

....

....

....

....

Father in heaven, thank You for Your Word. I know it's a
blessing and an invaluable tool as I walk out faith
every day. In the name of Jesus I pray. Amen.

Day 314
A New Story

Show me the way I should go, for to you I entrust my life.
Psalm 143:8 NIV

When we follow God, trusting Him with our entire lives, we begin to have a new perspective with new values and new dreams. Things we once thought were essential lose their importance, while other things we once considered silly or fanciful take on new substance. The world around us stops looking ordinary and flat as we perceive the radiance of hope shining through the most everyday features. We begin to see possibilities we never considered before.

But none of this will happen if we insist on holding on to our old values and dreams. We must be open to the new dreams that God is giving us.

....

....

....

....

....

....

....

....

....

....

....

Thank You, Lord of possibility, that Your dreams for me are far
greater and more beautiful than anything I could imagine.
I want to read Your new story for my life.

Day 315
Silent Prayer

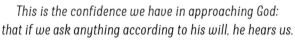

This is the confidence we have in approaching God:
that if we ask anything according to his will, he hears us.

1 JOHN 5:14 NIV

We all know that not every prayer is answered, at least not always in the way we'd like. Yet, every time we pray and ask God to move in a certain area, we are growing our hope. In this verse, John reminds us that prayer—like hope—requires that we surrender our me-first attitudes and replace them with a whatever-God-wants attitude. This means that prayer should not be just a list of things we want God to do, a long monologue where we seek to tell God what action He should take in the world. Instead, we might better make a prayer habit of first sitting silently in God's presence, asking Him to pray in and through us whatever He is waiting to pray.

So, if you feel tempted sometimes to give up on prayer when it feels as though you're just talking to empty air, try listening instead of speaking. Allow a silent, wordless hope to fill your time of prayer.

....
....
....
....
....
....
....
....
....

Show me Your will, Lord God. Pray Your prayers
through me. Remind me that all my hope is in You.

Day 316
Perfect Peace

You will keep in perfect peace all who trust in you,
all whose thoughts are fixed on you!

ISAIAH 26:3 NLT

Peace seems so far away sometimes—far from the world's situation, far from our communities, and far from own hearts. We respond to the circumstances around us with anxiety and fear, believing the dangers are insurmountable. We'd like to feel peace, but nothing we see tells us that peace is possible.

Peace, however, isn't an emotion we can work up in our own strength—and it doesn't depend on what we can see with our physical eyes. Instead, peace is one of the blessings God longs to give us as we begin to believe His promises. When peace seems impossible, all we need to do is focus our attention on Him rather than on the world around us. As we give Him all our worries, one by one, every day, He will do His part: He will keep our hearts at peace.

....
....
....
....
....
....
....
....

Jesus, I believe that You can fill my heart with
Your peace. I believe that Your peace has the
power to change me. . .and to change the world.

Day 317

Open Communication

An open, face-to-face meeting results in peace.
PROVERBS 10:10 MSG

As women, many of us believe it's more loving to avoid honest communication than to share what we really feel, think, or need. Inside, we may be smoldering with resentment, but we keep those feelings hidden. Sometimes the resentment comes out anyway—not directly but "sideways," through passive-aggressive comments and actions. We believe people (especially our spouses!) should pick up on these hints we're giving about our state of mind, and then we become even more frustrated and resentful when our message isn't heard. This approach almost always fails to bring the results we desire.

We need to believe in our own right to have our feelings heard, honestly and openly. Sharing our complaints directly without letting anger build up inside us, and encouraging others to do the same, allows God's peace to flow into our relationships.

....

....

....

....

....

....

....

....

Lord, I believe You value my feelings and opinions. Help me value them too,
while at the same time respecting others' feelings and opinions as well.
Teach me to communicate more clearly, with respect for both myself
and the other person. Bring Your peace to all my interactions.

Day 318
Goals

A longing fulfilled is a tree of life.
PROVERBS 13:12 NIV

In our hurry-up, goal-driven world, we often fail to take pleasure in the successes that come our way. Maybe we were longing to get our master's degree—but as soon as we got it, we instantly began longing for a better job. Or maybe we wanted a new house—and as soon as the papers were signed, we started planning a remodeling project. We thought we needed to be married in order to be happy—but once we were married, we believed we *had* to have children in order to find contentment.

Take stock of your life. What beliefs are shaping your attitudes about your achievements? Think about what you were most hoping to achieve a year ago or five years ago. How many of those goals have you achieved? Don't move on too quickly from one goal to the next, never allowing yourself to find the blessing God wants to reveal in that achievement. With each goal reached, His blessing is spreading out into your life like a tree whose branches grow ever wider.

....

....

....

....

....

....

....

....

....

I believe in the value of each of my life's achievements, Lord. May I
not discount or undervalue the goals You've helped me reach.

Day 319

The Blessing of Admitting Sin

When I finally saw my own lies, I owned up to my sins before You, and I did not try to hide my evil deeds from You. I said to myself, "I'll admit all my sins to the Eternal," and You lifted and carried away the guilt of my sin.

PSALM 32:5 VOICE

Sometimes we sin and don't even realize we're doing it. It's not malicious or deliberate disobedience, but it's sin nonetheless. Maybe it concerns our thought life or the shows we're binge-watching. Maybe it's an addiction or an idol. Or maybe we know we're sinning but don't think anyone—including God—knows it or sees it. We hide it out of embarrassment. Let's remember that the Lord is our safe place. We can bare our souls before Him and share every detail of our sin with Him. He knows it all anyway!

And when we admit our shortcomings, confessing our iniquities, the guilt and shame that often accompany them will be removed. It's a blessing that we can be real with God, knowing He won't turn away in disgust or walk away.

....

....

....

....

....

....

....

Father in heaven, thank You for promising to lift the guilt and shame I've been carrying. Thank You that I can share honestly with You about my sins. And thank You for looking at me through the lens of Jesus' blood rather than the wretchedness of my failures. In the name of Jesus I pray. Amen.

Let God Set Your Pace

Enthusiasm without knowledge is no good; haste makes mistakes.
PROVERBS 19:2 NLT

We live in a world that believes *fast* is better. Every day, we're bombarded with messages that say: *Hurry. Go faster. Accomplish more. Multitask so you get more done. Time's a-wasting.* Countless books have been published that focus on time management and promise to tell us the secret of how to do things faster and more efficiently so we can fit more into each day. But the promises those books offer are a mirage, because there are still only twenty-four hours in a day—and we're still not superwomen.

In 2013 researchers at the University of Toronto found that America's "fast-food mindset"—an impatient, ultraefficient culture that prioritizes speed over other values—interferes with our ability to appreciate small moments of pleasure. "Undermining people's ability to derive pleasure from everyday joys," the study concluded, "could exert a significant long-term negative effect on people's happiness."

Millennia ago, the author of Proverbs 19:2 already knew that speed is not the answer. God is never in a hurry—and He doesn't want you to dash through life and lose your way. Instead, He wants you to slow down and believe He will bless you in each and every moment.

....

....

....

....

....

....

Whenever I believe I have to go faster and faster,
remind me, Lord, that You want me to rest in Your
presence, relying on You to set the pace of my life.

Day 321
Keep on Trying

We confidently and joyfully look forward to sharing God's glory. We can rejoice, too, when we run into problems and trials, for we know that they help us develop endurance. And endurance develops strength of character, and character strengthens our confident hope of salvation. And this hope will not lead to disappointment. For we know how dearly God loves us, because he has given us the Holy Spirit to fill our hearts with his love.

ROMANS 5:2–5 NLT

Two thousand years ago, the apostle Paul understood that seemingly hopeless situations can help us grow when we have the right attitude. If we continue to persevere and have hope, we can create something incredible! Perseverance—when we keep trying despite difficulties, opposition, and even failure—can make us stronger, more hopeful people. As Christ's followers, we have a hope that will never let us down or disappoint us, because our hope is rooted in God's love, a love that will never fail us. As we act in that hope, who knows what seemingly impossible things we may accomplish?

....

....

....

....

....

....

....

....

God of love, thank You that You will never disappoint me or let me down. Give me the hope in You that I need to keep trying, even in situations that from my perspective seem hopeless.

The Song of Hope

*If all you want is your own way, flirting with the world every
chance you get, you end up enemies of God and his way.*

JAMES 4:4 MSG

When the Bible speaks of the "world" in verses like this one, it's referring to a system of thinking and living that is not based on hope in God's love. Down through the centuries of history, human societies have always created their own values, placing importance on things like material wealth, power, and fame rather than on the selfless love of Jesus. We easily absorb these values, even when we consider ourselves to be Christ's followers.

That is why James warns us not to "flirt with the world": the world's voice can easily drown out the Spirit's. When that happens, instead of surrendering our lives to God's love, we'll find ourselves right back where we started, with our egos at the center of everything. When we look at the world from this perspective, we often see only frustration and hopelessness. When we surrender to God's way of thinking, however, we can hear the song of hope.

....

....

....

....

....

....

....

....

Today, Spirit, open my ears to Your song of hope.
Teach me to ignore the world's voice.

When You Fall

Though the righteous fall seven times, they rise again.
PROVERBS 24:16 NIV

Sometimes we talk a lot about sin, encouraging each other to create habits of self-accusation and self-abasement. We may think that these habits will lead us to greater humility and dependence on God, but they are often another way for us to focus on ourselves. This route doesn't lead to hope. Instead, we become chronically disappointed in ourselves—not because we are humble but because we had wanted to excel and now our pride is wounded.

When we are truly humble, we focus all our attention on God, not on our sins and failures. When we do sin, we accept that we have fallen short of what God wants for us, and we give ourselves anew to Him so that we can go on with fresh hope and confidence in His power and love.

Help me, Lord, not to focus on my own flaws and mess-ups. When I
fall flat on my face, remind me to immediately look up at You.

He Came to Make Things Right

"God didn't go to all the trouble of sending his Son merely to point an accusing finger, telling the world how bad it was. He came to help, to put the world right again."
John 3:17 msg

We need to recognize the reason Jesus came to earth. Once we do, it sets our hearts right and brings a deeper understanding of His love. Think of the sacrifice God made because we matter to Him. Think of what Jesus endured to bridge the gap sin left. Scripture reminds us that He didn't come down here just to make us feel bad. Instead, He came with a grand purpose to right what had gone wrong. God commissioned Jesus because of His compassion for us. The thought of eternity without His beloved was unimaginable, so He made a way for us to be made right in His eyes. He blessed us! Let that sink in, then say a prayer of thanksgiving. Let Him hear your heart of gratitude for His great love and provision.

....

....

....

....

....

....

....

....

Father in heaven, my heart is so moved at the blessing of salvation. Forgive me for not taking the time to fully understand the gift of Jesus. It's hard for me to recognize everything that comes with His sacrifice, but I give You my heart of gratitude, hoping it delights You. I'm blessed by knowing I will be with You forever. In the name of Jesus I pray. Amen.

Day 325
Forgiveness

"If you see your friend going wrong, correct him. If he responds, forgive him. Even if it's personal against you and repeated seven times through the day, and seven times he says, 'I'm sorry, I won't do it again,' forgive him."

LUKE 17:3–4 MSG

The number seven in the Bible has a meaning greater than a mere numerical value. It symbolizes completeness, fullness, even eternity. So when Jesus spoke of forgiving someone seven times, He was using heavenly arithmetic. He was telling us that forgiveness should have no ceiling it can't reach beyond.

As humans, however, we tend to believe that forgiveness has reasonable limits. A person who repeats the same offense over and over can't be very serious when he asks for forgiveness, we tell ourselves. That just seems to make sense. And it *does* make sense from a human perspective. But luckily for us, God isn't reasonable. He forgives our sins no matter how many times we repeat them. His forgiveness is full, complete, endless. And He asks us to extend His heavenly arithmetic to others' faults as well.

....

....

....

....

....

....

....

Jesus, I believe You have forgiven all my sins; I believe Your forgiveness is absolute, without limits. Teach me not to set limits on my own ability to forgive. Teach me to believe love is strong enough to cover every failure and injury.

The Courage to Hope

I eagerly expect and hope that I will in no way be ashamed,
but will have sufficient courage so that now as always Christ
will be exalted in my body, whether by life or by death.

PHILIPPIANS 1:20 NIV

During the 1930s, Dorothy Thompson was an American journalist who was one of the first people to speak out against Hitler and his Nazis. She took a stand for what she knew was right. She understood that courage was not the absence of fear but the willingness to face any circumstance with boldness and faith in the truth.

The apostle Paul also had the courage to know that everything—even death—can be meaningful; even the worst situations are opportunities to allow Christ to use us and fill us with His Spirit. We often do not understand why certain circumstances are allowed to happen, but in Christ, we can still have hope for a better tomorrow.

Christ Jesus, give me the courage I need to hope even when I
don't understand what is happening, and may my hope give
me the courage I need to take a stand for You.

Courageous Hope

*Then she arose with her daughters in law, that she might return from
the country of Moab: for she had heard in the country of Moab how
that the Lord had visited his people in giving them bread.*

RUTH 1:6 KJV

Naomi was originally from Bethlehem, and when her husband died, she wanted to leave the home she had made with him in Moab and go back to her birthplace. She had been gone many years (long enough to raise sons to adulthood), and although there was a famine in Moab, her life there must have been familiar by this time—and yet when she heard that God was helping His people back in her homeland, she went. She didn't just hope that God would miraculously take care of her and her widowed daughters-in-law; she acted.

The Bible is full of stories like Naomi's, stories where, with God's help, women found their way against the odds. One daughter-in-law, Orpah, decided to go back to her people, but Naomi and her other daughter-in-law, Ruth, found their way by journeying into the unknown to Bethlehem. There they found new happiness and security. Ruth, the foreigner, married a Jewish man and became one of Christ's ancestors.

When Naomi heard a message about what God was doing, she made up her mind and took action. And her determination led to Christ.

....
....
....
....
....
....

Give me the courage and hope of Naomi, God.
May I go where You lead me.

Day 328
Believe in the Lord's Care!

*"The Lord will guide you always; he will satisfy your needs in a
sun-scorched land and will strengthen your frame. You will be
like a well-watered garden, like a spring whose waters never fail."*

ISAIAH 58:11 NIV

What do you believe God wants for your life? This verse from Isaiah tells you: God wants you to be healthy—not just physically but emotionally, intellectually, and spiritually as well. He wants to fill your life with all the things you truly need. The life He wants for you is not dry and empty and barren. Instead, it is lush and full of delicious things to nourish you. Like everyone else in the world, you'll have to cross life's deserts sometimes; but even then, you can be confident that God will supply what you need to reach the next oasis He has waiting.

....

....

....

....

....

....

....

....

....

Shepherd of my heart, I believe You are always guiding me,
even when my life is challenging. I believe You will care for
me and nourish me, no matter the circumstances of my life.

Day 329

When You Need a Reminder

The Eternal One bless and keep you. May He make His face shine upon you and be gracious to you. The Eternal lift up His countenance to look upon you and give you peace.

NUMBERS 6:24–26 VOICE

Everything about this scripture is a blessing. It's one of those passages that can bring tears to your eyes because you feel the weight of it. You see its importance. You feel the unconditional love. And it fills your heart with gratitude because it speaks right into those places of insecurity that say you are not enough.

Today's scripture has the power to make you feel significant and valued. As you reread it, what stands out to you the most? What connects with your weary heart? What brings encouragement? Let this be one of those verses you choose to memorize. Speak it over yourself anytime you're battling a sense of worthlessness. When you need a reminder that God cares, repeat it out loud so you can hear it. God has a lot to say to you through these words, and it will bless you to take them to heart.

....

....

....

....

....

....

....

Father in heaven, these three verses bring me to tears because they're not something I hear from anybody. I don't always feel loved or seen or known. I don't feel significant or important. But I know You're speaking directly to me through these words, and I need Your help to receive them. In the name of Jesus I pray. Amen.

Day 330
When We Need Saving

Give thanks to God—he is good and his love never quits. Say, "Save us, Savior God, round us up and get us out of these godless places, so we can give thanks to your holy Name, and bask in your life of praise." Blessed be God, the God of Israel, from everlasting to everlasting. Then everybody said, "Yes! Amen!" and "Praise God!"

1 CHRONICLES 16:34–36 MSG

Sometimes we need saving. We need rescuing from our circumstances. And there are times God is the only one who can pull us up as we're sinking. Maybe you're reeling from discovering that your husband's private life has been riddled with betrayal. Maybe you discovered the inappropriate things your child has been doing behind your back. Maybe you're a single mom trying to hold everything and everyone together. Maybe you are beginning to see your parents' health fail. Maybe life has exhausted you and you're feeling weary.

Friend, grab on to God and don't let go. He will bless you with strength, wisdom, endurance, and peace. The Lord will guide you through the messiness of life and into a safe space. And in the end, you will stand strong and thank God for saving you.

....
....
....
....
....
....
....
....

Father in heaven, hear my cry right now. See my burdened heart.
Step down and pull me from the waters that surround me. I am
desperate to be saved. In the name of Jesus I pray. Amen.

Day 331

Patience and Courage

*Wait patiently for the L*ORD. *Be brave and courageous. Yes, wait patiently for the L*ORD.*
P*SALM *27:14 *NLT

Patience is all about waiting things out. It's about holding on another moment longer. It means enduring hard times. As a younger person, you probably believed you couldn't possibly endure certain things—but the older you get, the more you realize that you *can*. If you just wait long enough, the tide always turns. Hold on. Be patient. Believe that, in time, your life will change. God will rescue you from today's circumstances—and that belief will empower you with both patience and courage.

....
....
....
....
....
....
....
....
....
....
....
....

Lord, strengthen my belief in Your power to save and help so that I can
have the patience and courage I need to endure my life's challenges.

Day 332
Feed My Lambs

When they had finished eating, Jesus said to Simon Peter, "Simon son of John, do you love me more than these?" "Yes, Lord," he said, "you know that I love you." Jesus said, "Feed my lambs."
JOHN 21:15 NIV

Peter had failed Jesus miserably when he publicly denied knowing Him. Afterward Peter must have wondered if Jesus would ever be able to feel the same about him. But Jesus did not criticize or scold Peter; He didn't ask Peter to try to do better in the future or embarrass him in front of the other disciples. Instead, Jesus talked to him one to one. First, He asked Peter to reaffirm his love—and then He told Peter to act on behalf of others.

Jesus still uses the same approach with each one of us. When we've failed Him, we often feel ashamed; we may want to give up trying. But Jesus doesn't want us to wallow in our shame and sadness. Taking action, getting involved, reaching out to those in need, and serving Jesus by loving others: that's how we regain our sense of hope and energy.

....

....

....

....

....

....

....

....

Jesus, we both know how many times I've failed You and how hopeless
and powerless that can make me feel. But I do love You. Show me
Your "lambs" who need my help. Restore my hope in You.

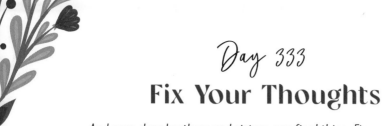

Day 333
Fix Your Thoughts

And now, dear brothers and sisters, one final thing. Fix your thoughts on what is true, and honorable, and right, and pure, and lovely, and admirable. Think about things that are excellent and worthy of praise.

PHILIPPIANS 4:8 NLT

Hope in God is easily eroded. It gets washed away in the onslaught of negativity that we read and hear every day. Here again, though, the Bible asks us to take responsibility for our thoughts.

Instead of dwelling on all that is cruel and unfair in the world, look for glimpses of God's justice and truth. Instead of focusing on all the things that irk you in another person, focus on seeing what is admirable in them. And most of all, instead of constantly pondering all that is wrong with yourself—all your failures and your flaws—look at yourself through God's eyes, seeing your own loveliness and potential. Focus on what lies ahead in hopeful expectation.

....

....

....

....

....

....

....

....

....

*May my thoughts be fixed on Your vision for me
and for the world around me, dear Lord.*

Day 334
Shalom

"May they have abundant peace, both near and far," says the Lord, *who heals them.*
Isaiah 57:19 NLT

The English definition of peace, according to the online Oxford dictionary, is "freedom from disturbance." The Hebrew word for peace—*shalom*—has a far deeper and more positive meaning, one that's not limited to the political world (as in the absence of war) or the social world (as in the absence of quarrels and disagreements). The Bible's concept of peace describes the reality that God is constantly calling into being, the kingdom of heaven. The word *shalom* contained all these meanings: completeness, safety, well-being, health, prosperity, contentment, friendship, wholeness, and perfection. *Shalom* is the concrete embodiment of our hope in God.

....

....

....

....

....

....

....

....

....

....

Lord, I want to work with You to create Your shalom in
the world around me. Help me to fix all my attention
and effort on this hope I have in You.

Day 335

Why We Care for the Poor

*Whoever cares for the poor makes a loan to the Eternal;
such kindness will be repaid in full and with interest.*

PROVERBS 19:17 VOICE

It is a privilege and a burden to love those in need. When we do, though, it delights the heart of God. He notices our generosity and kindness. As we bless others with our resources, it blesses Him. And that knowledge should bless us.

Isn't one of our deepest desires to glorify the Lord with our lives? When we care for the poor—be it the financially poor, confidence poor, bravery poor, health poor, joy poor—it stores up heavenly treasures for us. Every time we choose to stand in the gap for someone who's struggling, it's like making a loan to God. And that loan will be paid in full, with interest, when we see Him face-to-face.

Ask God to give you a generous heart so you can love others with purpose. Ask for compassion so you can see the need before you. Tell our gracious God you are ready and willing to take care of those He puts in your path.

....
....
....
....
....
....
....
....

*Father in heaven, I want my life to make a difference. I want my
life to glorify Your name! Open my eyes so I don't miss any
opportunity to help someone in need. Give me a heart
for the poor. In the name of Jesus I pray. Amen.*

Day 336
Saved by Grace

For it's by God's grace that you have been saved. You receive it through faith. It was not our plan or our effort. It is God's gift, pure and simple. You didn't earn it, not one of us did, so don't go around bragging that you must have done something amazing.

EPHESIANS 2:8–9 VOICE

What a blessing to realize we are unable to save ourselves by working hard. It doesn't matter how many hours you volunteer at the shelter. It doesn't matter how much money you donate to charity. It doesn't matter how many homeless people you feed in your community or the number of malaria prevention pills you provide for those living in Africa. You could attend church twice a week, lead a small group, sing in the choir, or rock babies in the nursery, but these things can't buy your salvation. Nothing you do makes it so. It is by faith alone that we are saved. We can't earn it. We can't buy it. We don't deserve it. God's grace has been extended to us through His Son, Jesus, and we're the ones to receive the blessing of eternal life. Thank Him right now.

....
....
....
....
....
....
....
....

Father in heaven, I am overwhelmed by Your kindness and generosity. I am deeply moved by the sacrifice of Your Son. And I am grateful my salvation doesn't hinge on anything I can do. In the name of Jesus I pray. Amen.

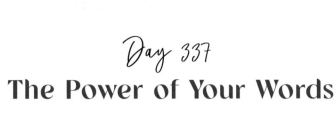

Day 337
The Power of Your Words

Wise words bring many benefits.
PROVERBS 12:14 NLT

Maybe you believe the things you say have very little importance in the grand scheme of things. If so, that belief might encourage you to be careless in your conversations. In reality, your words have power. They can tear down others, causing them to doubt themselves and God. Or your words can empower those around you with hope and a sense of their own potential. What you say makes a significant difference in others' lives in ways you may never realize. Your wise encouragement, concerned questions, and loving instruction will bring blessing into the lives of those with whom you interact.

....
....
....
....
....
....
....
....
....
....
....
....

God, I believe You can use my words to bless each person I encounter today. I ask that You fill my conversations with Your love.

Day 338
Dare to Dream

*"I will pour out my Spirit on all people. Your sons and daughters will prophesy,
your old men will dream dreams, your young men will see visions."*

JOEL 2:28 NIV

We sometimes think that dreams are impractical, a waste of time; but hope and dreams go hand in hand. Hope, like dreams, requires a sense of vision. In most cases, that doesn't mean God will send us into a trance where we have the sort of revelation He gave to the apostle John when he authored the book of Revelation. We can't literally see into the future. But hope gives us the ability to *imagine* a better future—and imagining something is the first step toward creating something new. Just remember that Reverend Martin Luther King Jr.'s dream helped usher in a new era of civil rights for all people.

What dreams do you have? What may God be calling you to imagine for the future?

....
....
....
....
....
....
....
....
....

Lord of possibility, may I dream Your dreams for the world. Give me a
vision of Your kingdom, and may my dreams and vision give me the
courage and the hope I need to do the work You call me to do.

Day 339
Justice

*"Be just and fair to all. . .for I am coming soon to rescue you
and to display my righteousness among you."*
ISAIAH 56:1 NLT

This verse links justice to the hope we have that God will rescue us from our troubles. Justice is an aspect of God's nature, and it is also something He expects of us. This doesn't mean, though, that we are to judge and punish others.

Typically, our concept of justice focuses on two questions: What law was broken? What punishment does the offender deserve? God's justice, however, focuses more on restoration than punishment. It asks: Who has been harmed? What do they need to be healed? What action can we take to bring that healing? This is the kind of justice God calls us to work for. It asks that we become sensitive to others' situations rather than focusing only on our problems and those of our immediate circle. It extends our vision of hope out into the communities around us. We do all that is within our power to bring justice, but we cannot be expected to right every wrong that we see or hear. We must do whatever we can and leave the rest to God.

....

....

....

....

....

....

....

....

*May my vision of hope, Lord, give me the energy to work
for justice for all who are oppressed and suffering.*

Come, Lord Jesus

*He who testifies to these things says, "Yes, I am
coming soon." Amen. Come, Lord Jesus.*
REVELATION 22:20 NIV

This verse comes at the end of Revelation, the last book in the Bible. The Bible's story ends with this promise—Jesus is coming soon—and our response should be "Yes! Come, Lord Jesus." As we affirm our willingness for Jesus to come, we are not speaking only of the end of time; we are saying we want Jesus to come now, come today, come into our world through us and in us. We are welcoming Him into our lives.

In this world, even the happiest stories end; but in the kingdom of heaven, where Jesus is always coming soon, there are no endings. As followers of Christ, that is the reality in which we live. Because of Jesus, hope goes on forever, a world without end. Amen.

....

....

....

....

....

....

....

....

Jesus, come today into my life. Tell Your never-ending
story of hope through me and in me.

Day 341
But We Will Not

We are cracked and chipped from our afflictions on all sides, but we are not crushed by them. We are bewildered at times, but we do not give in to despair. We are persecuted, but we have not been abandoned. We have been knocked down, but we are not destroyed.

2 Corinthians 4:8–9 voice

There is no doubt life is going to beat you up. Chances are it already has. We are going to face daunting and terrifying times. Our hearts are going to be broken in unexpected ways. There will be unforeseen tragedy that knocks on our door. People will criticize us for not being good enough. We'll be persecuted because we believe in God. We will be knocked to our knees by relational troubles, financial struggles, and health issues. We'll be caught off guard by evil more than once. But when we anchor our faith in God, these experiences will not crush us. We won't give in to despair. We'll know without fail that God hasn't abandoned us to figure things out ourselves. And we will not be destroyed.

What a blessing to have a heavenly Father who promises to sustain and restore when the storms of life hit.

....

....

....

....

....

....

Father in heaven, life is hard. Sometimes I battle fear and anxiety at overwhelming levels. Bless me with the reminder that You promised to save me. Knowing that keeps me from falling into despair. In the name of Jesus I pray. Amen.

Day 342
His Unfailing Love

I trust in your unfailing love; my heart rejoices in your salvation.
PSALM 13:5 NIV

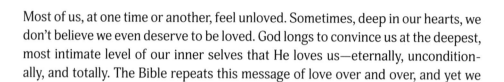

Most of us, at one time or another, feel unloved. Sometimes, deep in our hearts, we don't believe we even deserve to be loved. God longs to convince us at the deepest, most intimate level of our inner selves that He loves us—eternally, unconditionally, and totally. The Bible repeats this message of love over and over, and yet we hesitate to believe it.

Love is the reason Jesus came to earth. Love was the message He brought to us from God. Not a generic, all-purpose sort of love, but a unique love for each one of us, specific to our own hearts. We are each called by name, treasured and cherished.

The love of God is written into your very being. It is the force that connects the molecules of your body. It flows through your blood and sings in the neurons of your brain. And you see His love everywhere you look, for His love is what holds the world together. Believe in God's unfailing love—and your heart will rejoice!

....

....

....

....

....

....

....

....

God, I believe You love me. I believe my very existence
springs from Your creative love. Let no self-doubt of
mine interfere with the intimacy we share.

Desperate Times

Make the most of every chance you get. These are desperate times!
EPHESIANS 5:16 MSG

We might read this verse and think to ourselves, "If things are so desperate, what's the point of trying? I might as well give up." But that attitude can keep us stuck in old habits. It can also contribute to our world staying stuck in the old habits of violence, racism, and cruelty. There is an opportunity to find the good in every difficult situation. That's the attitude the apostle Paul is talking about in this verse from his letter to the church at Ephesus. There are opportunities for God's grace even in the most desperate times.

Holy Spirit, I know You are always working in the world. Remind me
that even the most challenging situations are filled with unseen
potential. When I encounter circumstances that seem hopeless,
give me the hope I need to act on Your behalf.

Day 344
A Mother's Love

*I've cultivated a quiet heart. Like a baby content in its
mother's arms, my soul is a baby content.*

PSALM 131:2 MSG

A sleeping baby lies completely limp in her mother's arms, totally trusting and calm. No worries about the future disturb her peace. No anxiety makes her doubt her safety in her mother's arms. That's the attitude we all need to practice. It won't happen automatically; we need to constantly cultivate the belief that God holds us secure in His love. With that belief firm in our minds, we can let ourselves relax in God's arms, wrapped in His grace. Life will go on around us with all its noise and turmoil, but we will be completely safe, totally secure, resting in trust.

Loving Lord, I believe You love me with a mother's love.
I believe I am wrapped in Your arms, forever safe, no matter
what is happening in the world around me. Bless me,
I pray, with peace and total confidence in You.

Day 345

Open the Curtains!

But whenever someone turns to the Lord, the veil is taken away. . . .
So all of us who have had that veil removed can see and reflect the
glory of the Lord. And the Lord—who is the Spirit—makes us more
and more like him as we are changed into his glorious image.

2 Corinthians 3:16, 18 nlt

Do you ever feel as though a thick, dark curtain hangs between you and God, hiding Him from your sight? Everyone has that feeling sometimes—but that's all it is: a feeling. It's not reality. We can still believe that the Spirit of God is with us, despite our feelings. The Bible says that all we have to do is turn our hearts to the Lord and that sense of a curtain between us will be drawn back, letting God's glory and grace shine into our lives. When that happens, we can soak up the light, allowing it to renew our hearts and minds and mold us into the image of Christ.

Holy Spirit, I believe You are always with me, even when I
can't see You or sense Your presence. Remind me to turn
back to You again and again throughout my day.

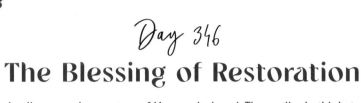

Day 346
The Blessing of Restoration

I will restore the captives of My people, Israel. They will rebuild their ruined cities and return to them. They will plant new vineyards and drink wine from them, and they will plant new gardens and eat the food they grow. I will plant them in their own soil, and they will never be uprooted again, for this is the land I have given them.

AMOS 9:14–15 VOICE

In the Bible, there are countless examples and stories of God restoring His people. He restored families, positions, lands, laws, groups, and individuals. He gave new names, drew new borders, created new hope, and gave new promotions.

God is in the business of restoration even today! He brings beauty from the ashes in our lives. He can heal marriages and make them stronger. He can reinstate courage and confidence so we can move forward. He can re-establish broken relationships with friends and family. God can rebuild our finances from dust. He can repair our broken hearts. He can bring back the peace and joy that our circumstances have drained.

Talk to the Lord with authenticity, sharing the shattered places you want pieced back together. Let Him bless you through restoration.

....
....
....
....
....
....

Father in heaven, thank You for being a God who restores.
Thank You for seeing the value in bringing important parts
of our lives back from the dead. You bless me in beautiful
ways. In the name of Jesus I pray. Amen.

Day 347

Where Will Your Focus Be?

You see, the short-lived pains of this life are creating for us an eternal glory that does not compare to anything we know here. So we do not set our sights on the things we can see with our eyes. All of that is fleeting; it will eventually fade away. Instead, we focus on the things we cannot see, which live on and on.

2 CORINTHIANS 4:17–18 VOICE

When you're facing tough times and difficult moments, what you focus on matters. And the choice is yours to make. You can focus on the mess you're in, staring into the face of all the worries and what scares you, or you can focus on God. You'll fix your gaze either on insecurities or on God's promises. Your sights will be set on everything that could go wrong or on the redemption coming your way as you place your faith in the Lord. It's up to you. Why not plan now what your focus will be for the next challenge you face? Choose today that you'll focus on God no matter what comes your way tomorrow, making an intentional plan to activate your faith over your fear.

....

....

....

....

....

....

....

....

Father in heaven, You are the one who calms the storm that rages in my heart. You are the one who replaces fear with peace and sadness with hope. You've blessed me before, and I know You'll bless me again. In the name of Jesus I pray. Amen.

Claim God's Promises

*"Look, I've given you this land. Now go in and take
it. It's the land GOD promised to give."*
DEUTERONOMY 1:8 MSG

The Bible is full of God's promises to us—but sometimes, because we don't totally believe, we neglect to claim these promises as our own. We read them, we hear them in sermons, we may even have memorized them, and yet, deep in our hearts, we're not convinced. As a result, our lives are not as full and rich as God longs for them to be. We leave those promises lying on the table, unclaimed; meanwhile, we experience needless pain and anxiety.

God yearns to give you so many blessings. Go ahead and believe in His promises. Take the gifts He's offering you. Believe—and begin to live a life of deep, wide, and endless blessing.

God, thank You for all You give me and for all You have
promised to give me. Let no disbelief of mine stand in
the way of Your love having full power in my life.

Day 349
There's No Such Thing as "Hopeless"!

"What do you mean, 'If I can'?" Jesus asked. "Anything is possible if a person believes."
MARK 9:23 NLT

Do you ever find yourself throwing up your hands and saying, "It's hopeless!" A painful situation you've struggled to improve may be frustrating you. It could be that you've tried to learn a new skill and it's just not coming easily. Or maybe it's a person in your life who seems hopeless to you because no matter how many times they promise to change, they always fall back into the same hurtful behaviors.

Everything is possible with God, but our own attitudes can get in the way, hindering the Spirit's movement in our lives and in the world around us. Things may not work out exactly as we hoped or as quickly as we wished—but with God, nothing is hopeless!

....

....

....

....

....

....

....

....

....

....

Jesus, the next time You hear me saying I think something is hopeless,
remind me that, through Your power, anything is possible.

Day 350

Believe in God's Renewal!

*Take on an entirely new way of life—a God-fashioned life, a life
renewed from the inside and working itself into your conduct
as God accurately reproduces his character in you.*

Ephesians 4:24 msg

Life is full of irritations and stress. Bills to pay, errands to run, arguments to settle, endless responsibilities—they all rub at our hearts until we feel old and worn. At the end of a long week, we sometimes feel tired and drained, as though all our creativity and energy have been robbed from us. Instead of believing the lies that exhaustion tells us, we need to use those feelings as wake-up calls, reminders that we need to open ourselves anew to God's Spirit so that He can renew us from the inside out.

God's love has the power to change our hearts and minds, filling us with new energy to follow Jesus. God will renew us. Day after day, over and over as we believe in His promises, His blessing comes to us, making our hearts fresh and green, giving our minds and bodies new energy.

....

....

....

....

....

....

....

Creative God, I believe Your energy has the
power to renew me—body, mind, and spirit.

Believe in the Still Point!

For Jesus doesn't change—yesterday, today, tomorrow, he's always totally himself.
HEBREWS 13:8 MSG

In one of T. S. Eliot's poems, he speaks of the "still point of the turning world." This is a place of stability and certainty, a place where our souls can find a sense of stillness and peace, even as the world continues to change around us. Meanwhile, of course, as human beings, we continue to live in the stream of time. Sometimes all the changes that time brings terrify us; sometimes they fill us with joy and excitement. Either way, we can believe in that still point: Jesus Christ, who never changes. His constant, steady grace leads us through all life's changes, and one day it will bring us to our home in heaven, beyond time.

....

....

....

....

....

....

....

....

....

....

....

Jesus, I believe You are the constant center of all life. When life is a whirl of change and challenge, I believe You will hold me steady.

God Will Never Walk Away

How blessed the man you train, GOD, the woman you instruct in your Word, providing a circle of quiet within the clamor of evil, while a jail is being built for the wicked. GOD will never walk away from his people, never desert his precious people. Rest assured that justice is on its way and every good heart put right.

PSALM 94:12–15 MSG

Chances are you've been rejected or abandoned in your life. Maybe a parent had no choice but to put you into the foster care system. Maybe you lost someone unexpectedly. Maybe a husband walked out on your marriage or a friend turned her back on you. Maybe a child no longer wants a relationship with you. Life on earth can beat you up, but not God. He never will.

There's nothing you can do to make God walk away from you. He's incapable of deserting you because His love won't allow it. Even at your very worst, when you're throwing a tantrum, spewing hateful words, or taking out your anger on others, God is right there with you. He's offering hope and help for the weary. Let Him be your safe space—a trusting place to be imperfect and honest.

....

....

....

....

....

....

....

Father in heaven, I am blessed and grateful for Your steadfastness to the ones who love You. Remind me that Your promise to love me forever is unshakable and nonretractable. In the name of Jesus I pray. Amen.

Day 353

Leaning on a Friend

Two people are better off than one, for they can help each other succeed. If one person falls, the other can reach out and help. But someone who falls alone is in real trouble.

ECCLESIASTES 4:9–10 NLT

Our society has deeply ingrained beliefs about independence and self-sufficiency—and those beliefs can make it hard for us to accept help from others. The Bible tells us over and over, though, that we are interconnected. We need each other. We cannot stand alone. And God uses our relationships with each other to speak to us and comfort us.

Have you ever noticed that in the best friendships, you take turns being needy? You're strong enough to help your friend one day—and the next day she's the one offering you comfort and help. Over and over, God uses our friends to make His love real in our lives, while He uses us to spread His love back to our friends. So stop believing that the only way to succeed is by "standing on your own two feet"—and don't be afraid to lean on a friend.

Beloved friend, I believe You put my friends in my life to show me Your love. Remind me not to be too proud or too independent to accept the blessings You long to bestow on me through my friends.

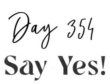

Day 354
Say Yes!

"I am the Lord's servant," Mary answered. "May your word to me be fulfilled."
LUKE 1:38 NIV

When the angel came to Mary with the news that she was to give birth to God's Son, she didn't say, "Aw shucks, I'm just not good enough, Gabriel." She simply said, "Yes"—and her *yes* allowed a brand-new reality to be born into our world.

The word *yes* can have the same power in our lives. I like to remember a quote that speaks of hope being available when we simply say yes! It's not always easy to do that, though. We are often so aware of our own limitations that we lack the confidence to say yes to God. We look around and see all the reasons why saying yes to God would make no sense (it would cost too much money; people might think we were being silly; we don't have time; we're not good enough, smart enough, or popular enough). Mary could easily have said those things too. Instead, she said yes! She just said yes—and her *yes* brought hope to us all.

....

....

....

....

....

....

....

....

....

....

Give me the courage, Lord, to say yes to hope—yes to
Your love, yes to Your power, and yes to Your will.

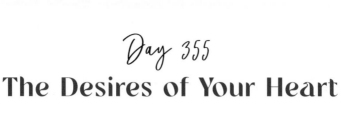

The Desires of Your Heart

Take delight in the Lord, and he will give you your heart's desires.
PSALM 37:4 NLT

What kind of God do you believe in? Is He loving and generous—or stingy and cruel? Do you ever feel as though He wants to deny you what you want, as though He's a tightfisted stepparent who takes pleasure in thwarting you? That image of God is a lie. God is the one who placed your heart's desires deep inside you. As you turn to Him, believing that He alone is the source of all true delight, He will grant you what your heart most truly craves. That's what His Word promises—and you can believe it!

....
....
....
....
....
....
....
....
....
....
....

I believe, Lord, that You gave me the desires I feel—the deepest and truest longings of my heart—and I believe that You didn't give me these yearnings to tease me or torture me. Thank You that in Your time and in Your way, as I find my delight in You, You will give me the fulfillment I crave.

Day 356

I Would Have Never Made It

Who stood up for me against the wicked? Who took my side against evil workers?
If God hadn't been there for me, I never would have made it. The minute I said,
"I'm slipping, I'm falling," your love, God, took hold and held me fast. When I
was upset and beside myself, you calmed me down and cheered me up.

PSALM 94:16–19 MSG

Have you ever said the words of the psalmist in the scripture above? *"If God hadn't been there for me, I never would have made it."* This sentence may be a staple in your responses to hard situations. You've probably seen the Lord show up in meaningful and unexpected ways before. What a blessing to have a testimony of His faithfulness!

Think back on the times God steadied you when something shook your foundation. Do you remember when a wave of peace washed over you in the middle of the storm or you had a sudden sense of joy overcome you? Keep these memories close, because in the future you'll need the encouragement they offer. Never forget the ways God has blessed you and those you love.

....

....

....

....

....

....

....

....

Father in heaven, I can remember the times You have helped me
when I was slipping and falling—the ways You were there to calm
me when I was upset. Thank You for blessing me with Your
compassion! In the name of Jesus I pray. Amen.

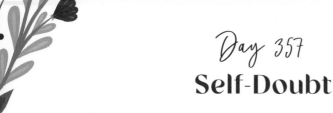

Day 357
Self-Doubt

She sets about her work vigorously; her arms are strong for her tasks.
PROVERBS 31:17 NIV

As authors Katty Kay and Claire Shipman interviewed some of the world's most influential and successful women, they noticed something odd: no matter how intelligent and talented these women obviously were, and no matter what they had objectively achieved, each of these women suffered from self-doubt. When Kay and Shipman decided to investigate further, they discovered that a vast gap separates the sexes when it comes to self-confidence. Compared with men, women don't consider themselves as ready for promotions, they predict they'll do worse on tests, and they tend to underestimate their abilities. Despite the progress women have made over the past century, Kay and Shipman concluded that today's women continue to face a crisis of confidence.

The woman described in Proverbs 31 has often been held up as a model for Christian women—but we don't always believe in the values this woman holds out to us. The Proverbs 31 woman is neither weak nor passive. She knows her own strengths, and she uses them efficiently and vigorously. She doesn't let self-doubt hold her back. She believes in herself.

....
....
....
....
....
....

God, I believe You have given me strengths and abilities You want me
to use for Your kingdom. May my belief in You help me believe
more in myself—so that self-doubt never gets in the way of me
doing and being all You have called me to do and be.

Salvation

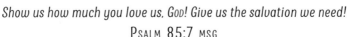

Show us how much you love us, God! Give us the salvation we need!
PSALM 85:7 MSG

In some churches, salvation in Christ is believed to be a crisis moment, a turning point, a dramatic Saul-on-the-road-to-Damascus conversion. But that's not what everyone experiences. Even if you did have that kind of dramatic conversion experience, Jesus' salvation is a steady, ongoing thing. Christ works in your life day by day, healing you, transforming you, and creating new life in you.

According to *Merriam-Webster's Dictionary*, the word *salvation* comes from the same roots as "safe," "make whole," "keep healthy," "make entire and complete." This is the salvation Jesus offers you. This is why He came to earth and died on the cross, so that He could offer you this ongoing health, this constant safety, this spiritual and emotional wholeness.

By His power, you become all you were created to be, whole and holy, sanctified and complete. You need salvation on many levels: spiritually, of course, but also at the ordinary, day-to-day level of your emotions, habits, and thoughts. Believe that Jesus is saving you, over and over, throughout every day!

....

....

....

....

....

....

....

....

Jesus, I believe in Your constant salvation. Thank You for blessing
me with wholeness and health, safety and fulfillment.

Treasuring Every Step

How blessed are those who make Your house their home, who live with You;
they are constantly praising You. [pause] Blessed are those who make You
their strength, for they treasure every step of the journey [to Zion].
PSALM 84:4–5 VOICE

Imagine treasuring every step of your journey, including your life right now. How do you cherish struggles in marriage? How do you adore the difficulties of parenting teenagers or toddlers? How do you value seasons of financial fear? How can you appreciate anxiety from your career or hold dear frustrations in friendship? Well, if we look at today's scripture, it says we can be blessed in these times by making God our strength. We can treasure them because we are walking with God, not alone. It means we lean on Him for hope instead of on ourselves. We press into His promises to save and restore. It means we adopt a position of praise, thanking God now for the faithfulness we'll see later. This is how we make Him our home. And when we find the courage and confidence to walk this out every day, the blessings will flow. We will come out as victors.

....
....
....
....
....
....
....
....

Father in heaven, bless me with Your strength so I can learn to
treasure whatever life brings my way. In the good times or the bad,
I know You will be with me. In the name of Jesus I pray. Amen.

Day 360
Patient Hope

If we hope for what we do not yet have, we wait for it patiently.
ROMANS 8:25 NIV

Hope is a form of patience that shines with confidence. It's not the kind of patience that just plods along wearing a dreary face, putting up with life's troubles with big sighs and no expectation that anything better will ever come along. Instead, hope *knows* that something better is up ahead.

Hope believes God will keep His word. Even though right now things may look frightening or sad, hope shines its light into our hearts, reassuring us that better times are yet to come. We can't see the future—but we believe God has amazing things planned.

....
....
....
....
....
....
....
....
....
....
....

Dear God, when I feel like giving up, give me new hope in Your promises.
Fill my heart with joyful expectation of all You will do both in my
life and in the world. And please, help me to be patient!

Believe in God's Plan!

Commit to the Lord whatever you do, and he will establish your plans.
P ROVERBS 16:3 NIV

When you don't understand what's happening in your life and you aren't certain what to do next, believe that God has a plan for your life. Give Him all the details. Consciously and prayerfully place in His hands every aspect of your life. Then take the next step you can see, even if it's only a very tiny step. Don't be paralyzed by fear. Do what is in front of you to do. Although you still don't know what your long-term future holds, walk through the doors of opportunity that open each day. In time, God will bring new clarity to your thoughts, and you'll be able to see the path ahead.

....

....

....

....

....

....

....

....

....

....

....

....

Lord, no matter how confused and lost I feel, I believe You have
a plan for my life. Show me the small steps I can take next.
Bless me with the certainty that You are leading me.

Day 362
God's Priority

Jesus said, "'Love the Lord your God with all your passion and prayer and intelligence.' This is the most important, the first on any list. But there is a second to set alongside it: 'Love others as well as you love yourself.'"
MATTHEW 22:37–39 MSG

Sometimes we believe God wants things from us that He never said He wanted. We think a certain kind of daily devotional practice is required, or we assume church has to be a priority in our lives. Spending time with God and His people *is* important—but it's important for our own spiritual well-being. God never said He needed us to do those things to make Him happy. He never said, "Thou shalt read one chapter of the Bible every day, and then thou shalt spend a half hour in prayer. And then on Sunday, thou shalt spend at least two hours in a church building."

Once again, those things can be helpful to our own spiritual journeys—but Jesus made clear what God's priority really is, and it's very simple: love. Daily devotions and Sunday church services are only important if they help us to better love God and others (and even ourselves).

Jesus, I believe love is Your number one priority for my life. May I stop putting the cart before the horse, believing I can please You by doing "religious" things. Let Your love shine through everything I do.

Day 363

Believe in God's Abundance!

From his abundance we have all received one gracious blessing after another.
JOHN 1:16 NLT

Some people only exist. They go through their days with their eyes on the ground, plodding along as though life were an endurance test. They believe their lives are dull and hopeless.

When you feel like that (and we all do, at one time or another), learn to look up. Believe that God has good things He's longing to give you. Don't overlook the small joys and tiny blessings He is showering into your life. It's easy to be so focused on the big things—financial challenges, your health problems, your loved ones' issues—that you forget to notice the many small ways God shows His love. Each new sunrise, each good meal, each warm bath, each good night's sleep—all send you love messages from your Father.

Cultivate the belief that each day that comes is a brand-new present from God to be unwrapped with joy. Hold out your hands. Accept His abundant blessings.

....

....

....

....

....

....

....

....

Abundant God, I believe You have blessings in store for me today.
May I not be so preoccupied with my problems that I fail to
see the grace and love You shower down on me.

Day 364
Those in Need

She opens her arms to the poor and extends her hands to the needy.
PROVERBS 31:20 NIV

Family, home, job, church, friends, personal and spiritual development—our days are so busy that it's hard to make time for anything extra. We believe we honestly care about those in need, but we only have so much time, energy, and money to go around. We truly believe we're doing all we can. But the Proverbs 31 woman once again challenges us to re-examine our beliefs. This woman took care of her family and herself; she was no self-sacrificing doormat. But she believed she was strong enough and rich enough in God's blessings that she had enough to share.

No one can do everything, and God doesn't expect us to be superwomen. But He does ask that we believe He'll use us to help those who are in need. The "poor" may lack financial resources, but they may also lack attention, love, physical energy, or skills. Look around you. See the people God might be asking you to reach out and help. Believe you can make a difference in someone's life—and God will use you and bless you.

....
....
....
....
....
....
....
....

God, I believe You want to use me to be Your hands, feet, eyes, and
mouth, spreading Your love and help to those who need it.

Day 365
Good News

The Spirit of the Sovereign LORD is on me, because the LORD has anointed me to proclaim good news to the poor. He has sent me to bind up the brokenhearted, to proclaim freedom for the captives and release from darkness for the prisoners.

ISAIAH 61:1 NIV

Sometimes, we may forget that the Bible brings us *good news.* We allow ourselves to be burdened with depression and frustration; we wear frowns more than smiles. Others watching our faces and hearing our words might not be able to tell we have something special in our lives. In fact, they might think we feel pretty much like the rest of the world often does—hopeless. In reality, the Bible has given us the best news ever: we are unconditionally loved and made whole for eternity; and so, even when the world seems the darkest, we have hope!

Sovereign Lord, remind me that frowns, gloomy attitudes, and angry words are not what it takes to draw people to You. Help me to change the world with the good news of the hope I have in You.

Scripture Index

OLD TESTAMENT

NEW TESTAMENT

Journal Your Journey of Faith

Pray More: A Devotional Journal for Women

This delightful devotional journal features daily readings and prayers designed to help you live your best life as you learn to place your trust in the almighty God, who gives you courage.

Hardback Cloth / 978-1-63609-912-5

Good Morning, God! An Encouraging Prayer Journal for Women

What better way to guarantee a good morning than to spend time in prayer? *Good Morning, God!* encourages you to do just that—to set aside a few minutes each day for quiet time with God. Nearly 200 faith-building devotional prayers are accompanied by inspiring scripture selections and journaling space.

Flexible Casebound / 978-1-63609-848-7